ARNHEM - THE FIGHT TO SUSTAIN

ARNHEM THE FIGHT TO SUSTAIN

The Untold Story of the Airborne Logisticians

Frank Steer

LEO COOPER

First published in Great Britain in 2000
and reprinted in this format in 2020 by
Pen & Sword Military
an imprint of
Pen & Sword Books Limited
Yorkshire - Philadelphia

ISBN 978 1 52679 193 1

A CIP record for this book is available from the British Library

Printed and bound in the UK
by CPI Group (UK) Ltd, Croydon, CRO 4YY

MIX
Paper from
responsible sources
FSC® C013604

Pen & Sword Books Limited incorporates the imprints of Atlas, Archaeology, Aviation, Discovery, Family History, Fiction, History, Maritime, Military, Military Classics, Politics, Select, Transport, True Crime, Air World, Frontline Publishing, Leo Cooper, Remember When, Seaforth Publishing, The Praetorian Press, Wharncliffe Local History, Wharncliffe Transport, Wharncliffe True Crime and White Owl.
For a complete list of Pen & Sword titles please contact
PEN & SWORD BOOKS LIMITED
47 Church Street, Barnsley, South Yorkshire S70 2AS, United Kingdom
E-mail: enquiries@pen-and-sword.co.uk
Website: www.pen-and-sword.co.uk

Or

PEN AND SWORD BOOKS
1950 Lawrence Rd, Havertown, PA 19083, USA
E-mail: Uspen-and-sword@casematepublishers.com
Website: www.penandswordbooks.com

Contents

List of Maps

Tables

Foreword

by

General Sir Rupert Smith KCB, DSO, OBE, QGM

I accepted readily Frank Steer's invitation to write this Foreword, for I know from experience how much a commander depends on his logisticians and administrators in achieving his objective. The essential endeavours of these most necessary men and units are often unrecorded. Usually their successes are obscured by the glow of triumph or the smoke of disaster, and their rare failures are examined in detail and without context in a search for the one to blame.

Frank Steer's excellent and very readable book tells the story of the airborne logisticians of British Airborne Forces and in particular their actions in support of the 1st Airborne Division at Arnhem. Here is an account of brave and resolute men of high morale. Men who, in battle with their plans awry and with grave losses of men and materiel, adapted to their new circumstances and continued to do their duty. Men who, in the face of defeat, fought and engaged the enemy closely to the end. The need for such men today is as necessary as it was then at Arnhem.

These men had devised a concept of the sustainment and maintenance of Airborne Forces in battle. This concept and the plans and organisation it spawned are explained simply and clearly by Frank Steer. The concept had the flexibility to stand the shocking proof of battle and in large measure remains in use today. Indeed much of what was achieved by those airborne 'sustainers' is of relevance today. One of the characteristics of our recent operations is the increasing threat to the rear of the force. There was no rear area at Arnhem, and as it was for the men at Arnhem so it is today: the need to sustain in adversity.

For those who wish to learn from the past, whether in the particular or more generally, I commend this book. Its pages contain an excellent example of the value of a sound flexible concept applied according to the circumstances by men of resource and indomitable will. Their example gives us goal to aspire to and an inspiration in adversity.

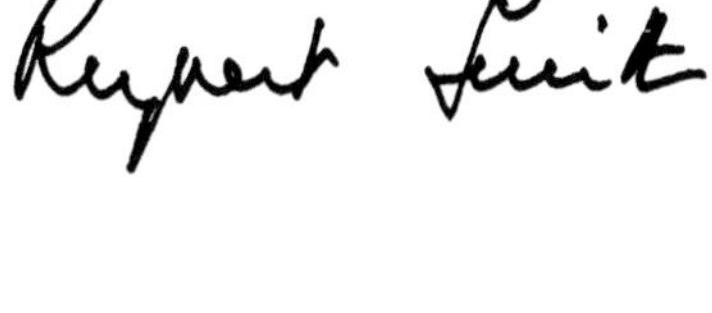

Preface

It all started in October 1998, in Robert Sigmond's[1] study in Renkum, just to the west of Arnhem. In the company of Drs Adrian Groeneweg OBE, Bob Gerritsen and others who work at or with the Airborne Museum 'Hartenstein', and weakened by too much Dutch hospitality, I agreed to investigate the prospect of writing something about logistics at the Battle of Arnhem. I thought a small pamphlet would suffice, involving not too much effort, and assumed it would be well documented in the plethora of books about MARKET GARDEN, the code name for the operation of which events at Arnhem, and in the nearby village of Oosterbeek a few miles to its west, were a part. All I would need to do would be to draw it together as a summary, and that would suffice.

Early investigations, however, showed that any readily available information was incomplete, and there was much that lay undiscovered or simply unreported. As I began to dig deeper, and made contact with some of the men who had served with the logistic units at Arnhem, it became obvious that there was a significant gap in the recorded history of the battle. When I suggested that the end product might be a book the veterans were unanimous in their delight that, at last, someone was going to tell their story; and very quickly it became clear that I was faced with a greater challenge than I might have first imagined. I knew that any attempt to withdraw from the project on the grounds that it was now much bigger than we had first thought would attract little sympathy from the inhabitants of the Hartenstein museum, but it was not that fear which drove me on. I realised that I had now undertaken an obligation to those who were there, those who survive to the present day and their families to set on record their achievements and their sacrifice, to relate their part in the Battle of Arnhem and, perhaps, to lay some of their ghosts. It is that, above all, which has motivated and sustained me throughout the long hours of research and writing this story of how logistic support was provided to 1st Airborne Division at Arnhem, and of the men who provided it.

It soon became clear that it would not be possible simply to start with the beginning of Operation MARKET GARDEN in September 1944. The development of logistic support policies, principles and practices, and the creation of the units which provided support to 1st Airborne Division, are inextricably linked to the development of British Airborne Forces themselves. Consequently, to tell the complete story it has been necessary to go back to the beginning, sketching in brief the building of Britain's airborne capability and weaving into it the development of the supporting logistic structure. The relevance, and importance, of this approach becomes clear as the story develops for it is as much from the development of the logistic concept that we learn lessons as it is from its eventual implementation and effectiveness. It is also helpful in trying to understand what those involved were planning to achieve and why, so that the impact of actual events on aspirations can be judged in the right context.

In setting the boundaries I chose to follow the current British Army definition of what is meant by 'Logistic Support'. It involves the supply of ammunition, fuel, food, spare parts, vehicles and a wide range of general stores; and their distribution throughout the Army. Also included are catering and the distribution of mail, as well as labour, provided by pioneers. I have not included equipment repair and maintenance or medical support, since they fall outside the scope of 'Logistic Support' as the term is currently used. Both these subjects are, in any event, covered in two excellent works: *With Spanners Descending* by Joe Roberts and *Red Berets and Red Crosses* by Niall Cherry.

During the Second World War, and up until 1965, the Royal Army Service Corps (RASC) was responsible for transport and distribution, of men and material, and also undertook other functions such as stock accounting in the field for ammunition, fuel and rations, and providing experts in the handling of fuel and food, including butchers and bakers. They also provided the Army with its military clerks for work in headquarters, and they were distinguished by the letter 'S' in their army number, as opposed to 'T' for other trades. Part of the distribution function also included air despatch of stores from Royal Air Force aircraft.

The Royal Army Ordnance Corps (RAOC) was the supply corps of the British Army, providing spares, clothing and other equipment from its depots, warehouses and mobile storage units. The Corps was also responsible for the quality, maintenance and repair of ammunition, and had specialists in these fields. The roles of the RASC and the RAOC were rationalised in 1965, with all supply and clerical functions, together with the experts in fuel and food, going to the RAOC. The transport and distribution tasks, including air despatch went to a new corps: The Royal Corps of Transport (RCT).

The Pioneer Corps (PC) was the labour corps of the Army. It comprised small units of just a few men capable of recruiting local civilian labour, as well as formed companies which provided a military labour force for, among other things, the handling of stocks in storage areas or the loading and unloading of aircraft. Consequently, there was an early synergy between them and the RAOC in particular. The Corps was not to become the Royal Pioneer Corps (RPC) until 1951. The Army Catering Corps (ACC), clearly, did the cooking, posted to units as individuals. There were no ACC units as such. The Royal Engineers Postal Section (REPS) ran the Army Postal Service, providing postal units for the handling and distribution of mail and post offices in the field.

In 1993 the four corps, together with the REPS (by then known as REPCS), were integrated into a single cohesive organisation, and the Royal Logistic Corps (RLC) was born. This, then, is the story of the provision of logistic support to 1st Airborne Division up to and during the Battle of Arnhem, by Corps whose heritage is carried today by the Royal Logistic Corps. It is told against the background of the development of the airborne forces they existed to serve, and of which they were very much a part. Information is drawn from a wide range of sources, including official texts, books about the battle and articles from journals. The Public Record Office, the Imperial War Museum, the Airborne Museum 'Hartenstein' at Oosterbeek, the Airborne Forces Museum at Aldershot, the Royal Air Force Museum at Hendon, the Museum of Army Flying at Middle Wallop, the Royal Logistic Corps Museum at Deepcut and the Bundesarchiv in Koblenz have all been supportive and helpful. I am most grateful to all of them for their help, and their permission either to use photographs or to quote from documents.

There are also a number of unpublished works, effectively diaries, written by participants and often containing a wealth of detail; and I was privileged to be able to interview a number of survivors. Since this is, above all, a story of the men of the five corps who took part in one of the great battles of the Second World War I have resorted extensively to anecdotes, quoting what they have either written or related to me, for who better to tell what really happened than those who were there; and without their contribution this work would be without colour.

It is perhaps worth acknowledging from the outset some of the challenges faced in compiling this story. Key among these was the disparate involvement of the five corps. The RASC had transport and air despatch units, for which there are histories, about which stories have been written and with survivors who can tell of the unit and the individuals who were part of it. The same is true, but on a smaller scale, for the RAOC. However, there were also RASC soldiers in other posts: each field ambulance had a number on establishment as drivers, there were RASC clerks in formation headquarters, there was even an RASC corporal acting as medical orderly for an infantry company. Tracking these individuals and others like them proved very difficult since nominal rolls for the units taking part were not complete, and many have disappeared. It has simply not been possible to compile much information about these men, and their stories must, for the time being at least, remain untold.

Cooks, of course, were posted as individuals on the strength of the units they served. Their exploits can only be uncovered if they featured in unit histories or anecdotes, of which there are very few - and the cooks do not often rate a mention. Yet they played their full part along with the rest, as witness the three who lie buried in the Arnhem-Oosterbeek War Cemetery. Furthermore, the ACC in 1944 was in its infancy, and not every cook wore the ACC badge. Many of them were 'regimental cooks', found from within the regiment to which they belonged, and wearing its cap badge.

The involvement of the Pioneers and the Postal Section was very small. Although they played their part they were not directly involved with 1st Airborne Division at Arnhem, but formed part of the support that flew in at the end of the battle.

Compounding the disparity in the level of involvement are the differences in the depth and detail of information. In some cases there is a great deal written by individuals in one unit, fighting beside another about which we know considerably less. For example, the accounts of the action at the Arnhem bridge by Private Ted Mordecai RAOC and Private Kevin Heaney RAOC, two of only six RAOC who reached the bridge, offer a mass of detail; yet I have been able to find comparatively little from the RASC platoon which also reached the bridge area, and which was almost forty strong.

A further complication lies with the memories of the participants. This is due, in part, to the time that has elapsed since 1944, but even very shortly after the battle differing perspectives of the same incidents were being given. This is inevitable, but on a number of occasions I was faced with descriptions that varied so significantly I was left wondering if we were all discussing the same event. I have sought, valiantly, to carve my way through all the detail of such incidents, trying to offer a balanced overview. It has, however, been one of the hardest aspects of this endeavour.

I would, therefore, entreat readers to be sympathetic, especially veterans, for it is their story I wish most of all to tell properly. I have tried to relate mention of corps, units and individuals in accordance with the degree of cap-badge involvement, but that has not always been possible because of the balance of information. If, from time to time, it appears that undue attention is being paid to a corps, a unit or an individual it is not a preference or a slight, but merely an indication of the facts available to me in trying to relate events in a way that reflects appropriately on all who took part.

The title[2] reflects the way in which the logisticians at Arnhem not only undertook their logistic tasks with courage and professionalism throughout the conflict, but also held on magnificently in the battle against a powerful and determined enemy. In so doing, they sustained not only those who depended upon them for support, but also their own individual contributions to the defence of the bridge and the Oosterbeek perimeter. The motto of the RLC today is 'We Sustain'. The manner in which their predecessors at Arnhem sustained the fight is a tribute to their courage and tenacity in everything they did, and is something of which the RLC today can be justly proud.

I could not have embarked on the task without considerable guidance, support, encouragement and patience from relatives, friends and colleagues. Drs Adrian Groeneweg OBE, vice-president of the Board of Trustees of the Airborne Museum 'Hartenstein', Robert Sigmond, Bob Gerritsen and Drs Jaap Korsloot have encyclopedic knowledge of events and people and their help has been beyond measure. They have all read my drafts with great patience and understanding, and the detail of their responses has made a huge difference to the accuracy of my work. To all four of them I offer my grateful thanks, not simply for starting me off on the project, but also for encouraging me, sorting some of my facts and providing constructive and positive comment and criticism. I asked not that they be kind, simply polite; and they were.

One of the joys of working with Dutch friends is their phenomenal hospitality, coupled with the gentle pity they bestow on anyone foolish enough to embark on a project such as this. Jook and Hanna van Slooten's home in Oosterbeek always provides an oasis of calm, of relaxation and of laughter, and I am most grateful for the bed they always offer whenever we visit. Even more so, I am grateful to Jook for his meticulous proof-reading of my work and, embarrassingly, his corrections to my English grammar.

Jan Hey's work in recording, diligently, the deaths of men involved in the Arnhem battle is outstanding. I have taken only the names of those killed and placed them in an annex, and have left all other detail to his Roll of Honour, a remarkable piece of work, compiled with great care and devotion, and which is available from the Airborne Museum 'Hartenstein'. Jan has given permission for me to reproduce what I require, and I remain in his debt. I have added some additional detail on air despatchers who were killed, and whose names appear on the Air Despatch Memorial in Oosterbeek, thanks to Wybo Boersma at the Airborne Museum 'Hartenstein', who drew on the unsurpassed knowledge about air despatchers of Mr Lex Röell.

Lieutenant Colonel Willy Carlisle RLC undertook, whilst commanding 47 Air Despatch Squadron RLC, to bring together details of air despatch operations in support of Operation MARKET GARDEN. I have drawn extensively on his work and thank him most sincerely for his permission to use it and for his support. Also on air despatch issues, if in doubt, I could always turn to Eric Pepper, whose knowledge of what happened to individual RAF aircraft and their crews is unrivalled. He was rarely stuck for an answer, and was always willing to help.

Lieutenant Colonel Derek Armitage at the Museum of Army Flying and Mr Alan Brown of the Airborne Museum in Aldershot have always been there to talk when I needed them, and Corporal Bob Hilton of the 2nd Battalion The Parachute Regiment has a database of invaluable detail on which he has kindly allowed me to draw. To them I offer my gratitude for their patience and their willingness to help and guide me.

Brigadier Mike Wharmby, late of the RLC and a former commander of the modern Airborne Logistic Regiment, Lieutenant Colonel John Arkinstall RLC, Major Tom Mouat RLC and Robert Robinson-Collins all read the first draft. Their comments were gratefully received, and helped me adjust text in order to make the book as palatable as possible across what I hope will be a wide audience. Lieutenant Colonel John Hambleton MBE, the Regimental Secretary of the Royal Logistic Corps, assisted me greatly in publishing the work, for which he knew he had my thanks. His untimely death, before publication, was a great sadness. I am also indebted to Lieutenant Colonel Mike Young, a fellow author and corps historian for his help.

General Sir Rupert Smith KCB, DSO, OBE, QGM, late of the Parachute Regiment and currently Deputy Supreme Allied Commander Europe, very kindly took time from his extraordinarily busy appointment to read my manuscript and write the Foreword. He knows how much I appreciate that, but, more importantly, he has reflected the importance of sound, flexible logistic doctrine and planning and the high quality of the soldiers needed to provide effective logistic support in war; as important now, for the RLC, as it was then for the forming corps. My thanks are not simply for his time, but also for the wisdom he has brought to my work.

No acknowledgment could be complete without mention of my wife, Virginia. Her support and understanding, taken together with regular supplies of tea, have been essential to the completion of this work. Long hours, late nights, extensive walks around the battlefield, ages talking to veterans and historians and reading source material have required more forbearance and patience than I am entitled to. A simple 'thank you' probably appears inadequate, but she knows how much I mean it.

Which brings me, finally, to the veterans; those who were there and have displayed such patience and understanding in responding to my letters, my telephone calls and my many questions. My gratitude to them is boundless. This, after all, is the story they wanted to be told; and it is my hope, above all else, that they are happy with it.

Brigadier F.R. Steer MBE
Andover
August 2000

1. Robert Sigmond is the author of 'Off At Last', the story of the 7th Battalion The Kings' Own Scottish Borderers, and the part they played at the Battle of Arnhem
2. I am indebted to the officers and warrant officers of 16 Regiment The Royal Logistic Corps for guiding me on the choice of title, during a tour of the Arnhem Battlefield in April 2000.

Abbreviations

AA&QMG	Assistant Adjutant and Quartermaster General – normally a Lieutenant Colonel
ACC	Army Catering Corps
ADOS	Assistant Director of Ordnance Services – normally a Lieutenant Colonel
AE	Ammunition Examiner
AEAF	Allied Expeditionary Air Force
AFDAG	Airborne Forward Delivery Airfield Group
AUCL	Administrative Unit Civil Labour
BOWO	Brigade Ordnance Warrant Officer
BRASCO	Brigade Royal Army Service Corps Officer
CRASC	Commander Royal Army Service Corps
CREME	Commander Royal Electrical and Mechanical Engineers
DAA	Divisional Administrative Area
DDST	Deputy Director Supplies and Transport – normally a Colonel or Brigadier
DZ	Dropping Zone
EFI	Expeditionary Forces Institute
FMA	Forward Maintenance Area
FMACC	Forward Maintenance Area Control Centre
GS	General Service
GSO 1	General Staff Officer Grade One – normally a Lieutenant Colonel
GT	General Transport
IOO	Inspecting Ordnance Officer
KOSB	King's Own Scottish Borderers
LST	Landing Ship Tank
NAAFI	Navy Army and Air Force Institute
NCO	Non-commissioned Officer
OFP	Ordnance Field Park
OO	Ordnance Officer
PC	Pioneer Corps – up until 1951
PIAT	Projector Infantry Anti-Tank
RAOC	Royal Army Ordnance Corps
RASC	Royal Army Service Corps
RCT	Royal Corps of Transport
RE	Royal Engineers
REME	Royal Electrical and Mechanical Engineers
REPCS	Royal Engineers Postal and Courier Service
REPS	Royal Engineers Postal Section
RLC	Royal Logistic Corps
RPC	Royal Pioneer Corps – after 1951
SDP	Supply Dropping Point
SHAEF	Supreme Headquarters Allied Expeditionary Force
SOP	Standard Operating Procedure
WO	War Office

Chapter One

In The Beginning

The Early Development of Airborne Forces

The impetus to create an airborne capability for the British Army came directly from Winston Churchill. Following the evacuation from Dunkirk, and conscious of the threat of invasion, the Prime Minister formed a view that a 'corps of parachutists' would offer a significant enhancement to the defence of the homeland. From this embryo of an idea were to grow the two British airborne divisions that were to wage war in Europe in 1944, in the very forefront of the assault on the occupied countries and Germany.

With an initial target strength of 5,000 men, the project suffered an inauspicious start. Having decided to pursue the concept, and with Churchill having directed its initiation on 22 June 1940, it became clear after just a few weeks that potential parachutists were not forthcoming in the numbers anticipated, and those there were could not be adequately trained due to a shortage of aircraft. Despite considerable pressure from the Prime Minister this was to remain a limitation for some time to come, for the Royal Air Force was loath to dedicate precious aircraft to a role which would deny their use as bombers. Initially, therefore, it was decided that parachuting could only take place from suitable, dual-roled aircraft with a bombing capability. One such aircraft was the Whitley bomber, and the original pioneers of parachuting had actually begun learning their art by standing in a Whitley's open tail, the rear gun turret having been removed, holding on to a bar. The parachute was then opened by a normal ripcord and the man was pulled off the aircraft by the slipstream. This exhilarating experience ceased when an American parachute superseded the RAF model. From then on, parachutists were to be treated to the joy of dropping through a round hole in the aircraft deck, with the parachute being opened by a static line attached to the hole's side. The hope was that the parachutist's face would not collide with the far side of the hole as he passed through. Not everyone was lucky.

With training commencing on 8 July 1940, the tragic distinction of suffering, on 25 July, the first fatality, went to the RASC. Driver Evans, attached to No 2 Commando, died when his rigging lines became twisted, preventing the canopy from deploying and making him the first airborne recruit to be killed on a formal military parachute training course.

Given the aircraft shortage and the technical difficulties, early thoughts for airborne operations soon began to give preference to gliders. They were felt to be safer, more flexible and capable of carrying better loads; and they could concentrate a force on the ground very much more easily than parachute formations.

There already existed a small basis upon which to develop early ideas and concepts. The Central Landing School had been formed at the start of the War to investigate the problems associated with parachuting and the carriage of troops by glider; and shortly after Churchill's pronouncement the Air Ministry decided on four types of glider and commissioned their construction, although the decision on what would finally be adopted would have to wait until prototypes had been tested.

In the early days no definite combat units were designated for the gliderborne role, with a general view pervading that anyone could do it with minimal training. It was accepted that units would need a lighter scale of vehicles, and would probably have to do with less equipment, but otherwise there was seen to be little difference from normal light infantry operations. The specifications put forward for the gliders made no allowance for the carriage of wheeled vehicles and the heavier weapons, such as guns or mortars, although one type was to be capable of carrying a light tank. Of the four types originally suggested, two were to be used in 1944: the Horsa, a twenty-six seater which could, as an alternative, carry a jeep and trailer with its crew or a 6-pounder anti-tank gun; and the Hamilcar, larger and developed as a weight carrying glider which could also hold up to forty troops.

However, a year of wrangling was to pass as the War Office and the Air Ministry postured for position over where responsibilities lay for the doctrine, training, command and control of airborne forces. It was the German invasion of Crete and firmly stated views by Mr Churchill that were finally to galvanise them into some form of action. The result was an agreement to press ahead with a programme for the development of airborne forces which would provide two brigades of parachute troops: one each for Home and Middle East operations. There would also be sufficient gliders and tugs for two airlanding brigades: again, one for Home and one for Middle East operations. To supplement these

Horsa glider, capable of carrying 26 troops, or a combination of jeeps and trailers. 3,655 were bu
Courtesy Museum of Army Flying

Hamilcar glider, designed to take a light tank or two Bren carriers and could carry 40 equipped men. Courtesy Imperial War Museum

forces there was also a requirement for sufficient aircraft for an airlanding brigade to operate in an airtransported role, wherever it might be required.

Despite the preference for gliderborne troops, it was a brigade of parachutists that was to be the first airborne formation in the British Army. July 1941 saw the creation of 1st Parachute Brigade, comprising a brigade headquarters, four parachute infantry battalions and a troop of Royal Engineers. There was an aspiration to provide other supporting troops, including a 'supply' unit of a type which was not determined, and the establishment of which was to be left until 'later'. From the outset, therefore, the problems of supporting, logistically, an operation, although acknowledged, were taking second place to the development of operational and tactical doctrine and methods.

By September 1941 the parachuting aspects of airborne operations were reasonably well organised, with advantage being taken of the early experiments and trials. However, with the commander of the 1st Parachute Brigade completely immersed in his evolving parachute capability, the responsibility for glider development still rested with the Royal Air Force; and still no gliderborne troops had either been allocated or trained.

Nonetheless, the War Office was of the view that troops carried by glider or aircraft would be necessary in order to support parachutists for all but the most limited of operations. Hence, on 10 October 1941, 31st Independent Infantry Brigade Group was selected as an airlanding brigade group. Recently returned from India, the Brigade had just completed mountain warfare training in Wales and, consequently, was already prepared to operate in a light role. The Brigade was given the task of undertaking the early investigation into the organisation, equipping and training of an airlanding formation; and they were to prepare for travel in both gliders and transport aircraft.

As a natural progression from the formation of the first brigade of parachutists, a headquarters was formed to oversee the further development of the airborne concept. On 29 October 1941 Brigadier F. A. M. Browning, commander 24 Guards Brigade, was selected to be commander Parachute Troops and Airborne Troops, in the acting rank of Major General. He took under his control 1st Parachute Brigade and 1st Airlanding Brigade, and set up a headquarters in King Charles Street in London. The staff he gathered around him were, for a considerable time, to play a major part in the development of airborne forces. One of their number was an Assistant Director of Ordnance Services (ADOS), Lieutenant Colonel G. M. Loring RAOC; and he was the only logistician on the staff in those early days.

It was not long before Major General Browning initiated the formation of an operational airborne divisional headquarters. He had two reasons: he judged that there was the potential for airborne operations on a divisional scale, for which a headquarters would be required; and, notwithstanding this, it would be bad for morale for any headquarters controlling combat troops not to be in a position to go into action. Thus it was, in November 1941, headquarters 1st Airborne Division was formed. The stage was set, the players were beginning to form up, and it now remained for the supporting cast, the logisticians, to come on board.

Airborne Logistics - Conception and Birth

Importantly, when 31st Infantry Brigade had been given the airlanding role, and then became part of the 1st Airborne Division, it had brought with it its full brigade logistic support package. This, ultimately, would provide the basis upon which the logistic support of the whole division would be built. There was one RASC company: 31st Independent Infantry Brigade Company RASC, commanded by Major Michael St J. Packe, and initially this was the only RASC support available to the Division.

Michael Packe, came to the Airborne Division as the Major commanding 31st Independent Infantry Brigade Company RASC, and was made Lieutenant Colonel and CRASC in 1943.
Courtesy Imperial War Museum

In addition there was 31st Independent Infantry Brigade Ordnance Workshop and Field Park RAOC, also a company sized unit. At that time the RAOC was responsible for supply of repair parts, clothing, tentage, general stores and a wide range of services, and for the repair and maintenance of Army equipment. Its soldiers were trained, among other things, as inventory control clerks, storemen, textile repairers, mechanics and technicians.

In May 1942 1st Airborne Division Postal Unit REPS appeared on the scene. A small unit, it comprised a junior officer, a sergeant and thirteen junior ranks. Its value was, of course, completely out of proportion to its size given the enormous importance attached by soldiers to an effective mail service. This wasn't simply to ensure they received regular deliveries, but also that they could have confidence that their own mail was arriving safely back home.

The service to be provided by these units was vital, but equally important was the quality of the men delivering it. Logistic support for airborne forces had to be provided by people who shared the ethos of the corps d'elite that Browning sought to build. It was his view that the airborne formations would be leading the assault on tasks that no other formation could accomplish. They should expect, as a matter of course, to be surrounded by the enemy, cut off for some time from all supply except by air and have to defeat a more heavily armed opponent before being relieved by ground troops. Throughout all this they would have to be sustained, taking with them all they could and relying on air resupply for the rest.

However, although a number of company and battalion sized raids were successfully mounted, it would be some time before airborne forces were deployed in anything like formation size, that is at brigade strength or greater. Indeed, it was not to be until the latter part of 1943, when 1st Airborne Division was operating in North Africa and 1st Parachute Brigade completed three parachute operations in five months with the 1st British Army. They captured over 3,500 prisoners and inflicted over 5,000 casualties; but at a cost to themselves of some 1,700 killed or wounded.

The Brigade carried with it on these operations the logistic shortcomings of the early days, where the aspiration to form support units at brigade level had been stated, but never realised. They had no supporting services of their own, of any sort, under command, and being too far from 1st Airborne Division's limited logistic capability were reliant for logistic support on neighbouring formations. It was the equivalent of living off the land with no guarantee that their requirements would be met, for they would need to be sure that equipment was of the same type, and that those upon whom they had to rely had sufficient

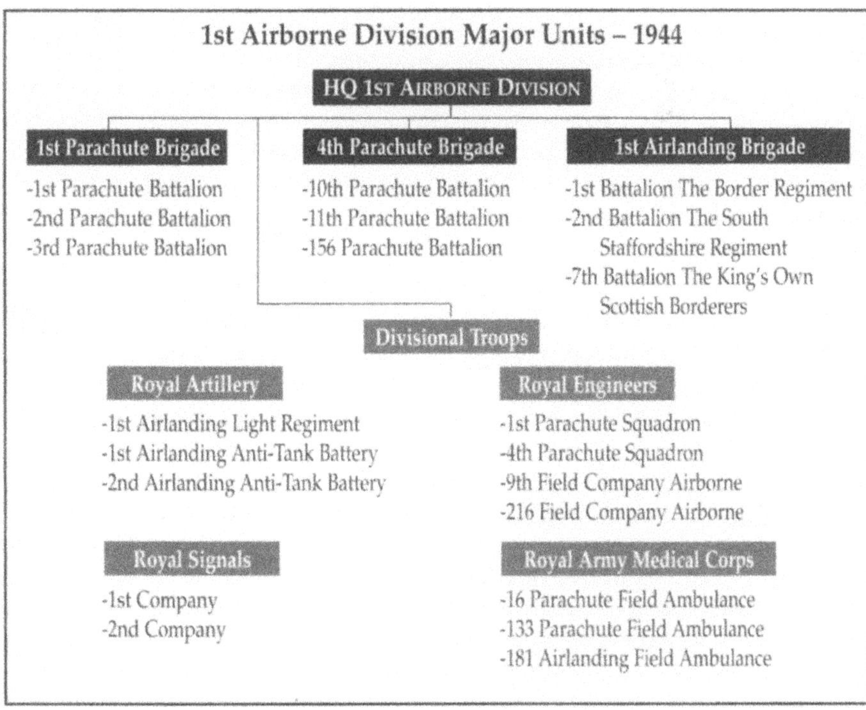

stocks to spare. It was a significant limitation on parachute operations, precluding the sustainment of independent activity, temporarily out of reach of ground forces, that Browning had envisaged as being the hallmark of his elite troops.

This key lesson proved that the aspiration to build direct logistic support into airborne formations had to become a reality, and with the capability to deploy close to the fighting elements. Work on designing an airborne logistic support concept was now accelerated, looking to develop a support package for the complete airborne division which would sustain a deployed, independent, isolated airborne force of any size up to divisional strength. This became the main driver in forming the concept of logistic operations and developing logistic doctrine.

However, the Division had been increased in size to three brigades. The 4th Parachute Brigade had formed up in the Middle East, and when 1st Airborne Division went to North Africa in 1943 the Brigade joined 1st Parachute Brigade and 1st Airlanding Brigade as part of the Division in May of that year. There was another difference: each brigade now comprised only three battalions, a reduction from the four with which 1st Parachute Brigade and 1st Airlanding Brigade had begun their existences. Taken together with the supporting arms and services the total was some 15,000 men and it was this order of battle for which logistic support had to be developed, organised and trained, and which would fight at Arnhem the following year.

The Royal Army Service Corps

Fortunately, a great deal had already been done by 1943, in most cases on the personal initiative of logistic commanders. Indeed, the early developmental work had commenced before 1st Airborne Division's deployment to North Africa, and very shortly after the formation of the divisional headquarters. For example, by May 1942, 31st Independent Infantry Brigade Company RASC had become 250 Airborne Composite Company and, initially, was the 'catch-all' for all the RASC transport and distribution tasks, including air despatch, in the Division. In this new role it had begun experimenting from the very outset with air delivered stores, and initially this had involved glider packing and then packing containers into the bomb bays of Whitleys for delivery by parachute.

Driver Jim Wild RASC of 250 Company found that all the drills, even the role for which they were training, seemed to be based on trial and error; and they were expected to pack and despatch stores as well as carry out the normal RASC ground duties. He spent some four weeks just packing panniers to the correct weight to be suitable for carrying in aircraft, experimenting with various methods and trying out different ideas. At some stage it was decided that soldiers undertaking air despatch duties needed to do four parachute jumps, and Jim went to Hardwick Hall to do his. He was fortunate; the programme, eventually, would not cover all air despatchers and many were to have their first parachuting experience jumping from doomed aircraft on an operation. In Jim's case the training was never put into effect as he would eventually go to Arnhem in a glider.

> *Everything we did was new, and even the officers were feeling their way round everything.*
>
> Driver J. Wild RASC, 3rd Parachute Platoon 250 Airborne Light Company RASC

However, given the wide range of its responsibilities, its enormous variety of equipment and the constant ground transport tasks, taking soldiers to airfields all over the country for training, it soon became clear that one small RASC company would not be enough to service the needs of the entire division. Early in 1943 Michael St J. Packe was promoted to Lieutenant Colonel and made Commander RASC (CRASC), thereby becoming the divisional commander's advisor on all RASC matters and the commander of RASC troops in the Division. His command was increased from one to three companies. Of these, the original company, specially trained and equipped with jeeps and trailers and known as the Light Company, was to provide an airborne detachment on operations. This detachment would be trained to jump in with the parachute brigades, or land by glider, to provide immediate support to troops in battle whilst they awaited the arrival of reinforcements. Once implemented, this concept would overcome the lack of immediate logistic support felt so keenly by 1st Parachute Brigade in North Africa.

For 250 Company this meant that the forward parachute and glider element was configured into three platoons, each commanded by a captain, with a jeep section in each platoon commanded by a subaltern, and with five jeeps each towing two trailers full of supplies. Each of these two parts of the platoon had a sergeant as second-in-command.

The remainder of the Company comprised the headquarters and workshop personnel, plus two further light jeep platoons. These two jeep platoons would normally expect to travel as part of the Seaborne Echelon,[1] except that if there was any spare room on the air lift they would fly in as additional support elements. Consequently, they were as well trained as the other three platoons. Additionally, the training of the headquarters elements included packing and despatch of panniers and containers from aircraft.

The forward parachute platoons would be designated to a particular brigade and provided limited sustainability for airborne troops to take with them, typically two days supply of ammunition, plus, perhaps, food or fuel. Once on the ground their operational function was to mark out a Supply Dropping Point (SDP) when required, then to retrieve all supplies dropped by air, predominately ammunition, and distribute them to the brigade in need of them. The resupply was normally despatched in panniers from the doors of Dakota aircraft and also in containers held in the bomb bays or under the wings of dual-roled bomber aircraft.

When not being used in this role the platoons were organised to act as an additional brigade headquarters defence platoon. This meant they had to be

The first complete RASC parachute stick, 3 October 1942. Taking part: Back Row, L to R: *SSgt Myers APTC, Capt D T Kavanagh, Capt F G Bate, Dvr Bryce, Sgt Odell, Major M StJ Packe.* Front Row L to R: *LCpl Stanley, Capt J H Gifford, Sgts Walsh, Chedgey, Whitehead.* Courtesy John Gifford

skilled in infantry tactics and in the handling of infantry weapons. They undertook field firing in Yorkshire and on the Pennines in Derbyshire and rough-riding on jeeps and motor cycles on Salisbury Plain. They also practised river crossings, night navigation and night fighting. They had to be able to drive a Bren carrier[2] and to fire every weapon up to 6-pounder[3] anti-tank guns; and they were taught how to use Nobel's explosive to make Gammon bombs.[4]

> *All the men went through the parachute course, and some trained to be specialists, such as medics or signallers. Everyone was highly trained in a variety of weapons: mortars, PIATS[5] etc; and of course had to be proficient as drivers of a range of vehicles. Overall a great deal of emphasis was placed on physical fitness. My platoon once marched thirty-five miles in a day for six consecutive days straight down the Pennines from Scotland to Edale.*
>
> Captain W. V. Gell RASC, Officer Commanding 3rd Parachute Platoon 250 Airborne Light Company RASC

With the formation of a full RASC Column[6] the other two companies were able to take much of the load of air despatching and general transport from the Light Company, and the structure was very much more balanced and effective. 93 Airborne Composite Company RASC was a normal transport company, providing heavier lift and greater bulk carrying capability. Given the size and numbers of its vehicles it would normally expect to travel as part of the Seaborne Echelon.

253 Airborne Composite Company RASC was to provide, essentially, the Division's air despatch capability. However, it was very much more than simply

air despatch, for the unit had to look after the reserve dumps based in the United Kingdom, pre-packing panniers and containers, carrying out maintenance and configuring loads. Their responsibility for loading aircraft began when they examined the rollers and other equipment in the aircraft to ensure that they were correctly fitted and in working order. Lieutenant Colonel Michael Packe provided divisional RASC staff for each dump for stock control, security and load preparation.

Packe regarded his problems in supplying the Division as two-fold: how to get stocks in and then how to distribute them once there.

> *As regards delivery of stocks, after a good deal of more or less technical discussion and an experiment involving a few hearty explosions but, happily, no loss of life, it was decided that the commodities should be pre-packed by the RASC and held by them at a base until an operation started. Some were to be in the cigar-shaped containers which could be dropped by parachute from the bomb racks of heavy aircraft; others, in rectangular wicker baskets (light and resilient) which were to be parachuted by despatching crews of RASC personnel from the doorways of Dakotas fitted with metal roller conveyors.*
>
> Lieutenant Colonel M. St J. Packe RASC, HQ 1st Airborne Division

Lieutenant Colonel Packe modestly omits to point out that the wicker basket was his idea. Seeking, in the early days, ways to drop loads undamaged, and thinking about it whilst at home, his eye had fallen upon the family laundry basket. Realising its qualities of strength, resilience and lightness he had returned to 250 Company, which he commanded at the time, and trials had subsequently proved the success of his concept.

Panniers and containers were pre-packed in certain standard loads identified by code serial numbers and labels. Detailed lists of these standard packs were issued to all concerned so that any formation requiring stores had only to quote the code serial number and the amount for their requirements to be met.

For an operation 253 Company would be faced with the task of collecting the pre-determined loads from the dump areas, driving to the appropriate airfields, loading the aircraft, undertaking the mission, and then, on return, driving back to their own base before repeating the whole thing again the next morning. It made for a full day, and when they weren't busy they undertook normal ground transport duties, ferrying troops and loads of stores. It is worth noting that the

Douglas C47 Dakota. Courtesy Museum of Army Flying

Containers could be held for dropping beneath either the belly or the wings of aircraft. Courtesy Imperial War Museum

Wicker baskets were used to despatch stores from Dakotas via the side-door, or through the bomb bays of dual-roled bomber aircraft, such as the Stirling used at Arnhem. Courtesy Imperial War Museum

Containers could be utilised for a range of stores, including ammunition and spares. This standard 'F' type is carrying weapons. Courtesy Imperial War Museum

Special containers were manufactured for the carriage of specialist equipment, such as radios. Courtesy Imperial War Museum

eventual bill for supporting an airborne division with aerial resupply would be calculated at two hundred and seventy tons, and this would require at least one hundred and thirty five aircraft. 253 Airborne Composite Company's strength was such that it could only man fifty aircraft with four-man crews, and this was a serious weakness in sustaining any operation above brigade level beyond forty-eight hours.

The problem of ensuring proper distribution and support was considered by Packe also to have a significant human dimension. The ethos was established by the divisional commander who was determined that his force would go into battle accompanied by sufficient detachments of all arms and services to make it completely self-contained. He was also clear that all units under his command, without distinction, would be very much in the airborne family as envisaged by Lieutenant General Browning. Lieutenant Colonel

Packe, therefore, ensured that the RASC was well equipped, imbued with a very high morale, smart and soldierly, strictly disciplined, observant, healthy and above all trained as fighters with every conceivable weapon under all imaginable conditions. In return for these extreme standards of conduct, they received small privileges: extra week-end leaves, airborne pay, immunity from the more frustrating type of regulations, the chance to win the parachute wings; and the red beret.

> *Plans for operational resupply must be flexible, and those responsible for delivery resourceful. This at once became the keynote of the RASC elements in 1st Airborne Division when it was raised in 1942.*
>
> Lieutenant Colonel M. St J. Packe RASC

The Royal Army Ordnance Corps

The Ordnance Workshop and Field Park, commanded by Major C. C. Chidgey RAOC, had moved at the end of 1941 into Barton Stacey Camp, near Andover. It was during this time that parachute training, glider loading and flying experience were undertaken. The 1st Battalion The Border Regiment (1st Border) part of the 1st Airlanding Brigade, shared the camp, and was very helpful in providing high-quality infantry training to the unit. It mattered not where one served in the Division's logistic support elements, the ethos was the same: be the best as a tradesman and as a soldier – there was no compromise.

In November 1942 the Corps of Royal Electrical and Mechanical Engineers (REME) was formed, removing from the RAOC the responsibility for repair and maintenance and leaving it purely as a supply corps. Consequently, the workshop element was detached to form a separate unit, leaving Major Chidgey with the balance of the unit now re-titled as 1st Airborne Division Ordnance Field Park[7] (OFP). The senior RAOC officer was the ADOS, Lieutenant Colonel G. A. Mobbs RAOC, and he controlled the activity of all RAOC soldiers in the Division. The role of the OFP was to support the 1st Airborne Division with its requirements for 1st and 2nd line[8] technical spares and assemblies plus all clothing and general stores. It also held large quantities of lashing equipment for gliders and for packing stores to be dropped by parachute.

General stores, such as tentage, rope, camp stores and the like, and clothing, were issued to the OFP in bulk and reissued by breakdown into brigade lots by the Brigade Ordnance Warrant Officers (BOWOs) attached to each of the brigades, and providing brigade commanders with their Ordnance advice and expertise. To help him in this task Major Chidgey had a sergeant and four RAOC soldiers from divisional headquarters permanently attached, and they were reinforced, as necessary with staff provided by the ADOS.

It was the difficulty faced by 1st Parachute Brigade in North Africa that caused Major Chidgey to appreciate the need to have vital support close to hand, and led him to develop the concept of a forward deployable element of the OFP, similar to the forward support sub-units being created by the RASC. He sought to achieve

1st Airborne Division – The Logistic Chain of Command

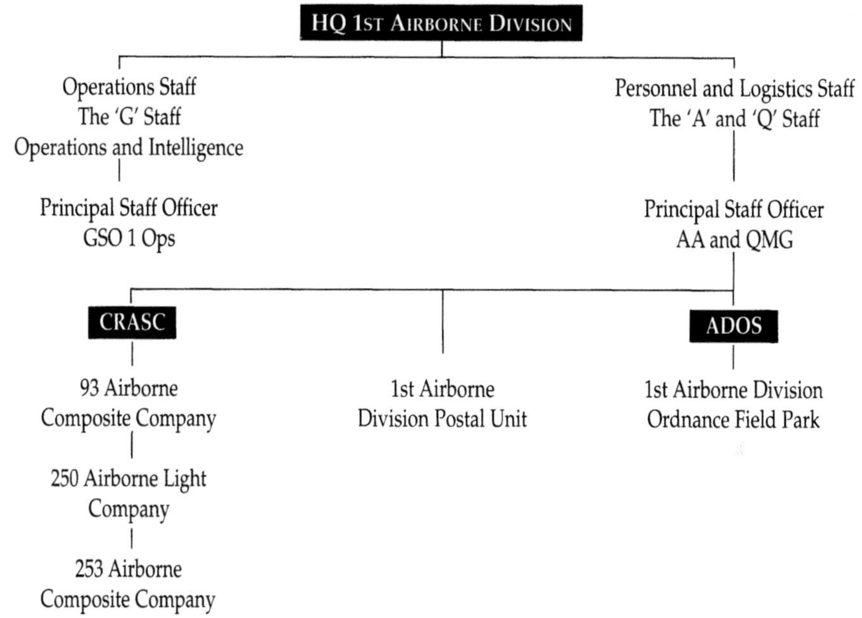

this by using his parachute trained personnel and specially adapted jeeps and trailers. The trailers were configured such that bins lined the sides and the front, facing outwards, and their shelves held the smaller, detailed items of stock. For slightly bulkier stores there was a gap running the length of the trailer between the backs of the bins and it was in here that larger items could be fitted. Typically, these were most likely to be weapons, such as rifles, Sten guns[9] and 2" mortars.[10]

> *Glider troops received a shilling a day, parachutists two shillings and sixpence. But a parachutist only received parachute pay if he was filling an establishment slot designated for parachuting; otherwise he only received the shilling. I had six men per brigade annotated as parachutists. Rank in these cases was less important than being able to do the job, although I did have four sergeants or staff sergeants who were parachute trained and could go anywhere.*
>
> Major C. C. Chidgey RAOC, Officer Commanding 1st Airborne Division OFP

The OFP's total unit vehicle strength, including the airborne detachments, comprised some fifty-five 3-ton and 15-cwt[11] trucks, jeeps, trailers and motor cycles. Altogether some 8,000 different lines of stock were carried, only about 250 of which went with the forward detachment. Some of the 3 -tonners were fitted with racks and bins to hold the range of stores, and the storeman was usually the driver as well. He had to maintain his stock and his vehicle, park it, camouflage it and defend it. Stock control was managed by a card index system called 'Bizada', derived from a commercial application known as 'Business Aid' and which was to be used by the RAOC until 1979 when it was replaced by a computer.

Early 1944 - A Logistic System in Place

Thus it was, by the early part of 1944, 1st Airborne Division possessed a well trained, competent logistic support organisation based on a divisional structure, but capable of providing forward support to brigades operating either independently or as part of a larger airborne operation. It comprised an RASC column of three companies for the transportation and distribution of supplies by air or overland, an OFP to provide spare parts and other stores, both of these units with a forward deployment capability, and a Postal Unit REPS. It was a structure that had developed over some two and a half years and had been built around some hard operational lessons, not only from North Africa, but also from operations undertaken by 1st Airborne Division, or elements of it, in Sicily and Italy.

The logistic units were restricted in what they could carry into battle and there was heavy reliance on a limited air despatch capability. However, as final plans were being laid for the invasion of Europe, to take place in June 1944, 1st Airborne Division was capable of sustaining operations for two days without resupply before it would have to rely on an aerial resupply system manned by 253 Airborne Composite Company RASC which, although well trained, could only deliver what were probably inadequate volumes of stock.

1. There was a considerable amount of an airborne formation's equipment which could not be transported by air, and there were elements of the formation whose presence might not be considered vital in the early days of battle and for whom it would be inappropriate to utilise valuable aircraft space. These would all expect to travel overland to support the formation once relieved by ground troops. There are a number of names shown for this element of the Division: for example Seaborne Echelon in the war diary and Seaborne Tail in the post-operational report. The term chosen for this book is the one that was used predominantly, and appears in the war diary: Seaborne Echelon.
2. The Bren Carrier: a tracked vehicle, open topped and capable of carrying some ten men with a machine gun mounted. It was air transportable in a Hamilcar glider.
3. The 6-pounder: a towed anti-tank gun with a crew of five and capable of firing armour piercing shot for the defeat of armour, literally by punching a hole through it, and high explosive which gave it a limited anti-personnel capability.
4. The Gammon Bomb: The Grenade Hand No 82. It comprised a No 247 Fuze, known as an Always Fuze as it would detonate whichever way it landed. Attached to the fuze was a stockingette bag into which plastic explosive could be crammed, making it a blast grenade of use against tanks where its detonation on the outer armour would peel off flakes of metal inside which then flew around, white hot and at great speed, to the acute discomfort of the occupants.
5. PIAT: Projector Infantry Anti-Tank. This was a shoulder fired, short range anti-tank weapon. A spring loaded spigot fired a light bomb allegedly out to a range of one hundred yards, but that was very much a pious hope. Engagement ranges were very much shorter, and usually measured in a few tens of yards. A shaped charge in the warhead projected a white hot stream of molten copper through the armour, and additional damage to the crew was caused by over-pressure inside the vehicle, to say nothing of the risk of fire from fuel or ammunition.
6. 'Column' was a traditional term, and was used to describe a unit comprising a number of RASC transport or distribution companies in support of field formations; effectively an RASC battalion.
7. Ordnance Field Park: A 'Park' is a storage area in the open, and both the RAOC and the Royal Engineers had them, in the latter case to hold engineer stores. 'Field' shows that the storage area is for the support of a field force formation. Hence 'Ordnance Field Park', a deployable unit holding Ordnance Stores.
8. 1st Line support is essentially that provided by the unit, its quartermaster and any attached tradesmen, such as armourers or mechanics. 2nd Line support is more sophisticated and usually provided to a fighting unit by a separate logistic unit at brigade or divisional level with more equipment and better working facilities.
9. A 9mm calibre sub-machine gun, its ammunition was interchangeable with the German Schmeisser.
10. A small mortar, capable of being fired by one man, it fired a variety of bombs, including High Explosive, Smoke and Illuminating rounds.
11. Cwt: A hundredweight, equivalent to 112 Lbs. 15-cwt refers to a small load carrying vehicle.

CHAPTER TWO

The Preparations Continue

The Further Evolution of Airborne Forces

On 6 June 1944 Allied Armies mounted their assault on occupied France across beaches on the Normandy coast. This seaborne lift was preceded by an airborne assault, dropping at night, with the British contribution being made by 6th Airborne Division, the sister division of 1st Airborne Division.

By now Major General Roy Urquhart was commanding 1st Airborne Division, which had been back in England since the beginning of 1944 from a nine month sojourn in the Middle East and the Mediterranean Theatre. It was located principally in the north and north-east of England. Browning had been promoted to Lieutenant General with the formation, in April 1944, of an airborne corps headquarters to command the two British airborne divisions. The role of 1st Airborne Division during the invasion of Europe was to remain in England, frustrated, as a reserve for 21st Army Group fighting on the continent. 4th Parachute Brigade was at a particularly high state of readiness in case it was required at short notice to reinforce a beachhead in an operation code-named TUXEDO; but, as was to prove the case with other operations over the weeks and months to come, the call never came.

Just before D-Day, on 2 June 1944 the Supreme Headquarters Allied Expeditionary Force (SHAEF) had issued outline proposals for the formation of a combined British and American headquarters for the control of airborne troops, to be considered after the Normandy landings had taken place. On 20 June the headquarters was formed, and its purpose was to generate joint planning between troop carriers and airborne forces, joint training, coordination with ground and naval forces and sufficient technical equipment and supplies both in type and quantity to sustain anticipated operations. Eisenhower was of the view that the whole activity had been 'too loosely organised' and he wanted 'to tighten it up'.[1]

This initiative laid the foundation for the formation of 1st Allied Airborne Army. It was to include 1st British Airborne Corps, which comprised 1st and 6th Airborne Divisions, 1st Special Air Service Brigade and 1st Independent Polish Parachute Brigade. The Americans provided XVIII US Airborne Corps, with 17th, 82nd and 101st Airborne Divisions together with some airborne aviation engineer battalions, and IX US Troop Carrier Command. 38 and 46 Groups RAF would come under operational command of the headquarters when so placed for specific operations by headquarters Allied Expeditionary Air Force (AEAF). In practice 1st Allied Airborne Army would have priority call on these two groups during any major airborne operation.

In addition, though not officially part of 1st British Airborne Corps, 52nd Lowland Division, which had been training as a mountain division before 6 June, was shortly afterwards reorganised as an air-transportable division to support airborne forces once airfields capable of accepting aircraft had been secured.

Browning was made the Army's deputy in addition to commanding his Corps, although it would be August before the Army Headquarters could be placed on anything like an operational footing. And whilst the top-level structure was being put in place 1st Airborne Division continued to train hard for whatever might come its way.

> *Gliders were awful. They gave you sick bags as you got on and once one started to throw up they all did. You were always buffeted in the tug's slipstream. On my first flight it was the pilot's first flight. There were tiny windows and you couldn't see much; and the training was for thirty hours. A mate told me to go parachuting instead, so off I went to Ringway.*
>
> Private F. R. G. Pugh RAOC, 1st Airborne Division OFP Forward Parachute Detachment

> *I was the Company HQ Sergeant for a long time and didn't join 2nd Parachute Platoon until just after D Day when the existing incumbent broke his collar bone. I was the sergeant for the Jeep Section, and very shortly after taking over lost my officer in a traffic accident near Swindon, so I ended up doing both his job and mine. I have a strong memory of glider training and the attempts made to cure air sickness. We went to Newbury race course with the thirty blokes most susceptible to the problem and kept sending them up with different tablets and timed the time to sickness. It was horrible.*
>
> Sergeant W. H. Chedgey RASC, 2nd Parachute Platoon 250 Airborne Light Company RASC

Major C.C. 'Bill' Chidgey RAOC, Officer Commanding 1st Airborne Division OFP.
Author's Collection

Sergeant William Chedgey RASC, pronounced 'Chidgey', and Major C.C. Chidgey RAOC, commanding the OFP, were, coincidentally, both known as 'Bill'. When asked how an officer with the initials 'C. C.' came to be called 'Bill', Major Chidgey was wont to reply, occasionally sternly: 'If your names were Cecil Cyril, you'd be called Bill too!'

To ensure that the Division could be properly sustained for whatever operation it undertook there was, in addition to the intense training programme, a great deal of activity: planning proceeded apace; air despatch resources were enhanced and additional ground logistic support assets were developed and deployed.

Logistic Planning

As the role of 1st Airborne Division after 6 June 1944 was to stand by to carry out at short notice operations of widely varying natures anywhere in France or, later, the Low Countries, any administrative plan had to be flexible in order to cope with the different types of operation, changing orders of battle and varied numbers of aircraft. It also had to be simple, as time for briefing and implementation would be short. Continual planning and subsequent cancellation of operations was demoralising, but at least had the saving grace that people were constantly being briefed and brought up to date and the administrative drills were well understood by all.

All administrative orders[2] for 1st Airborne Division operations were based on two comprehensive administrative instructions issued prior to 6 June. For operations planned subsequently the only details to be sent out were allotments for transit camps and aircraft, resupply details, the locations of the Divisional Administrative Area (DAA)[3] and prisoner of war cage, and money exchange arrangements.

Based around these instructions Michael Packe developed his own ideas, seeking to reduce as much as he could to drills and set procedures in order to minimise briefing for short notice operations, and to remove, as far as possible, the nebulous fog of war once battle was joined. In his Standard Operating Procedure (SOP)[4] of 8 August 1944 he set the template for the deployment of divisional RASC.

He saw three particular commitments. Prior to launching an airborne assault they would have to carry the Division to airfields, transit camps and billets in the south, from where aircraft ranges to the continent were shorter; and they would have to provide the administrative services necessary to launch the airborne element of the Division. Then he would need to provide a full airborne element from HQ RASC and 250 Airborne Light Company RASC to accompany the Division on Scale 'A',[5] as they had practised on exercises. Finally, he would need to make available the maximum number of aircrews for air resupply from 253

King George VI being shown panniers by Captain W.V. Gell RASC, commanding 3rd Parachute Platoon, 250 Light Company. Lieutenant Colonel Packe is in the background. General Urquhart is 'whited out' for 'security reasons'. Courtesy Imperial War Museum

Captain Gell explaining containers to the King. Courtesy Imperial War Museum

Composite Company RASC. To achieve this he required a very small headquarters element, comprising himself, his second-in-command, a clerk and a driver. 250 Company was to detach 1st, 2nd and 3rd Parachute Platoons with their jeep sections to accompany their respective brigades in the 'usual manner'. These platoons would move to airfields under brigade direction, with the jeep sections going in the glider element convoys.

He would have to provide a Seaborne Echelon comprising the balance of HQ RASC, 93 Composite Company RASC complete, and the residue of 250 Airborne Light Company which had not been delivered by air. He planned for his seaborne lift to leave after the airborne element, and to include forty-seven vehicles from 253 Company to supplement unit 1st line transport. He was clear, however, that if sufficient aircraft were available, he would fly in the balance of 250 Company up to the maximum airlift available.

For the task of moving and launching the Division, he was allotted the services of 518, 634 and 636 General Transport (GT) Companies RASC, giving a total of 400 vehicles when added to his own divisional lift.

His policy for loads in the Seaborne Echelon was that 93 Company would have two platoons carrying 2nd line ammunition for the Division based on a predetermined scale. The third platoon would carry one day's compo,[6] plus some additional stores as required. Full AFG1098[7] equipment was to be carried as well as NAAFI packs; and motor cycles were to be carried in the backs of load-carrying vehicles. Interestingly, there is no mention of fuel lift, and Packe notes that any remaining space would be offered up to Divisional Headquarters for any additional stocks they might wish to load.

Similarly, 250 Company's Seaborne Echelon, in addition to the residual, individual, equipment of those going by air, would take only NAAFI packs and AFG1098 equipment. Technical trailers[8] and motorcycles were to be loaded on 3-ton vehicles, although the reason why the trailers were not towed is unclear. Presumably it was to do with a shortage of towing vehicles.

A 'normal' allotment of gliders for the RASC airborne element was expected to be one for HQ RASC, fifteen for the jeep sections of the parachute platoons and up to ten for any additional 250 Company elements that might go by air. Were he to be given additional gliders for 250 Company, Lieutenant Colonel Packe's first priority would be to get the workshops platoon embarked, before Company Headquarters and then additional load carriers. He determined the basic load of a glider as a jeep and two trailers, with its driver and spare driver. A third passenger would normally be a member of a platoon headquarters. This would offer a spare capacity in each glider of 1,000 lb for the carriage of additional stores. In the first glider this would be utilised to carry 250 Company's AFG1098, and all subsequent loads would be made up with artillery ammunition.

Other planned glider allocations were three each for the ADOS[9] and the Commander REME (CREME).

Apart from Packe's well written instructions there appears to have been a dearth of orders on administrative issues. One reference only could be found, in 4th Parachute Brigade, to an administrative order for Arnhem, comprising a half page of typescript covering the operation. It referred to orders issued for Operation LINNET and covered some specific detail about casualty evacuation for the forthcoming operation. Operation LINNET was a corps level operation involving broadly the same force levels as would be used at Arnhem, designed to secure a bridgehead over the Escaut Canal at Tournai. It was never executed.

Resupply from the Air

Much of the developmental work in resupply by air, or air despatch, had come from the Far East where the paucity of overland routes and the nature of the terrain made it a major element in the sustainment of ground forces. In the European Theatre, supply and maintenance by air were planned only as emergency measures rather than as a routine part of the normal system. Given the huge size of the ground force elements, and the daily consumption tonnages of ammunition and fuel, to say nothing of the rest of a major ground force's requirements, aerial resupply could only ever deliver a small fraction of what was required.

There was another difference in the European Theatre: enemy opposition from the air and the ground was much more intense and this had considerable influence on the technique for dropping which was designed to eject the whole load in a single run over the DZ. At Arnhem the Dakota and the Stirling were the two aircraft used for aerial resupply. To discharge panniers from a Dakota, the

RAF pilot would select the course and fly his aircraft at the lowest possible speed and at an agreed height. This gave the crew of four air despatchers, usually commanded by a corporal, the stability and time they needed to despatch their load in one run. The drill entailed dropping sixteen panniers in eight to twelve seconds, and instant obedience to orders from the pilot was essential. The signal was a green light and constant training was required in order to get it right; and it could only be done by working very closely as a team with the RAF crew.

In the case of the Stirling, one of the two air despatchers was hooked into the intercom for the signal to drop. The smaller despatching crew in the Stirling was due to the fact that much of the load was in containers which were dropped from the bomb bay, and this was controlled by the aircrew. Panniers were dropped through the hole in the deck when the bomb doors were open, and with less room and fewer panniers only two men were necessary. However, whilst the Dakota ejected its load by use of a quite sophisticated gravity roller system out through the side door, the air despatchers in a Stirling had to manhandle their load to the hole in the deck and drop it through. It was very hard work, and great dexterity was required to avoid despatching oneself.

For their safety air despatchers used the observer's parachute. They were worn in front and operated by pulling a ripcord, using a 'D' ring. However, in order to avoid the risk of pulling the cord, and hence deploying the parachute, whilst despatching they were kept in a corner of the aircraft until needed. As the air despatch organisation grew in numbers there was less and less opportunity for air despatchers to avail themselves of the parachute training which had been available to Jim Wild and his colleagues in the early days, and many would receive none at all.

The 3-tonner was backed up to the fuselage and the load manhandled on board before pushing it up the gravity rollers of the Dakota. Courtesy Imperial War Museum

> *We had no parachute training at all. When they were issued from stores we were told to strap it on, pull the ring, turn our head to one side, count ten and hope.*
> Driver H. C. Simmonds RASC, 253 Airborne Composite Company RASC

Prior to takeoff the despatching crew would have loaded the aircraft. There was no materials handling equipment to assist them, so the 3-tonner was backed up to the fuselage and the load manhandled on board before pushing it up the gravity rollers of the Dakota, or into the belly of the Stirling. The angle of a parked Dakota was thirty degrees, which made it a very hard uphill push.

Stores to be despatched by air were held in dumps, controlled for 1st Airborne Division by 253 Airborne Composite Company RASC. Packing the loads in the dump areas was a considerable skill and the packers required knowledge of the stresses which would be suffered by loads, and had to assemble them to certain ruling dimensions. Paramount in all this was speed and safety, and the result had to be panniers and containers of a size and weight to exit the aircraft freely, but not so heavy as to damage the load on impact with the ground. Added to this were the precautions which had to be taken when dropping certain kinds of ammunition. Some fuzes could arm under the impact of sudden shock, and the advice of RAOC IOOs[10] and AEs[11] was invaluable here; and for this reason they were attached to air despatch units.

Whilst there was a great deal of work going on to refine despatching drills and procedures and to train crews to work closely with the RAF, there was a significant shortfall in the volume of supplies that could be delivered by the airborne composite companies in each of the two British airborne divisional RASC columns. Then, in the spring of 1944, 21st Army Group, commanding British operations in Europe, set a requirement for a resupply capability by air for its ground forces for 350 tons a day air landed, and 3,000 tons a day air dropped. It was only possible for 253 Company to crew fifty sorties per day, eighty-five crews short for just their own division's requirements; and the same was true for its sister company in 6th Airborne Division, 63 Airborne Composite Company RASC. To meet the 21st Army Group requirement a new and separate capability was required for the support of ground forces.

This entailed a huge expansion of air despatch resources, and three companies were formed, a total of twelve despatching platoons with each platoon comprising seventy-four soldiers of all ranks. They were re-roled from two other units and on 3 May 1944 Lieutenant Colonel L.W. Walsh, commanding No 8 Training Battalion RASC, called together his officers and men to introduce his namesake, Lieutenant Colonel S.W. Walsh, the Commanding Officer of No 36 Lines of Communication Transport Column. Lieutenant Colonel S.W. Walsh had instructions to bring the two units together and to form and command 48 Air Despatch Column. The Training Battalion was to break up to become 799 and 800 Air Despatch Companies, whilst 223 Air Despatch Company formed from the Lines of Communication Column. They were stationed in the south of England, 223 Company at Burford, 799 Company at Stratton St Margaret and 800 Company at Down Ampney. The Column Headquarters was at Ashton Keynes,

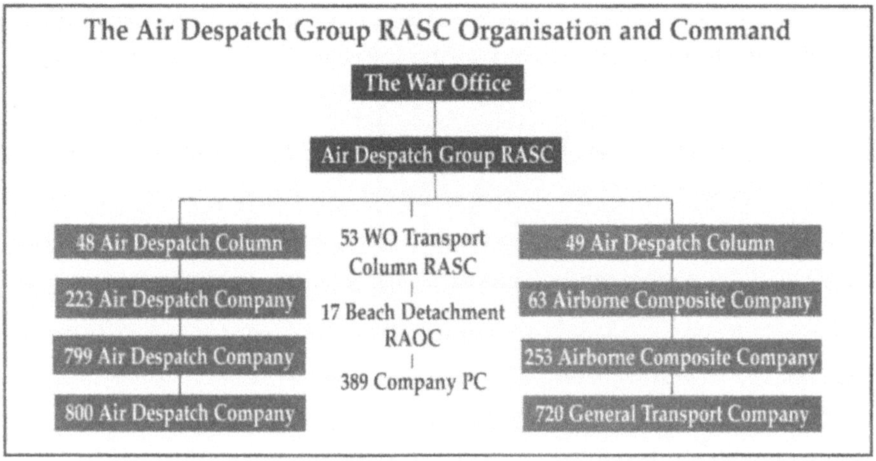

controlled directly by the War Office and not by headquarters Airborne Forces.

The outcome of all this was a split in responsibility, with two organisations involved in air despatch. In the Airborne Corps, 253 and 63 Companies were controlled by the Deputy Director Supplies and Transport (DDST)[12] Airborne Troops, Colonel T.H. Jeffries. Formerly in 1st Airborne Division, and Michael Packe's predecessor as CRASC, he was a man immersed in airborne logistics. The two airborne composite companies were not organised as a special establishment as were the air despatch companies in 48 Column, but were composed of a headquarters, three transport platoons, a composite platoon and a workshops platoon. It was the drivers in the transport platoons and relief driver increments who were intended to undertake the onerous task of driving to the airfields with their lorries loaded with stores for the aircraft, accompanying the stores in flight, despatching them from the air and then returning to their airfields and their lorries and driving them home. They had no general transport support, and had to do just about everything themselves.

Colonel Jeffries understood very clearly that the air despatch support to each of the airborne divisions was inadequate, and that if Browning's vision of a divisional operation, cut off from ground support for several days, was to be sustainable he would need the additional support of the new air despatch column. He negotiated with the War Office to obtain agreement, but had to accept that there would have to be a rationalisation of air despatch resources. The outcome was to form the two airborne composite companies into a second air despatch column, and to reinforce them with a general transport company to help relieve some of the pressure. Thus was borne 49 Air Despatch Column, comprising 63 and 253 Airborne Composite Companies and 720 GT Company RASC. The airborne composite companies each controlled a dump of five days stocks of supplies, and 720 Company's job was to transport them from the dumps to the airfields. A commanding officer was appointed to 49 Column, and he came, initially, under Colonel Jeffries' control. Headquarters 49 Column was located at The Piggeries, Down Ampney.

The next logical step was to draw the two air despatch columns into a single, cohesive organisation. This led to the creation of an Air Despatch Group, which also took command of 53 War Office Transport Column for the carriage of supplies from, to and between dumps and airfields. The commander was also made administratively responsible for 17 Ordnance Beach Detachment RAOC, not for beach operations, but to help manage control of stocks. Finally, he took under command 389 Company PC as a labour force. With the formation of the Air Despatch Group the War Office undertook responsibility for the maintenance by air of all formations, ground and airborne, including the Special Air Service. Consequently, control of its own air despatch support was removed from Headquarters Airborne Forces. Lieutenant Colonel S.W. Walsh RASC, the founder of 48 Air Despatch Column, was promoted into the role of Air Despatch Group Commander.

There was an essential difference between the two air despatch units. 48 Column was brought into being purely for the air despatch role, and its air despatchers were trained accordingly. The two air despatch companies in 49 Column, however, were airborne soldiers, glider and parachute trained, entitled to wear wings, the Pegasus badge of airborne forces and the coveted red beret; and trained to a high pitch in many more skills than air despatching. They considered themselves different, behaved as if they were different and were determined to be treated differently; with all the privileges that went with being a part of Britain's airborne forces.

This then was the final shape of an organisation which came into being on 18 August 1944, and which would support Operation MARKET GARDEN.

Developments in the Overland Resupply Situation

Watching events in France, and concerned at its own inactivity, the frustrations began to build in 1st Airborne Division as it was warned for operation after operation, only to have them cancelled as the reasons for them were overtaken by events on the ground in Europe. The benefit, however, of the Airborne Corps' staff reviewing their plans each time an operation was in prospect should not be overlooked. It gave them the chance to identify shortcomings in their planning and organisation and implement remedies, given time. One outcome was the realisation that there was no airborne forces logistic support other than that within the two divisions with nothing at corps level. Browning realised that he had a significant capability gap: there was nothing to deliver ground resupply into a deployed division, either from a captured airfield or from other, conventional, ground formations. Furthermore, with 52nd Lowland Division now allocated as an air transportable formation, he knew that if it flew into a captured airfield he had nothing with which to undertake airfield clearance or to provide other support which might be necessary.

Consequently, in July 1944, he obtained agreement from 21st Army Group to form an Airborne Forward Delivery Airfield Group (AFDAG). Its task was to receive troops, transport and stores arriving by air on one or more airfields. It was also to receive and hold stores of all descriptions and forward them to the fighting elements; and to take in, hold and return to the United Kingdom all casualties and salvage; and it was to be able to take control of the whole airhead. It was to train in order that it could function equally well on an airfield which had been constructed as it could on a firm, permanent base. However, since there was no British airborne engineer airfield construction capability, operating on a damaged or non-permanent airfield could only be done with US assistance using their gliderborne engineers.

It was Operation TRANSFIGURATION that was to provide the impetus for the bringing together of the units to form the AFDAG, and for the Seaborne Echelon to embark for the continent. The operation, planned to take place between 7 and 17 August, would have involved the 1st British Airborne Corps deploying two divisions and the Independent Polish Parachute Brigade. TRANSFIGURATION was to have been undertaken in conjunction with Operation LUCKY STRIKE B, a plan for a sweeping armoured movement around the southern flank of the German forces in Normandy. Operation TRANSFIGURATION envisaged the capture of an airfield which, once made serviceable by a US airborne aviation engineer battalion, would have been used to land 52nd Lowland Division, thereby providing a forward base and pivot from which Allied armour could go forward into Paris.

In the firm belief that TRANSFIGURATION would take place and not be subject to cancellation, headquarters 1st Airborne Division ordered, on 12 August, units of the Seaborne Echelon to begin leaving their peacetime locations. They were to move to the continent so as to be in position to provide support when the airborne landings took place. 250 Airborne Light Company's base was at Branston in Lincolnshire, except for 2nd Parachute Platoon, commanded by Captain Desmond Kavanagh, known to many as 'Paddy', which was in Nissen huts at Oakham, and which was designated to support 4th Parachute Brigade. The Company was commanded by Major John Gifford. He had been with the unit since the very early days when it was part of 31st Independent Infantry Brigade Group. When Michael Packe had been promoted to become CRASC it had been John Gifford, who had moved up to fill his place. He deployed with the Seaborne Echelon of 250 Company, in accordance with Michael Packe's vision for the use of RASC assets in support of a divisional operation. With his three parachute platoons well dispersed supporting their brigades he would be able to serve the Division best bringing the whole company back together once the Seaborne Echelon had joined up. Consequently, he took his headquarters, his workshop platoon and two light jeep platoons overland, leaving the other three to go and join their brigades, ready to fly.

Major John Gifford RASC, Officer Commanding 250 Airborne Light Company RASC
Courtesy Imperial War Museum

Major R. Tompkins commanded the much larger 93 Airborne Composite Company. He left Hartsholme Hall, near Lincoln, on 13 August with, among other things, some seventy 3-tonners, seven 15-cwt trucks and twenty-eight motorcycles. Departing early, he arrived in his transit camp at 8.30 p.m. that night.

At 7.00 a.m. on the same morning Warrant Officer Class One (WO1) Don Eyres was surveying the OFP seaborne party as it paraded in the playground of Spitalgate School, in Grantham in Lincolnshire – just near the railway station. The unit had been billeted there since Christmas, on its return to England from the Mediterranean. Don Eyres was to take with him thirty-eight soldiers from the OFP, together with a warrant officer and ten soldiers from the ADOS' staff at Divisional Headquarters. Bill Chidgey had decided that he would best serve his unit's role if he were to deploy with the airborne party, and therefore would remain in England. He had only two other officers: Captain Bernard Manley and Lieutenant Duncan Bell. He required Bernard Manley, a parachute trained officer, so that he could, if necessary, deploy an advanced parachute detachment with an officer, which meant keeping him back in England. As to Duncan Bell, it was Bill Chidgey's view that he did not have the technical experience to provide the OFP Seaborne Echelon with the guidance it required in order to function effectively. In any event, he had complete faith in WO1 Eyres

> *Don Eyres was a man who looked like nothing, and who did everything.*
> Major C. C. Chidgey RAOC, Officer Commanding 1st Airborne Division Ordnance Field Park

However, to offset the lack of an officer in the OFP Seaborne Echelon, Lieutenant Colonel Gerry Mobbs RAOC, the ADOS, detached his Ordnance Officer (OO), Captain Wally Gratrix, to the Seaborne Echelon headquarters and placed him in charge of the RAOC elements.

At Don Eyres' word of command the drivers started their engines, moving out of the school and turning right towards Grantham High Street and the start of their long journey to the Port of London. The convoy included ten binned 3-tonners, four GS 3-tonners,[13] one 3-tonner for battery charging and another for battery storage. There were also two 15-cwt GS vehicles and a 15-cwt water truck, two jeeps each fitted for carrying four stretchers, thirteen 4x4 5-cwt vehicles, ten binned trailers and six GS trailers. Twelve hours later, tired and in need of a meal and some sleep, they arrived at their transit camp.

Captain Wally Gratrix RAOC
Courtesy Imperial War Museum

Loading day was 14 August, and at this stage Operation TRANSFIGURATION was running to plan. Loading, therefore, commenced early that morning at East and West India Docks and the Victoria and Albert Docks.

At about the same time as loading was beginning in the Port of London, Major G F Patterson of the Royal Sussex Regiment, commanding 8 Forward Maintenance Area Control Centre (FMACC) in France, received a telephone call. He was operating as part of XXX Corps and his 8.00 a.m. telephone call from XXX Corps Rear Headquarters[14] advised him that he was to move by air to England at 1.00 p.m., in five hours time. He was ordered to take no stores or equipment with him and had no idea that he was to form the headquarters of

Lieutenant General Browning's AFDAG. With his second-in-command, Captain G.B. Sacher RASC, a sergeant, a corporal and five drivers he set off. Their journey was beset by difficulties over aircraft and it was in two parties that they eventually arrived at RAF Northolt, on the western edge of London. At 6.00 p.m. that day, just ten hours after the telephone call, he was in Rickmansworth at Headquarters 1st Airborne Corps where the outline of the role of the AFDAG in support of airborne operations was explained to him and his bemused staff.

Meanwhile, loading the Seaborne Echelon continued apace. It was a considerable task, with the total strength being some 84 officers, 2,180 non-commissioned ranks and 1,100 vehicles. Major R.D. Sellon of the 7th Battalion The King's Own Scottish Borderers (7th KOSB) commanded the whole Seaborne Echelon and they took with them 2nd Line ammunition and explosives, two days' compo rations for the whole division, fifty miles of petrol for every vehicle and the large packs containing the personal kit of the men in the airborne element, as well as cooking and office equipment. In addition, it was appreciated that supplies of 75mm ammunition for the divisional artillery might be difficult to obtain overseas and consequently each vehicle carried twelve rounds, giving a total of 4,500 rounds over and above normal 2nd Line allotments.

93 Company divided into two parties for loading on two transport ships, T298 and T299, embarking at 6.30 p.m. The OFP, however, had to wait and the soldiers returned to the transit camp that night. Don Eyres was a little perturbed as he left the docks, since earlier that afternoon, at 4.00 p.m., a binned 3-tonner carrying vital wireless spares had been dropped from a crane onto the edge of a hatchway during loading. The lorry had been hauled up to find that the prop shaft had been bent and would require replacement. It had been left on deck in order that repairs could be carried out, but there was no spare immediately available. An urgent demand had been sent to the huge Ordnance Depot at Bicester, near Oxford, seeking the swift delivery of the required part. The courier arrived at midnight, but, with an almost farcical inevitability, the item he delivered was found to be the wrong one for the vehicle. The item was redemanded, and arrived at 7.00 a.m. the next day. The repair was effected, and the vehicle successfully loaded.

WO1 Don Eyres RAOC. Author's Collection

On 15 August the Seaborne Echelon was on the high seas, crossing the Channel and heading for the invasion beaches in Normandy, just as Major Patterson and the AFDAG's new headquarters moved to Newcombe Barracks at Larkhill on Salisbury Plain. One early decision, however, had detached the 1st Airborne Division Postal Unit to the AFDAG, and Lieutenant J.E. Morris REPS, with a sergeant and thirteen junior NCOs and sappers moved to Larkhill. They were not to see the Division again until 26 September, at the end of the Arnhem operation.

The AFDAG was beginning to assemble with some speed. 165 Company RASC (Airborne Light), a newly-formed unit, equipped with fifty-five jeeps and eighty-one trailers, was among the first to arrive. At about the same time the advance party of 277 Company PC appeared, the balance of the unit having remained, for the time being, in France, where it had landed on D Day. At 3.00 pm some jeeps and unit equipment were obtained by Major Patterson's headquarters, and at 6.00 p.m. that evening the operation order was received. They were to be prepared, with everything at six hours notice to move with effect from 9.00 a.m. on 17 August, just fifteen hours later. And just as they were as ready as they could be the operation was postponed.

The postponement, however, came too late for the Seaborne Echelon for they were already disembarking onto Juno Beach and moving up to the Goldsmith Assembly Area prior to moving on to the area around the town of La Mine. For most units the move into their new locations was simple, but the area selected off a map for the OFP proved unsatisfactory. After a short reconnaissance a most suitable orchard was found and by 10.00 p.m. they were in place and the whole organisation was settled for the night.

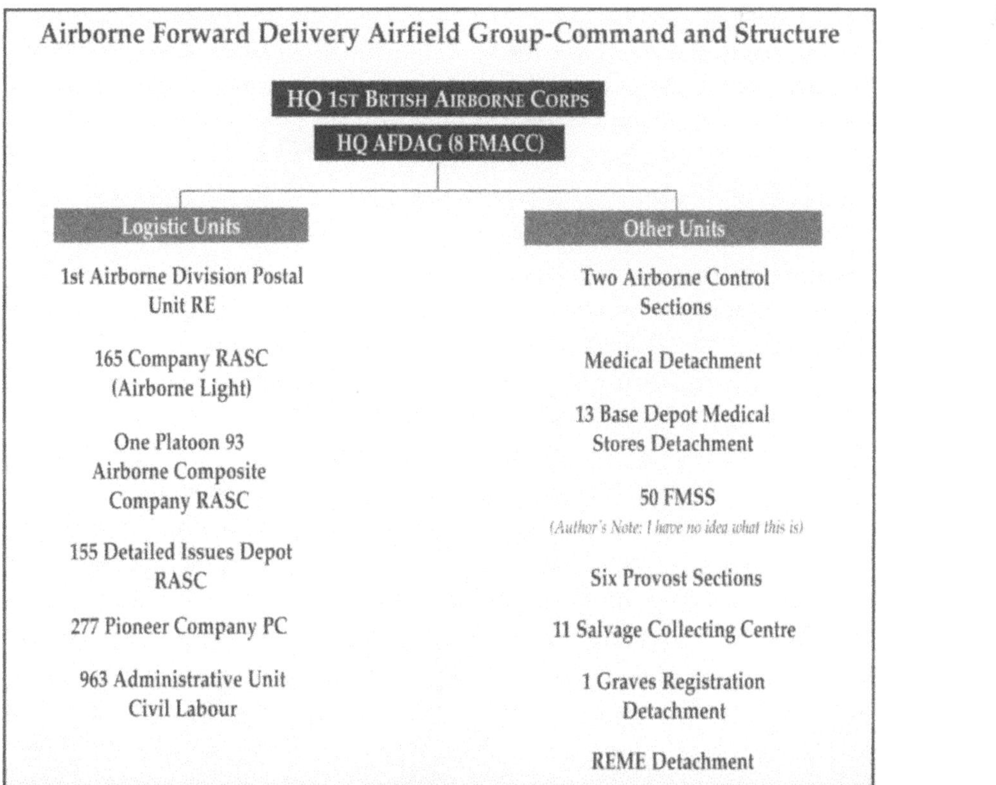

There was great excitement among the units spending their first night on the continent, with their brethren left behind in England poised, so they thought, very shortly to be a part of a decisive attack on the Germans in Europe. Lieutenant Richard Adams summed up the mood:

> *Although there was not yet a lot to do and not a lot to see except for the partly tidied up wreckage of the early battlefields, we were all strung up to a pitch of excitement which even the coolness of John Gifford could not altogether dispel. The Division was going into action at last! We had grown tired of khaki-bereted louts outside pubs at closing time shouting 'Yah! airborne - stillborn!' and similar witticisms. 6th Division had been the flower of the invasion; we felt sure we were to be the flower of the final victory.*[15]
>
> Lieutenant R. G. Adams RASC, OC C Platoon, 250 Airborne Light Company RASC

However, their enthusiasm was to be tempered by the cancellation of the operation on 18 August, and on the 19th the AFDAG HQ was sent on forty-eight hours leave. Meanwhile, in La Mine a mobile NAAFI, provided by the Expeditionary Forces Institute (EFI),[16] was attached to the Seaborne Echelon. Whilst they were in La Mine it was decided that OFP stocks would remain frozen in order to preserve its holdings for when they were needed by 1st Airborne Division. All demands from seaborne echelon units were to be referred to 17 Advanced Ordnance Depot at 'Red Hot' priority for immediate issue to the demanding unit.

As the training and preparation went on 1st Airborne Division was faced with the fact that much of its logistic support was on the other side of the Channel and virtually incommunicado; 21st Army Group was faced with a Seaborne Echelon on the continent for which it had no apparent short or medium-term role; and the AFDAG was faced with nothing to do. In the latter case, the problem was resolved by sending the headquarters back to France into its original role as an FMA Control Centre. It left on 23 August to be told, on arrival at XXX Corps Rear Headquarters, that it was to coordinate an Army 'roadhead cushion' northeast of Falaise.[17]

Meanwhile, in France, almost inevitably, petty disruptions were being visited on the Seaborne Echelon. Given the acute shortage of transport for the support of the ground forces, the bulk of this inconvenience fell on 93 Company whose size and shape made it invaluable as a general transport resource. For example, the Company was told to be ready to move by 10.00 p.m. on 21 August, prior to which they had been hoping to watch a film entitled *Dangerous Blondes* in the recreational tent. However, the tent leaked, the film was damaged, and the showing, and all subsequent shows, had to be cancelled. The next morning the move was cancelled, and arrangements were made for use of the Company's transport by 5 Lines of Communication Sub Area, which was operating from La Mine. 93 Company would spend the rest of August being messed around in a similar fashion, and undertaking general transport tasks in the Normandy area.

Oddly, although the AFDAG was now leaderless with its headquarters back in France, units were still being posted to join it. On 28 August 963

Administrative Unit Civil Labour (AUCL), a small unit of five from the Pioneer Corps, was warned to go to Bulford. Its role would be to recruit and administer local civil labour in support of AFDAG activity once it deployed on operations. Of the two officers, one, Major S. Clapp PC, was the OC, whilst Lieutenant H.S. Thompson PC was the Pay and Supervising Officer. The remainder comprised a sergeant and two private soldiers.

The AFDAG headquarters was off somewhere else in Le Mesnil at this stage, but not for very long. Indeed, the very next day, 29 August, at two in the morning, Major Patterson was ordered to proceed, with his headquarters, and with almost indecent haste, back to England. He was given until 5.00 p.m. that afternoon to make the journey. He was less than happy, and by 9.30 that morning was in XXX Corps rear headquarters advising the AA&QMG that he was: 'Far too old for this sort of thing'. It was to no avail, and very shortly he was on his way back to England to retake control of the AFDAG.

In England, as plans were continually being made for a range of airborne operations, and the logistic support arrangements constantly reviewed, it was most inconvenient having such a large slice of the Division's logistic assets on the far side of the Channel; and redistributing and reallocating them to meet changing circumstances was a complex and time-consuming affair. However, notwithstanding this, Major John Gifford was ordered to send three jeep sections back to the UK, and gave the task of selecting them to Lieutenant Richard Adams, commanding C Platoon.

> *There was no section of the seven in the Platoon with which one would seize the opportunity to part. Sergeant Smith, Sergeant Potter and I decided to put seven bits of paper into a beret and draw three out. The three names which came out were Corporal Baxter, Corporal Pickering and Corporal Hollis. Level-headed and cool, they got their men together and were off within the hour, eventually to go to Arnhem in a glider. I was not to see them again until well after the war.*[18]
>
> Lieutenant R. G. Adams RASC

This left Lieutenant Adams with four sections, commanded by Corporals Rawlings, West, Simmons and Herdman.

Meanwhile, the build-up of the AFDAG continued. The balance of 277 Company PC left France from Mike Beach on an LST[19] and went to Bulford, near Salisbury, in the south of England, to Tented Camp 5, and joined its advance party which had been there since 19 August. With a strength of 260, the Company was commanded by Major F.B. Wooding PC.

> *On arrival in Bulford they were issued with the familiar red berets and paratrooper smocks, and the excitement was terrific, although we had no idea what sort of operation was planned and less than five percent of the unit had ever been in a 'plane'.*
>
> Major F. B. Wooding PC, Officer Commanding 277 Company PC

Jeeps with trailers were also issued to 277 Company, the Company's normal heavy transport, with their accompanying stores, having remained in France and been sent to join the Seaborne Echelon.

The next day the FMA Control Centre arrived in Fargoe Camp, Larkhill as HQ AFDAG where it was to stay until 18 September. Meanwhile, 963 AUCL was ordered to proceed to No 5 Tented Camp in Bulford.

> *September sunshine found five puzzled members of 963 Administrative Unit Civil Labour frantically packing kit. They had been informed that they were part of 1st Airborne Division and that they were already a day late in joining their new formation at an airfield. Arrival at Bulford did nothing but add to the puzzle. After two hectic hours they found themselves in red berets and smocks and were the proud possessors of a jeep, trailer and parachute helmets. Here too they met their comrades, including 277 Pioneer Corps Company. This company had been recalled to England from Normandy after taking part in the land assault. They had been told they were wanted for a 'special task', which later turned out to be work with the Airborne Forward Delivery Airfield Group, loading stores and establishing dumps.*
>
> Major S. Clapp PC, Officer Commanding 963 AUCL

Also allocated to the AFDAG was 155 Detailed Issues Depot RASC, commanded by Captain L.I.M. Bruce-Vickers RASC. There were two other officers,

Major John Gifford's hand-drawn map of the route followed by the Seaborne Echelon to the Dutch Border.
Courtesy John Gifford

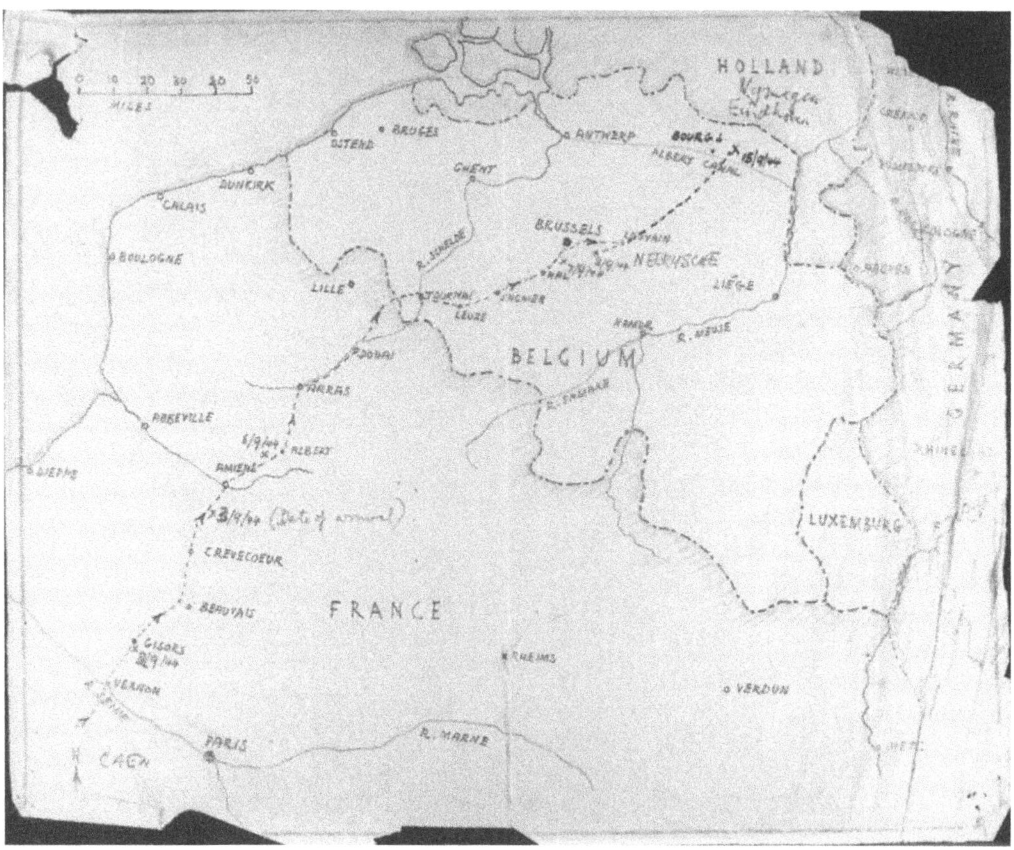

Lieutenants D.J. Lacey and M.B. Aston, in the unit with thirty-four soldiers and on 1 September they commenced drawing their airborne equipment. The unit's role would be to break down bulk fresh rations into detailed lots for issue to individual units. Once they had drawn their equipment they were to spend the rest of their time split between Lutterworth Camp and Spanhoe Airfield, practising loading jeeps and trailers into aircraft. They were helped in this by the soldiers of 277 Company PC.

And, as further reinforcement for the AFDAG, a transport platoon of 93 Airborne Composite Company, commanded by Captain Naylor RASC, returned from France to join 165 Company RASC (Airborne Light). Comprising fifty-eight soldiers in addition to the officer, they travelled in a jeep and two 3-ton trucks.

Very early in September it began to seem more and more likely that 1st Airborne Division might be used, and the pace and intensity of preparatory activity became intense. The Seaborne Echelon was ordered to move from its location in Normandy north to Cisars. In accordance with SOPs, supplemented by local instructions issued at the time, haversack rations were taken, tentage was struck and handed back to the OFP, slit trenches and latrines were filled in and the locations of latrines were marked as 'FOUL GROUND'. All unit signs and evidence of occupation were removed before locations were vacated. There was a clear sense of urgency in the Seaborne Echelon:

> *Well, then it came time to follow up, along with 2nd Army's pursuit. And my God, did we move. 1st Airborne might drop at any time and its seaborne tail was required to be in the van, close behind our tanks and infantry. We crossed the Seine on a Bailey Bridge at Vernon and after that it was simply a question of keeping going night and day. Sleep when you can, eat when you can. I got so sick of Spam that I could be really hungry and still be unable to face another plate of it.*
> Lieutenant R.G. Adams RASC

The Tide of Battle Turns

Meanwhile, in Europe things were changing. The advance of the Allied armies after the breakout from the Normandy beachhead had exceeded planned times and distances beyond belief. Paris was liberated on 25 August and Brussels on 3 September. The Germans were in headlong and disorganised retreat and the Allies seemed unstoppable.

It was then, at this critical moment, that logistics, and the limitations they impose on the aspirations and plans of even the greatest of field commanders, began seriously to impact on operations. With Allied Armies on the Franco-German and Dutch-Belgian borders it was 400 miles from the invasion beaches to the front line. For as long as the Germans held channel ports such as Calais, Dunkirk and Boulogne it was across these beaches that all supplies had to come, and from there be transported to the battle front.

There was simply insufficient transport to meet the needs of the armies. Fuel was a major problem: over a million gallons a day were required and only a fraction of that was getting through. The British left an entire corps west of the Seine simply to use its transport in order to supplement the overall lift; and an American armoured division was halted for four days, starved of fuel.

The Allies were slowing; it was perceptible, indeed obvious, and the Germans were not slow either to spot or to capitalise on it. Yet, even as German defences began to strengthen and the advance on Germany faltered, and then halted, the circumstances were evolving that would give the men of 1st Airborne Division what they believed would be their day.

1. General Dwight D. Eisenhower in a letter to General George C. Marshall Chief of the General Staff, United States Army, 28 July 1944.
2. In the British Army an administrative order, or the administrative element of an operation order, covered, inter alia, all logistic support matters. 'Administration' was the 'catch-all' word for logistics and personnel issues.
3. DAA: an area, usually in the rear of the divisional area, where the logistic units were gathered and logistic stocks were dumped or held on wheels.
4. Standard Operating Procedure: orders or instructions, almost always written and well practised, for standard procedures. The purpose was to simplify matters in the heat of battle.
5. It has not been possible to ascertain what is meant by Scale A, but it is presumed to mean two days of supply for ammunition, rations and fuel for a particular level and intensity of operations.
6. Compo: composite rations. See Annex 8.
7. AFG1098 is the book (Army Form G1098) which records the unit's account of its equipment. Consequently, it has been taken into common usage as the 'collective noun' for a unit's equipment; often referred to simply as the 'Gee Ten'.
8. Technical Trailer: a 'normal' trailer which had been adapted for the carriage of specialist equipment or stores. Typically, with stowage bins fitted to hold spare parts, or with, say, a generator, power tool or test set mounted.
9. Of the three logistic service heads in a division, two (RASC and REME) were 'Commanders' and one (RAOC) was an 'Assistant Director'. This was a historical hangover from the days when the RAOC was considered 'non-combatant', unlike the RASC which had always enjoyed 'combatant' status. The anomaly was removed by Army Order 179 of 22 October 1941, declaring the RAOC a 'combatant' service. REME, forming out of the RAOC in November 1942, went straight to 'combatant' status.
10. IOO: Inspecting Ordnance Officer, the forerunner of today's Ammunition Technical Officer. He was a specialist in ammunition, having undertaken a course of approximately a year in order to qualify.
11. AE: Ammunition Examiner, the forerunner of today's Ammunition Technician, the non-commissioned equivalent of the IOO.
12. Deputy Director Supplies and Transport: a senior RASC officer, normally a Colonel or Brigadier, depending on the headquarters in which he worked. He was the senior RASC officer in the formation, and in this case, as DDST 1st Airborne Corps, he was Lieutenant Colonel Packe's technical/functional superior.
13. GS means General Service, and denotes a vehicle or equipment which has a general use, and is not modified for a special purpose.
14. Rear HQ is one of the segments into which a formation HQ might break down. Main HQ would be where the General Officer Commanding (GOC) would normally be found, and he might also have a Tactical, or Tac, HQ. Rear HQ is normally run by the senior logistics staff officer, some distance in rear of Main HQ and was where most of the logistic staff and the service branches, such as RASC and RAOC, would be found. Rear HQ commands the DAA.
15. From 'The Day Gone By' by Adams, Hutchinson, London 1990, for this and all quotes from Lieutenant R.G. Adams RASC.
16. Expeditionary Forces Institute: NAAFI, the Services' canteen and shop provider is a civilian organisation. Many of its personnel, however, volunteer for service as in the Expeditionary Forces Institute; essentially NAAFI in uniform. They have Territorial Army status, are currently part of the RLC, and in 1944 wore the RASC cap badge.
17. 'Roadhead cushion' is a gathering of vehicles pending further moves much as a railhead for rail traffic.
18. All those missing from C Platoon after the battle were found to be prisoners of war.
19. LST: Landing Ship Tank, a flat-bottomed boat which could run up onto a beach and could be used for short sea crossings, such as the Channel.

Chapter Three

Beyond the Point of No Return

The Germans Begin to Steady

Field Marshal Model was desperate. The third commander of the German armies in the west in just two months, his line was crumbling everywhere and his pleas to Hitler for reinforcements grew daily more frenetic. His greatest concern was that Antwerp, were it to be captured, would provide the Allies with the port they required to shorten their over-extended lines of communication. His requests were unreasonable, and went unheeded: Germany could not provide the twenty-five divisions and an armoured reserve of five or six Panzer Divisions he sought.

Antwerp did in fact fall, on 4 September, to the British 11th Armoured Division. However, the Division's commander, Major General Roberts, had only been told to take the port. He did not exploit further to secure the north bank of the River Scheldt, thereby denying the Allies the use of Antwerp for so long as the river remained under German control, and alleviating Model's concern by an accident of oversight.

The British failure to dominate the whole of the port of Antwerp was a major strategic blunder. Lieutenant General Sir Brian Horrocks, commanding the British XXX Corps, of which 11th Armoured Division was a part, was later to admit that he had been concentrating so much on trying to get across the Rhine he had failed to appreciate the significance of the Scheldt's north bank. This was despite the huge logistic difficulties facing the Allies, and which were already impacting directly on his own corps' operational capability. It was a failure the Allies would live to regret.

On 1 September, Model had been replaced as the German commander in the west by Field Marshal von Rundstedt, who was returning to a post from which he had been sacked only two months earlier following a disagreement with Hitler on how to conduct the defence of Germany's western borders. Model moved down a peg, to take command of the northern sector of von Rundstedt's command, a task to which he was ideally suited. His last act, however, before moving to his new headquarters, was to order II SS Panzer Corps commander, Lieutenant General Wilhelm Bittrich, to take his two battered divisions somewhere quiet in order that they might repair and refurbish as much as they could of the damage they had suffered in battles in France. Accordingly, they agreed that the 9th SS (Hohenstaufen) and 10th SS (Frundsberg) Divisions would go into billets just north of the peaceful Dutch town of Arnhem.

Von Rundstedt's arrival back in the headquarters of Oberbefehlshaber West (OB West)[1] coincided with the slow down in the Allied advance, and gave him the time he needed to thicken up his defences on the Dutch-Belgian border.

General Student's 1st Parachute Army, a scratch force mixing a few veterans with the scrapings of various elements of the Army, Air Force and Navy, was in place within four days. Von Zangen's 15th Army was moved north across the Scheldt from its positions in the Pas de Calais in a remarkably skilful operation, taking some two weeks. Between them, these two generals began to develop the beginnings of a defence against an Allied assault into the Netherlands from Belgium.

Meanwhile, von Rundstedt put in place mechanisms to slow the headlong retreat of German soldiers through and out of Holland. With remarkable speed a coherent defence began to take shape, weapons and men began to arrive from Germany and daily, hourly, the Allied task was being made more and more difficult. Von Rundstedt was certain that the slowdown was not simply a pause, but a virtual halt, and he exploited every moment it offered.

Discord Among the Allies

Field Marshal Montgomery had for some time been proposing a narrow thrust into the very heart of Germany, taking the Ruhr, thereby destroying Hitler's industrial base, and striking for Berlin. His vision was for a force of forty-two divisions, twenty of which would be an armoured spearhead; and he would command it. Given all the resources the Allies could throw at it, he believed that such a thrust would overcome the logistic shortcomings they were experiencing, and shorten the war significantly.

Eisenhower's instinctive preference was for a broad approach, advancing simultaneously across a wide area and exploiting German weakness by not allowing them to concentrate. The debate about narrow and broad fronts was to be a major cause of disagreement between Montgomery and Eisenhower, and the other army commanders. Eisenhower simply could not agree to Montgomery's narrow front suggestion – the American public would not stand for huge numbers of Americans being under a British commander who found little favour with them and the British would be seen to be taking the credit in a war which had cost the US so much in men and material. Operationally, he was also concerned that the Germans, so swift and powerful in the counter-attack, might cut off Montgomery's thrust and there would be little left in reserve with which to rescue it.

Montgomery, chafing with frustration, was not to be put off. He continued to believe passionately in the potential for success of his narrow front vision. He pressed it with Eisenhower to the point of greatly angering the Supreme Commander, and even volunteered to operate under the American General Bradley if it would make Eisenhower see Montgomery's version of reason. This however, would have been as unacceptable an outcome to the British public as the prospect of Montgomery running it would have been to their American counterparts. Eisenhower was not to be swayed: for political and operational reasons he held to the view that the advance had to continue across a broad front.

However, on 7 September 1944, during a visit to his HQ by Prince Bernhard of the Netherlands, Montgomery announced that it was his intention to liberate the Netherlands, and that he was planning an airborne operation ahead of his ground troops. He had, some days earlier, been given command of 1st Allied Airborne Army, which was Eisenhower's only theatre level reserve; and it seemed he intended to use it. Certainly, something must have been in the wind, at least for a few days, to have caused the frenetic rush to the middle of Belgium experienced by the Seaborne Echelon of the 1st British Airborne Division.

It was to be Sunday, 10 September before Montgomery was able to explain his plan to Eisenhower at a meeting on board the Supreme Commander's aircraft at Brussels airport. His idea was to lay a 'carpet' of three airborne divisions over the waterways in Holland, to seize all the bridges between just north of Eindhoven, through Nijmegen and on as far as Arnhem, on the Lower Rhine. The British XXX Corps would advance up the road, across the captured bridges and then

Operation Market Garden: The Plan. Courtesy John Waddy

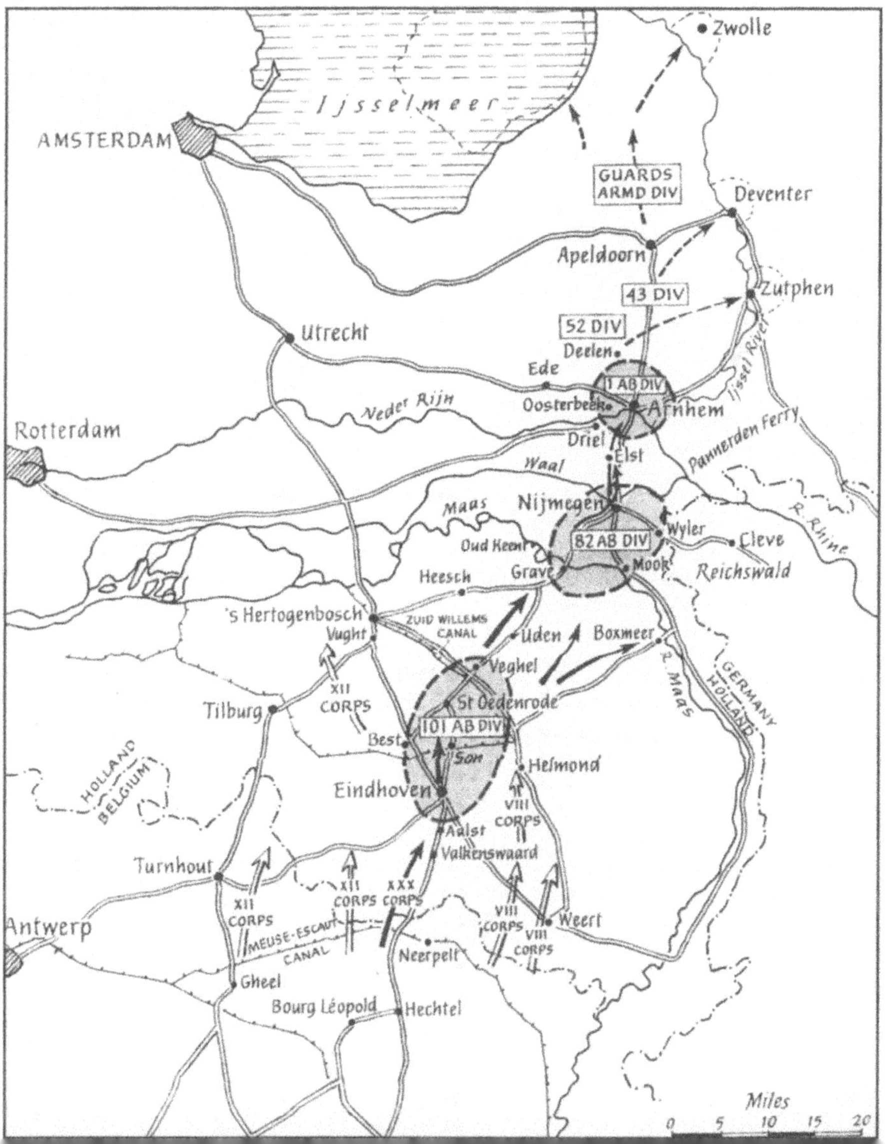

break out beyond Arnhem into northern Holland and the North German Plain. After some discussion Eisenhower agreed. He did so for a number of reasons: he was under pressure to use the highly trained, and very expensive, airborne army currently sitting in England and making no contribution to the war effort; the plan, if it worked, would have a major impact in shortening the war; and V2 rockets had begun to fall on London on 8 September from sites in western Holland. It may have been this last factor above all others that influenced him to take the risk, for once beyond Arnhem his armies could easily destroy the launch sites.

He gave his sanction to the plan, with the limitations that there would be no move beyond Arnhem until the situation had clarified, and Montgomery would receive no logistic priority. However, Montgomery had enough, despite the constraints. Planning, which had already started, accelerated and Browning was briefed. He had seven days in which to prepare the largest airborne assault of all time. His Corps, comprising the 82nd and 101st US Airborne Divisions and the 1st British Airborne Division, reinforced by 1st Independent Polish Parachute Brigade, would deploy onto its objectives in The Netherlands on Sunday 17 September.

Whilst Montgomery and Eisenhower were having their discussions at Brussels airport, the Seaborne Echelon, which had ceased its frantic rush north on 8 September, was enjoying life east of Brussels, billeted between the lovely old town of Leuven and the delightful village of Tervuren, with its beautiful parks and gardens. The headquarters was at Tervuren Monastery, and it was a time to relax. Soldiers were permitted trips into Brussels, and set about enjoying the delights available locally. Life, however, was not completely idyllic: a driver from 250 Airborne Light Company negligently discharged his weapon, and in so doing killed a Belgian civilian. He would, subsequently, receive ten days field punishment.

Preparing to Go

In England the first warnings of what was to happen were already being briefed to senior officers, and the outline plan was already taking shape; but there were complications. In delivering 1st Airborne Division to the bridge at Arnhem, the RAF would not accept the risk of dropping the force near the bridge. They were concerned about heavy anti-aircraft fire to the north and congestion with the American lifts to the south; and they could not afford losses given the paucity of transport aircraft. There was also a view that the soft polder just south of the bridge was unsuitable for parachute landings, and for gliders. Consequently, the DZs and LZs selected were on open heathland west of Arnhem, beyond the village of Oosterbeek in the area of Renkum and on the Ede-Arnhem road at Ginkel Heath. They were perfect for the task, but they were some eight miles from the objective.

It was to be a daylight operation, a situation caused largely by the lack of time to train pilots in such large numbers for the much more complex, not to say dangerous, business of dropping so many men by night; and there had been some bad experiences in the past. It had the advantage, however, that pinpointing DZs and LZs would be much easier and it allowed the RAF escorts to deal with enemy fighters much more easily than at night: the German night fighters were a real menace. Also, since anti-aircraft guns were radar controlled the threat from them was the same by day and by night. A more serious problem was that the shortage of aircraft would mean three lifts, spread over three days. This would cost the Airborne Corps the crucial advantage of surprise whilst its strength was building up, and was to prove a major weakness once events began to unfold on the ground in the Netherlands.

Two brigades of 1st Airborne Division would deploy on the first day, together with divisional headquarters. After landing the 1st Parachute Brigade would make straight for the bridge in Arnhem and hold it. The task of the 1st Airlanding Brigade was to remain on the DZs and LZs in order to secure them for the landings on the second day. On Monday, 18 September 4th Parachute Brigade was to drop onto Ginkel Heath and the 4th Brigade gliders would land on 1st Parachute Brigade's DZ of the day before, as would the balance of divisional headquarters' gliders. Both brigades would then march on the town to take up their positions around the bridge, which by then would be held by 1st Parachute Brigade. On the third day the 1st Independent Polish Parachute Brigade would land just south of the bridge, on the polder, whilst its gliders with their heavy equipment would come in to the north-west of Arnhem to link up later.

Urquhart was faced with little choice, but the air plan presented him with huge difficulty. Dropping so far from his objective he would lose the advantage of surprise, essential if lightly armed airborne troops were to have a chance of success. The arrival of his force was spread over three days, with only one quarter available to seize the objective. The second quarter was required to defend the DZs and LZs for the drop the next day of the third quarter, namely 4th Parachute Brigade. It would not be until the third day when he would be complete with the 1st Independent Polish Parachute Brigade on the ground.

Major General R.E. Urquhart, Commander 1st Airborne Division.
Courtesy Imperial War Museum

It was far from ideal, but Urquhart made the best of it that he could. He planned to send the three battalions of 1st Parachute Brigade on three separate routes into town. On the southern route, a narrow, minor road running alongside the Rhine, would go 2nd Parachute Battalion, commanded by Lieutenant Colonel John Frost. With him he would take the Brigade Headquarters and some of the support elements of the Brigade. The 3rd Parachute Battalion would also proceed to the bridge, on a more central route, which would take it through the centre of the village of Oosterbeek, whilst the 1st Battalion would move north of the railway line that cuts through Wolfheze, head alongside it into Arnhem and take up position in the town to the north of the bridge. Preceding all this, Major Freddie Gough's Reconnaissance Squadron, comprising jeeps fitted with

Vickers K machine guns and supported by a detachment of 9 Airborne Field Company RE, would rush to the bridge, seize it in a coup de main operation and then await the arrival of their more slowly moving infantry colleagues.

The Logistic Plans

Much of the planning activity for logistic support was based on earlier models, developed for the many cancelled operations. The plan was for the leading elements of XXX Corps to reach the Arnhem bridge within two days. Browning's estimate was that it might be held for four, but nothing could be certain. Erring on the side of caution, arrangements were made for automatic maintenance for four days, with options to stretch it longer if necessary. However, the difference between British and American ammunition and stores entailed an entirely separate organisation for packing and transporting supplies to be dropped by air. For this reason the US divisions would have to make their demands direct on XVIII US Corps in England and 1st Airborne Division would demand on Headquarters 1st Airborne Corps (Rear), which was also in England. These headquarters would then set in motion their own existing machinery for dropping pre-packed stores. Apart from 75mm ammunition, used only for the 1st Airborne Division pack howitzers, 9mm small arms ammunition, 6-pounder guns and ammunition, compo, fuels and oils, and jeeps, there were no other items that could be used by both nations.

The availability of aircraft was such that on the second day of the operation, Monday 18 September, only thirty-five Stirlings would be available to resupply 1st Airborne Division. However, having only landed half the Division, and with

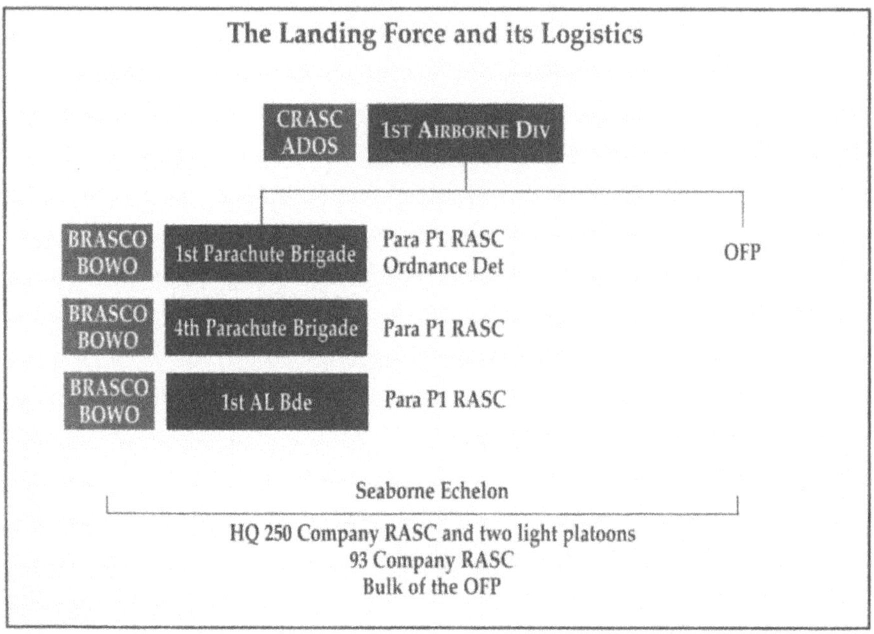

forty-eight hours' supplies having been carried in, only some top-up was necessary. Thereafter, provided there were no losses, there would be sufficient Stirlings and Dakotas to meet both the British and American requirements. To compensate for the initial shortage of resupply aircraft, and seeking to ameliorate the effects of bad weather and disruptions to the line of communication or other unforeseen difficulties, the 'Q' staff[2] in 1st Airborne Division tried an experiment. Carrying supplies in jeeps loaded in gliders did not make best use of all the carrying capacity in the glider. This was mainly a question of volume rather than weight, but they were also aware of the vagaries of wind and weather in scattering air-dropped loads and making them difficult to recover. Concentrating a consignment in a number of glider loads would greatly ease collection and movement to the DAA.

They arranged, therefore, for three pre-loaded Hamilcar gliders carrying composite loads of ammunition and stores to be flown in with the second lift. The range of stock, other than ammunition, included engineer stores for defensive works and some thirty panniers of Ordnance Stores[3] of an unspecified nature, although they were probably a mix of clothing, bulky items, weapons and general stores. In addition, an extra fourteen-man box of compo was put into every glider.

The vast bulk of the Hamilcar, capable of carrying a small tank, made it a perfect choice for carrying stores. The Bren Carrier, as shown here, was used at Arnhem. Courtesy Imperial War Museum

It was always clear that once a link-up had been made with XXX Corps, 1st Airborne Division would have to be administered entirely by XXX Corps as, except for the AFDAG organisation, 1st Airborne Corps had no administrative resources of any kind. To this end a close AQ[4] and Services[5] liaison with XXX Corps had been established during the week preceding the operation. In addition, arrangements were made to forward up the line of communication 110 tons of Ordnance Stores divided into three equal 'bricks'. These 'bricks' were intended to meet the requirements of 1st Airborne Division for recuperation after the battle, and would avoid placing what might well be a heavy and unforeseen load on the Ordnance resources of XXX Corps. Additionally, 1,000 stretchers and 2,600 blankets were to be flown in with the AFDAG.

The RASC Concept is Adapted for Arnhem

Michael Packe already had his plans laid in embryo, based on earlier planned deployments using similar force levels. Two parachute platoons of 250 Light Company would fly in the first lift, each attached to its parent brigade. They would be under command of the Brigade Headquarters, where RASC interests would be represented by the Brigade Royal Army Service Corps Officer (BRASCO). For 1st Parachute Brigade this was Captain P.G. Mortlock RASC, and the 1st Airlanding Brigade's BRASCO was Captain L.A.C. Lockyer RASC.

Once the immediate objectives had been gained and any stocks carried in the gliders had been collected and handed over, the parachute platoons would return to the SDP which should by that time have been captured and consolidated. They were then to man, lay out and prepare the SDP. Packe's second-in-command, Major D.G. Clarke RASC, who would go in on the first lift, was also to employ them for requisitioning, by force when necessary, all types of supplies and, especially, transport in the captured town. This was a lesson learned from the Taranto operation in September 1943, when, landing without any vehicles, 250 Light Company had acquired a number from the Italians. Working with requisitioned spares in their own workshops platoon they had very soon had enough transport running to sustain the force they were there to support.

In the second lift the CRASC with his skeleton headquarters would land, together with the third of the parachute platoons, their jeeps and trailers fully loaded. Ferrying extra supplies from the three Hamilcars, abandoned gliders and parachute containers they would begin to build up stock in the DAA. This was to be a well dispersed site immediately accessible to SDPs. On the third day the first supply drop would come in, and thereafter collection and issue to units from the DAA would follow normal routine until the land forces arrived and the reserve stocks carried by the Seaborne Echelon were available for use. The DAA, which was run exclusively by the RASC, and for which CRASC was responsible to the Q Staff, handled all sorts of commodities: Ordnance, Medical, REME and RE stores being included.

RAOC Support

Captain Bernard Manley, officer-in-charge of the OFP advanced parachute detachment.
Author's Collection

Lieutenant Colonel Gerry Mobbs RAOC, ADOS 1st Airborne Division.
Author's Collection

In Belgium, the OFP Seaborne Echelon, ensconced in a convent in Leuven, replenished all its stocks from the Corps Troops OFP of XXX Corps. As soon as they had come within range of each other the two OFPs had been in touch, with the small airborne OFP feeding off its much larger counterpart so as to preserve its own stock levels for the operation to come. The Corps Troops OFP had been a tremendous support, meeting all demands and routing spares from base depots via the local railhead. It was a great help in maintaining 1st Airborne Division's sustainability prior to the move of the Seaborne Echelon, on 16 September, north to Helchteren.

Back in England Major Bill Chidgey had also decided on his plan. He proposed to send Captain Bernard Manley and five parachute-trained soldiers with Headquarters 1st Parachute Brigade to go directly to the bridge. Their role would be to reconnoitre the bridge area, seeking locations for the OFP when it arrived, for use as storage areas, and to make arrangements for a vehicle park. This would be used to hold requisitioned vehicles which would then be issued once entitlements were determined, and to offset losses. From the balance of the OFP, still in Grantham, he selected ten soldiers to accompany him in gliders with four jeeps each towing a binned trailer containing stores. Lieutenant Colonel Gerry Mobbs, the ADOS, and WO1 (Sub-Conductor)[6] Gordon Jenkins, his chief technical clerk, would go in the same lift, but in different gliders. Staff Sergeant Brown, the divisional AE, was attached to the OFP party, as was a group of three soldiers, commanded by Sergeant Colin Bennet, from ADOS' headquarters staff. Their task was to break down bulk stock into detailed lots for issue to units. It is presumed that the thirty panniers on the Hamilcars were destined to receive their attention. The RAOC element would, therefore, be twenty-seven, including the bridge party and the three BOWOs: WO1 (Sub-Conductor) Halsall for 1st Parachute Brigade; WO1 (Sub-Conductor) Higham for 4th Parachute Brigade; and WO1 (Sub-Conductor) Eastwood for 1st Airlanding Brigade.

Away at Last

Throughout 16 September the final briefings were being given in England under a strict cloak of secrecy. CRASC briefed his officers on the operation at midday, and the second-in-command repeated the briefing for the soldiers at 6.00 p.m., after which the camp was sealed. The RAOC briefings were just as detailed, and were broadly the same for everyone. Sand tables and models were used, accompanied by aerial photographs, and there were street maps to show people their exact positions in the town. Everyone knew what they had to do, equipment was ready, they were fired up to go. Nothing, nothing whatsoever, could stop them now – and it would end the war by Christmas.

> *We were confined to camp from reveille. The briefing took place at 6.30 p.m. We studied maps, air photographs, etc. Rendezvous for various sections were pinpointed and studied. All personnel fully understood their orders, etc. Ammo and plastic high-explosive was issued, 24-hour rations and cookers were issued. Kits packed and to bed.*
>
> Lance Corporal J. L. Hughes RASC, BRASCO's Clerk,[7] 4th Parachute Brigade

Sunday, 17 September 1944 dawned a pleasant day with the prospect of warm sunshine. Breakfast was available and substantial for those who could face it; daunting for those prone to air sickness. The RAOC bridge party went to Barkston Heath aerodrome, collected their parachutes and prepared to go whilst the balance of the unit remained behind in Grantham ready to emplane the next day. Staff Sergeant Harry Walker, known as 'Mick',[8] was second-in-command of the party. A first-class soldier, he had joined the RAOC in 1939, before transferring to the Army Physical Training Corps in 1940. He attended parachute training at Ringway and then became an instructor, a role he carried out until the RAF took over parachute training in 1942. He was, eventually, to return to the RAOC in April 1944. Supremely fit and a battle-hardened soldier, Major Bill Chidgey had selected him specially to be part of his forward detachment. The other four soldiers in the team were Privates Ted Mordecai, Kevin Heaney, Mac McCarthy and Ron Pugh. Each had been chosen for their balanced mix of trade competence and toughness. They would fly in a Dakota with members of the 1st Parachute Brigade Defence Platoon, and with Bernard Manley nominated as the stick[9] No 1 and Harry Walker the No 2 they would be among the first to exit the aircraft.

From 250 Airborne Light Company, 1st Parachute Platoon, with 1st Parachute Platoon Jeep Section, was commanded by Captain Jack Cranmer-Byng RASC, whilst Captain Bill Gell was in charge of 3rd Parachute Platoon and its Jeep Section. Their aircraft allotment was two parachuting aircraft and ten Horsas, and an extra two gliders took additional elements of 250 Company.

From airfields all over England the vast armada took off. As it passed over the peaceful green fields, the small villages and the towns of a country going about its lawful business on a quiet Sunday morning the roar of the engines drowned out everything below. Normal conversation was impossible. Everywhere, people stepped out into the streets, looking up in wonder, and asking what it might mean.

Private Ron Pugh had been with the OFP since its time at Barton Stacey, before 1st Airborne Division's North African deployment in 1943. Whilst there he had formed an association with a young lady from Winchester, and they had stayed in touch despite the long separation. But on this day the young lady was not in Winchester.

> *I was staying with an aunt in Godalming when they flew over. The noise was terrific. As I looked up I knew my Ron was up there.*
>
> Freda Burgess, later Mrs Ron Pugh

Marie Manley was living at the time in Bexleyheath, with her two small children.

She too was aware of what was going on, and watched in awe as the huge numbers of aircraft roared overhead in a seemingly never-ending stream, taking her husband to war.

It was a good crossing. There was some turbulence over England, but once across the Channel it smoothed and the flight was quite comfortable. Looking down they could see the V-shaped trails of Air Sea Rescue launches waiting to collect anyone sufficiently unfortunate to have to land in or on the water. However, not everyone travelling in the air armada was a legal passenger.

During the early summer of 1944 a new draft arrived at Easton Hall, and among them was a replacement corporal cook. We had no particular expectations from him, but were pleasantly surprised. Corporal Menzies, an unassuming Scot, was great and it became a pleasure to sit down in the dining room. Nothing seemed too much for him, and what we fondly imagined was stewed gas cape before turned out to be cabbage. There was always a good, honest brew of tea going in the cookhouse and the pinched and hungry faces soon disappeared. It was not until the day before Arnhem that we really found out what a fantastic man Jock was. The Army Catering Corps, which Jock served with, were of course only attached to the Parachute Regiment, and were non jumpers.[10] *On this particular evening as we were talking in the cookhouse, Jock said: 'You blokes aren't leaving me behind, I'm coming with you.' We then had to bribe the stick sergeant in the aircraft and smuggle him on board. We were all impressed by this quiet man, who,*

Boarding at Barkestone Heath, Privates McCarthy (1), Mordecai (2) and Heaney (3) RAOC.
Courtesy Imperial War Museum

with no parachute training whatsoever, jumped for the first time in his life into what proved to be one of the bloodiest battles of the war. Luckily, he escaped death and was made POW.

Ron Holt, 2nd Parachute Battalion[11]

As they reached the coast and began to pass over the Netherlands they could see the effects of floods below where the Germans had breached the dykes as part of their efforts to defend the area. The flat, soaking land reflected up the glare of a September sun, and aircraft despatchers began to warn of twenty minutes to go. Men began to check their equipment, tension began to rise. This, then, was it.

Ahead of them they knew had already flown a force of pathfinders. The task of 21st Independent Parachute Company was to fly in advance of the main force in order to mark the dropping and landing zones in preparation for the main force, and to give the pilots something to home in on. This was done with a mix of visual and radio signals, with Eureka Beacons set up to provide a radio 'track' along which aircraft could fly. In addition, 1st Parachute Brigade's DZ was marked with its identifying letter in large white panels, together with a 'T' shaped symbol, with the stem of the letter pointing in the direction of the wind. The LZs for the gliders had only the identifying letter.

It was precisely 12.30 p.m. when the six officers and 180 soldiers of the pathfinder company jumped from their Stirling bombers, having taken off earlier that morning from RAF Fairford, in Gloucestershire. Some care had to be exercised when parachuting from the Stirling in order to avoid smacking one's face on the far side of the exit hole in the aircraft's belly - a process known as 'ringing the bell.' Whether there was undue apprehension among the pathfinders, crammed sixteen to an aircraft, as they contemplated this prospect is hard to say. Sitting in the first of the twelve aircraft Major 'Boy' Wilson was more concerned with ensuring his company landed accurately, with each of the three platoons hitting their allocated DZ or LZ correctly. There was no room for mistakes, since the main force would be just thirty minutes behind them and the markers had to be in place straight away.

Further down the aircraft, with his mind on other things, Private Frank Dixon ACC waited to jump into his third operational theatre, having previously seen active service with the Company in North Africa and Italy. Like the rest of them, he was among the elite of the elite; trained in all the skills needed to be an effective member of the Company and to undertake any duties – and he could cook.

Frank Dixon was a damn good cook, and, as subsequent events showed, he was an equally fine soldier.
Private A. Dawson, 21st Independent Parachute Company

Being in his company commander's aircraft, Frank Dixon was one of the very first to land in occupied Holland, in his case just near Reijerskamp Farm, in the centre of the Company's area of operations and on what would become the Landing Zone for 1st Airlanding Brigade. There were other cooks in the Company, but not every one of them in those early days was a member of the ACC. Units regularly had a mix of ACC and regimental cooks,[12] and it was one of these, Lance Corporal Sid Smith, who described the 'funny feeling' he experienced coming down on a parachute over enemy territory in bright sunshine on a Sunday afternoon and feeling 'a bit of a target.'

There were also soldiers in the 21st Company who had a link with the Pioneer Corps. Often, refugees from occupied Europe, on reaching England, aspired to join the Forces, seeking to do something to recover the situation in their homelands. Many of these men were placed in the Pioneer Corps, for reasons which remain unclear, although it is assumed that a mix of security concerns and language barriers were the most likely causes. However, feeling that linguists would make an essential contribution to their role, these soldiers, rather

21 Independent Parachute Company preparing to board their Stirlings at RAF Fairford. Private Frank Dixon ACC is circled. Courtesy Imperial War Museum

unkindly labelled 'aliens', were a natural source of talent for the pathfinders. Twenty-seven of them were taken from the Pioneer Corps and subjected to the phenomenally difficult training package that would grant them not simply entry to airborne forces, but to the highly specialised, supremely skilled pathfinder force. Having qualified, they were, of course, completely a part of airborne forces, but their passing remains a small, yet important, part of the history of the Pioneer Corps. Nine of them landed at Arnhem, three would not return.

By 1.00 p.m. they had done their job. All the markers were in place, everything was set. There had been a couple of skirmishes with some Germans with a couple of prisoners taken, but, given where they were and what they had achieved, it was remarkably peaceful. Then they heard in the distance the sound of the engines. Muted at first, it grew in strength as the huge numbers of aircraft bringing in two airborne brigades and their divisional headquarters approached.

All hell was about to be let loose in this quiet corner of this most peaceful country, and no one, not least the Germans, had any idea what was coming.

1. The German Army Headquarters fighting in the west.
2. Q Staff: In modern parlance: G4 staff, responsible for logistic matters.
3. Ordnance Stores: This was a 'catch-all' term used to encompass the complete range of stores supplied by the RAOC.
4. AQ Staff: In modern parlance: G1/G4 staff, responsible for personnel and logistics.
5. RASC, RAOC, PC, ACC, REME, REPS.
6. The appointment of 'Conductor' was, for an RAOC Warrant Officer Class One, the pinnacle of achievement. Granted only to selected, high calibre men it conferred on them the distinction of holding the most senior Warrant Officer appointment in the British Army. With its origins in the fifteenth century, it harked back to the days when individuals of quality and experience were needed in Ordnance appointments, requiring the intelligence and acumen normally associated with an officer. However, the structure of the Army in those days did not easily permit that they be commissioned, hence the appointment of Conductor. It gave to the WO the responsibilities of a junior officer, and entitled him to take the place of a subaltern officer on parade; but it conferred none of the other privileges of commissioned rank. The appointment has been retained with the formation of the Royal Logistic Corps, it goes to very few, it remains a prized honour, and Conductors to this day may take the place of a subaltern officer on parade, wearing officers accoutrements. The use of the term 'Sub-Conductor', as in WO1 Jenkins' case, used to mark the fact that a WO1 had achieved high status in his trade. However, it carried none of the privileges of being a Conductor, and was taken out of use in 1965 when the RAOC merged with part of the RASC.
7. Author's note: I have deduced this as being Lance Corporal Hughes' appointment from his diary, but cannot be absolutely certain.
8. A common nickname for anyone named Walker.
9. Stick: The name given to a group of parachutists when on board an aircraft from which they were to jump.
10. There clearly were parachute trained ACC, for many of them jumped at Arnhem, as their casualty list shows. Corporal Menzies had simply not done the course.
11. As told in 'Without Tradition 2 Para 1942 - 45' by Robert Peatling.
12. This was a situation that would prevail long after the war, and into the sixties.

CHAPTER FOUR

Liberation – Or So It Must Have Seemed

The Landings

They came in from the south-west, whispering silently on the wind as they swooped in along the line of the woods, before taking the sharp left turn that would allow the pilots to mark their spot easily and bring them in to land neatly on Landing Zone S. The gliders carrying 1st Airlanding Brigade had been released about two and a half miles out, at a height of 3,500 feet. With a sink rate of some 400 feet a minute they could choose when to kick in full flaps and make the steep dive that took them swiftly through potential enemy opposition. Straighten up, pick the spot and level into the landing zone to hit it at about eighty-five miles an hour, to bump and judder across the field before halting.

Nineteen minutes after the arrival of the 1st Airlanding Brigade the gliderborne elements of the 1st Parachute Brigade and Divisional Headquarters put down on Landing Zone Z. It was harder for these pilots as they ran straight into the LZ directly off their approach from the south-west with no chance to make a turn, slow the aircraft and get their bearings. The tendency was, therefore, to overshoot a little. With gliders coming in to the northern end of the LZ first and further and further to the south as wave after wave eased down from the sky, a number of the early arrivals misjudged their landing and ended up in the tree line at the top end of the LZ.

The landing was harder still for the large Hamilcars. They had no nose wheel, and the soft soil of the fields presented the pilots with something of a challenge, and one for which they had not had the opportunity to train. When the two landing wheels, located on either side of the fuselage under the wings, sank into

A successful Hamilcar landing. Note the nose, opened to remove the aircraft's load. Courtesy Airborne Museum 'Hartenstein'

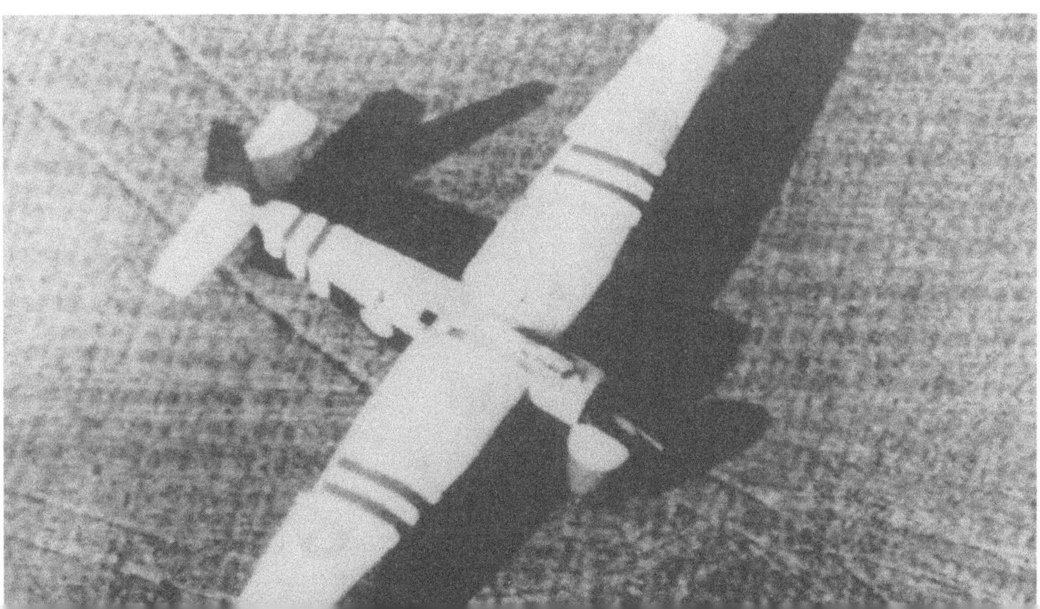

the ground the aircraft would pivot forward, the nose would dip, the tail was forced up and, in a number of cases, the glider was forced over in an ungainly forward roll onto its back. Given the heavy loads, including 17-pounder anti-tank guns and Bren Carriers, many of the passengers were badly hurt in these crashes – often with serious crush injuries. The pilots, with the cockpit on top of the aircraft, were particularly vulnerable; and some were killed.

Hamilcars had a problem landing. I saw a man screaming from his injuries following a bad landing. I gave him morphine and left him. It was all I could do for him.

Sergeant N. G. Griffin RASC, Staff Clerk, HQ 1st Airborne Division

'Bill' Griffin, as he was known, had been in one of the very early gliders to leave from Fairford with the tactical element of Divisional Headquarters, accompanying the AA&QMG and the ADMS.[1] Bill's real name was Neville, but living in India as a child the Afghan cook had never been able to get his tongue round 'Neville' and it had always come out as 'Bill'. He had been, for a time, General Urquhart's shorthand writer and was one of fifteen RASC clerks in Headquarters 1st Airborne Division. Bill's memory is that his own boss in the AQ branch was Warrant Officer Class 2 (WO2) George Fairhurst, with Staff Sergeant John Spencer as his deputy.

Lieutenant Colonel Preston, the AA&QMG, a South Lancashire Regiment officer, insisted I go with him in his glider as he wanted me to take his little black leather office box. We were the second glider out of Fairford, and I did not enjoy the ride.

Sergeant N. G. Griffin RASC

Part of the reason for his lack of enjoyment lay with the flak[2] his glider encountered crossing Holland. As if that were not enough, just as they were coming in to land another glider went straight past their front. Bill's glider, in which there was a jeep and trailer in addition to its passengers, veered and they landed hard on the nose. The pilot was all right, but the tail was in the air, with Bill's typewriter lost in the wreckage. They went into the woods near the Wolfheze asylum and opened up the Q cell.[3] The Germans soon located them and began mortaring so they moved and set up again under a Hamilcar wing.

Whilst those who had come in by glider were sorting themselves out, the relative calm of a glider landing was shattered by the noise of approaching aircraft carrying parachutists. From the south-west, following the same course as their gliderborne counterparts, Dakotas appeared on the horizon, little specks at first, growing larger as the formation drew closer and closer. Inside the aircraft men were standing, shaking down their equipment, taking a last pull on a cigarette. Many occupied themselves with checking kit they had checked many times already, others looked round, trying to find something in the eyes of others to help calm their own concerns. Some just stared ahead.

Given the despatcher's[4] warning at the ten minute point they made final checks and stood in line ready to exit the aircraft. They closed right up in order

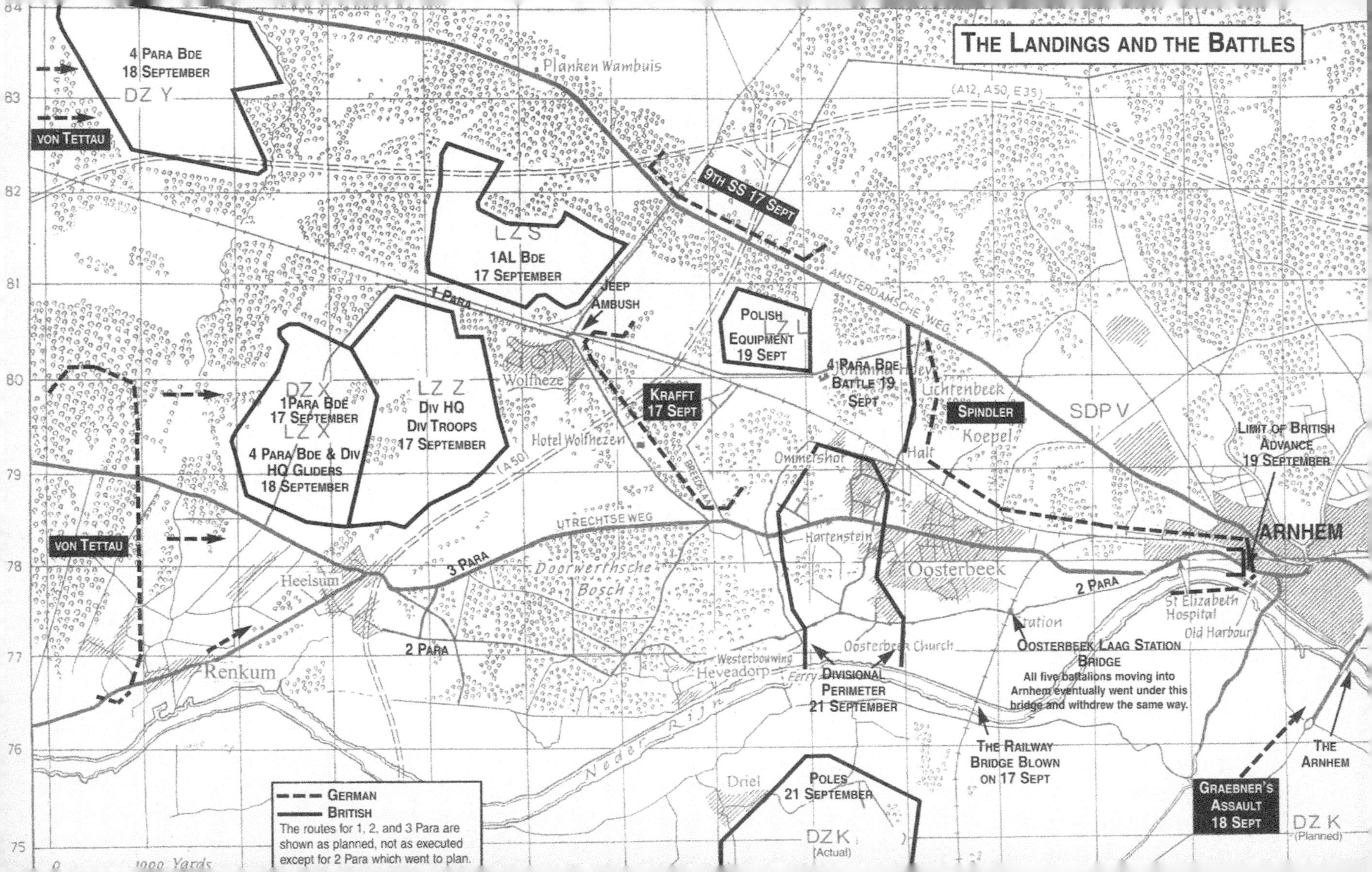

The Landings and the Battles
4 Para Bde
18 September
DZ Y
von Tettau
Planken Wambuis
(A12, A50, E35)
9th SS 17 Sept
LZ S
1AL Bde
17 September
Jeep
Ambush
1 Para
Amsterdamsche Weg
Polish
Equipment
19 Sept
LZ L
4 Para Bde
Battle 19
Sept
DZ X
1Para Bde
17 September
LZ X
4 Para Bde & Div
HQ Gliders
18 September
LZ Z
Div HQ
Div Troops
17 September
Wolfheze
Hotel Wolfhezen
(A50)
Krafft
17 Sept
Breedelaan
Lichtenbeek
Spindler
SDP V
Koepel
Halt
Limit of British
Advance
19 September
Ommershof
Utrechtse Weg
Hartenstein
ARNHEM
von Tettau
3 Para
Doorwerthsche
Bosch
Oosterbeek
Heelsum
2 Para
St Elizabeth
Hospital
Old Harbour
Station
2 Para
Oosterbeek Church
Oosterbeek Laag Station
Bridge
All five battalions moving into
Arnhem eventually went under this
bridge and withdrew the same way.
Renkum
Westerbouwing
Heveadorp
Ferry
Divisional
Perimeter
21 September
The Railway
Bridge Blown
on 17 Sept
The
Arnhem
Neder Rijn
Driel
Poles
21 September
DZ K
(Actual)
Graebner's
Assault
18 Sept
DZ K
(Planned)
German
British
The routes for 1, 2, and 3 Para are
shown as planned, not as executed
except for 2 Para which went to plan.
1000 Yards

to make sure they could leave as swiftly as possible, thereby avoiding undue dispersion on the ground. Then, suddenly, they were there. The aircraft ran in at 600 feet, their speed so slow they were virtually in a gliding stall. Parachutists were dropped the other way round from their gliderborne colleagues, the first coming down at the southern end of the DZ, with successive aircraft dropping their loads further and further north, taking their line from the road, Telefoonweg, which bisects Renkum Heath. By the time the last parachutist jumped, the aircraft's very slow speed had brought its height down to 500 feet; and everywhere there was the roar as pilots put on full throttle to lift away, their passengers discharged, to make their left turn and then head south, back home.

> *The last thing I remember was the despatcher's 'best of luck, cheerio.' He was all right, he'd be back home for tea.*
>
> Private E. V. B. Mordecai RAOC, 1st Airborne Division OFP, Forward Parachute Detachment

Bernard Manley, standing in the door of his aircraft, was concerned about the quality of the pilots, having had an earlier, and discouraging, experience during training jumps.

> *The pilot gave us the green light early. This was the second time an American pilot had done this to me, the first being on a training flight. The man behind me said 'green on.' I said 'not likely' and held a few seconds so I could be certain we would land in the right spot.'*
>
> Captain B. V. Manley RAOC, Officer-in-Charge, 1st Airborne Division OFP, Forward Parachute Detachment

Behind Bernard Manley, Harry Walker, unsure of what was happening had called that the green light was on and that they should be jumping, and he was being forced from behind by the press of soldiers. Bernard Manley was probably shoved through the door, but his delay had achieved his aim, and they landed as planned.

> *It was a first class jump. The pilot was super and got us in spot on. The RV was marked with blue smoke.*
>
> Staff Sergeant H. W. Walker RAOC, 1st Airborne Division OFP, Forward Parachute Detachment

> *As my parachute opened my helmet fell off and it landed before me. I thought: 'this is a good start.' However, when I landed the helmet, slightly dented, was only about ten yards away and, after taking off my harness, I picked it up and was able to wear it quite satisfactorily. We then made our way quickly to the rendezvous point. There did not appear to be any urgency; the sun was warm, everything was peaceful – had we really dropped into enemy territory?*
>
> Private K. J. Heaney RAOC, 1st Airborne Division OFP, Forward Parachute Detachment

The landing bore all the hallmarks of an exercise in England. Warm and sunny, it seemed a perfect drop with no problems. To many it seemed all that was needed was a NAAFI wagon for char and a wad,[5] before boarding transport back to barracks. However, it was not completely successful for everyone.

The parachutists followed the gliders in, many of them landing among stationary aircraft – some of which have already had their tails removed to exit the load. Courtesy Imperial War Museum

> *Overhead the Dakotas were still spilling out their contents and above them some Spitfires were circling the DZ. It was then I saw our first casualty. A chap was coming down with a kit bag dangling below him. I think it must have contained mortar bombs already fuzed up because as the bag hit the ground it exploded with a mighty bang. As he was only about twenty feet above it he caught the full blast and there wasn't much left of him.*[6]
>
> Private E. V. B. Mordecai RAOC

And there is no clear explanation of what caused the body of Sergeant R D Greenhalg RASC to be found in the Wandelpark in Tilburg. A twenty-nine year old staff clerk attached to Headquarters Airborne Troops, it had been thought he had been flung out of an aircraft without a parachute whilst over the town. Subsequently, research has indicated that he was probably on board a glider that made an emergency landing near Dongen and was killed shortly afterwards.[7]

Staff Sergeant Harry Walker RAOC, a picture taken when he was with the APTC. Author's Collection

Gathering together quickly, the RAOC party made for the blue smoke that marked their rendezvous with the Brigade Headquarters, in a wood near a small cemetery at the south-eastern corner of the DZ. Meanwhile, the parachute platoons of 250 Company RASC were gathering. The gliders having landed before the parachutists meant that 3rd Platoon, in support of 1st Airlanding Brigade, was down first. Being in gliders, which landed exactly as planned, the whole platoon, including its jeep section, was concentrated together and ready to go in very short order. Moving swiftly, it was very soon waiting at its rendezvous point. However, 1st Parachute Platoon, whose parachute element had been dispersed on landing, was having trouble coming together in order to go into town with 1st Parachute Brigade. The two platoon commanders discussed what to do for the best, not having access to Michael Packe's second-in-command, Major D.G. Clarke, who was nowhere to be found.[8] They made a decision that would have a profound effect both on them and their men.

Not long after 1st Parachute Brigade had landed I came across Jack Cranmer-Byng whose platoon had been widely dispersed. As 2nd Parachute Battalion together with 1st Parachute Brigade Headquarters were already heading for the bridge we decided to change places and I went immediately to follow 2nd Battalion towards the bridge where, after only a minor skirmish, we arrived late in the afternoon.

Captain W. V. Gell RASC

We should have gone to the bridge, but the Platoon suffered some casualties on the drop, and the senior captain kept us back on the DZ and sent 3 Platoon instead. Both platoons had the same rendezvous, just outside Heelsum.

Driver J. A. Taylor RASC, 1st Parachute Platoon, 250 Airborne Light Company RASC

The decision was not, apparently, affected by the scalings they carried since each of the parachute platoons were configured with the same loads, despite the difference in size between a parachute and an airlanding brigade. The latter was very much larger, with double the number of mortars and Vickers machine guns, and two platoons of 6-pounder anti-tank guns in each of the three battalions.[9] In any event, both officers must have assumed that the divisional plan would work and by the following evening they would be together in a DAA within the perimeter thrown round the Arnhem bridge by 1st Airborne Division.

Having consolidated, 1st Parachute Brigade began to head off towards the town, whilst 1st Airlanding Brigade set about digging in and preparing the defence of the DZs and LZs for the following day's landings. Freddie Gough's jeep squadron roared off with great pace and panache en route to the bridge, but there had been a delay and it was late. The landings had been complete by 2.10 p.m. At 3.00 p.m. 2nd and 3rd Parachute Battalions had moved off, followed at 3.30 p.m. by 1st Parachute Battalion. At 3.20 p.m. it was reported to Urquhart that the Reconnaissance Squadron had failed to arrive due to difficulties with its gliders, but this was not true. However, it was to be 3.35 p.m. before they departed on a task which had been imbued with such urgency in the planning of the operation.

The Germans React

The German reaction was swift. In the woods just east of Wolfheze, Major Sepp Krafft had positioned, coincidentally, two companies of his SS Training Battalion. Located in the countryside around Arnhem and Oosterbeek, its task was to train

SS soldiers, and many of its NCOs were battle-hardened veterans. On this peaceful Sunday some were relaxing in the late summer sunshine and others were conducting low-level training when life suddenly took a swift turn for the worse. However, having trained in countering airborne operations, Krafft knew that the basic principle was to advance straight into the teeth of an airborne drop, regardless of disparity in size, to throw the airborne units off balance in the very difficult consolidation phase following a drop. Bringing up his reserve company into a depth position, he positioned his other two companies further forward in a blocking line, running south from the area of Wolfheze along the line of Wolfhezerweg, slightly east of south in the direction of Utrechtseweg. He then sent out aggressive patrols to cause disruption and to gather intelligence. It was on Utrechtseweg that Krafft had his left flank, and it was along Utrechtseweg that 3rd Parachute Battalion was to march into Arnhem.

Concerned about his right flank, and unable to see over the high bank along which the railway ran from Wolfheze to Oosterbeek, he placed his reserve platoon north of the railway, partly on the embankment and partly on a piece of high ground just on the other side of a dirt track. It was the dirt track along which Freddie Gough's jeep squadron was to travel to the bridge, and along which Lieutenant Colonel Dobie's 1st Parachute Battalion planned to march; and Sepp Krafft had it straddled in less time than it was taking the Reconnaissance Squadron to prepare to move.

Field Marshal Model had only just moved to his new headquarters in the Tafelberg Hotel in Oosterbeek. Urquhart did not know it, but one of Germany's most able army commanders was on the spot to deal with the unexpected arrival of his division. On hearing of the landings, the Field Marshal immediately ordered the Tafelberg to be evacuated and made straight for Lieutenant General Wilhelm Bittrich's headquarters north of Arnhem in order to get the counter-strokes under way. As he did so, Major General Kussin, the Arnhem town commandant, was heading west into the woods to inspect Sepp Krafft's battalion.

Bittrich, in the meantime, was reacting swiftly. From his headquarters in Doetinchem he worked out the likely enemy aim and decided that Arnhem and Nijmegen were key objectives. He therefore ordered Lieutenant Colonel Harzer's 9th SS Panzer Division to undertake reconnaissance of both Arnhem and Nijmegen, whilst Major General Heinz Harmel's 10th SS Division was to move south to the Nijmegen area and secure a bridgehead on the south bank of the River Waal. Both commanders had a considerable amount of work to do to get their equipment, much of it in a poor state of repair, ready to move; but they set to with a will. Within two hours Captain Graebner's 9th SS Reconnaissance Battalion had some forty armoured cars and personnel carriers ready to go.

Everywhere there was a great sense of urgency. The SS placed great reliance on the quality of its junior officers and NCOs, and trusted them to make on-the-spot decisions and then act on them. The instructions were simple: move now, orders on the objective – wherever that might be. Graebner headed south to see what was happening in Nijmegen.

Model, arriving at Bittrich's headquarters at 3.50 p.m. confirmed his satisfaction with the measures being taken, and established headquarters II SS Panzer Corps as being in control of operations in the Arnhem-Nijmegen area.

1st Parachute Brigade Moves Towards Arnhem

Racing along the track just north of the railway, running east from Wolfheze, No 8 Section of Freddie Gough's squadron bumped into Sepp Krafft's reserve platoon, which was in a perfect ambush position. The two vehicles in the section were shot up and the crews either killed or wounded, with the latter, save one, being taken prisoner. As the ambush struck, Gough was heading back to see his Divisional Commander, Urquhart having asked to hear from him about the missing vehicles; which were not missing. He left his Squadron at a critical time. Meanwhile, Lieutenant Colonel Dobie at the head of 1st Parachute Battalion, decided not to follow his planned route along the same line as that being taken by the Reconnaissance Squadron, and on which they had been ambushed. He chose instead to head further north and make his way into Arnhem along the Ede-Arnhem highway.

On the river route 2nd Parachute Battalion was making good time, unhindered save for the excited local population who wished only to greet their liberators, not realising, perhaps, the imperatives driving Lieutenant Colonel John Frost and his men.

> *As we marched crowds of Dutch people came to the roadside, cheering and waving flags. I felt as if I was now swaggering, grinning away, sleeves rolled up, almost believing we deserved the cheers. After all, the people were now free.*
> Private K. J. Heaney RAOC

In addition to taking the main road bridge in Arnhem, Frost had some secondary tasks. On route to the town he was to seize the railway bridge and the pontoon bridge, both of which spanned the Rhine just west of the main road bridge. The task of taking the railway bridge went to Major Victor Dover's C Company. Moving at the rear of the column, he peeled off and set his company up to cover the attacking platoon. The Platoon Commander took a section with him, and was almost halfway across the bridge when it blew up in their faces, causing slight casualties. The loss of surprise had given the Germans all the time they needed to prepare the demolition charges. Watching the span settle in the river, Victor Dover felt a pang of apprehension as he pondered on the best laid plans of mice and men, and moved off with his company to his secondary objective: the German headquarters in the town, near the Gemeente Museum.

> *A Company was in front of us, and C Company behind. By this time it was getting dusk and as we marched along by the river road we heard an explosion and we were told that the railway bridge had been blown by the Germans.*
> Private E.V.B. Mordecai RAOC

Bernard Manley remembers a 'hard and busy' march. There were numerous delays, caused by enemy action at the head of the column, and boisterous Dutch civilians seeking to press everything on the soldiers, from kisses, through cakes to coffee. A number recall passing a German armoured car, smashed by the soldiers of 2nd Parachute Battalion, with the driver hanging dead out of the door. As he marched Captain Manley considered the role of his small party when they arrived at their destination. Major Bill Chidgey had an idea they should be looking for accommodation for some 150 vehicles, several large garages, a workshops and a storage area for bulk spares. This assessment was based on what he considered to be the full divisional requirement once the Seaborne Echelon arrived, including storage for requisitioned vehicles. Bill also took account of what he had been led to believe was the Division's next task: a move to seal the Dutch coast; and he needed the ability logistically to support this. Bernard Manley, who had joined the RAOC as a clerk at the outset of war, had been commissioned in 1942 before volunteering for airborne training. He spent a short time with 6th Airborne Division before joining 1st Airborne Division, and had age and experience in his favour. In sending the 34 year old Manley with the advance elements, Bill Chidgey was seeking to ensure the RAOC voice was heard when logistic requirements were being discussed.

> *I was told to commandeer any usable vehicle I could find. The intention was to create a vehicle park.*
>
> Captain B. V. Manley RAOC

Brigadier Gerald Lathbury had spent the first part of the advance with Frost's battalion, with his Brigade Headquarters included in the Battalion's order of march. Having seen the failure of the attempt on the railway bridge he had encouraged further haste before moving north to see what was happening to 3rd Parachute Battalion on the central route through Oosterbeek. Urquhart, himself seeking to find out what was going on had also come forward to 2nd Battalion, had missed Lathbury, and before following him north urged yet more haste on Frost. Gough, seeking his Divisional Commander, not knowing his squadron had withdrawn from the ambush and was not proceeding to the bridge, also followed the 2nd Battalion route, but missed Urquhart as the General went in search of the Brigade Commander.

Lieutenant Colonel Fitch's 3rd Battalion had been making good time until its leading elements reached the junction of Wolfhezerweg with Utrechtseweg. There, the lead platoon had bumped into General Kussin, returning from his visit to Sepp Krafft, and had riddled his car with bullets, killing all the occupants. The bodies would remain there until buried the next day by Padre Pare, attached to the Glider Pilot Regiment, and many survivors have memories of passing the car with the dead hanging out of it. Shortly after this, 3rd Battalion hit opposition, partly from Sepp Krafft, and by now both Lathbury and Urquhart were with the CO. In a much criticised decision, never fully explained, they decided to halt the Battalion as it was getting dark and move on the next morning. Fitch, had, however, sent C Company on a flanking move to the north to see if they could find another route into Arnhem. He was never to see them again, but the Company did get to the bridge that night and, although depleted, was to provide Frost with a much needed boost to his fighting power. Urquhart and Lathbury both remained with 3rd Battalion, neither of them in touch with their respective headquarters, neither headquarters knowing the whereabouts of their respective commanders.

With C Company on its march into Arnhem was Corporal Gerald Roberts RASC. Born in Leeds, he had only been with the Company a week, as its medical orderly. He had completed his parachute course, and had been posted to 16 Parachute Field Ambulance as a driver. Being a qualified medic, he had been of more use for these skills than for his driving attributes, and he had thus been selected to be the C Company medical orderly.

> *Corporal Roberts was with the Company headquarters and the remnants of 9 Platoon in a schoolhouse from the Sunday evening to the Wednesday evening, together with some Sappers under Captain Eric MacKay of 1 Parachute Squadron RE. Corporal Roberts set up the aid post there. The house was built into the embankment on the eastern side of the bridge, so with the house facing the road it formed a sort of semi-basement. Roberts was ably assisted by Sapper Pinky White, but it was Roberts who took complete control of our medical support and who ran it throughout. He was a first class chap.*
>
> Lieutenant L. W. Wright, Officer Commanding 9 Platoon, C Company, 3rd Parachute Battalion

On the northern route, 1st Parachute Battalion had never quite made the Ede-Arnhem road. The lead company had bumped into German opposition moving down from the north: the forward elements of 9th SS, probing to identify who the enemy were and what they were up to. Heavily armed with machine guns, and light armoured vehicles, they were more than a match for the lightly equipped airborne troops. Dobie decided to change plans yet again, and moved to his right, into the woods paralleling the road and began to make his way through the trees towards the town. The going was very much slower and it was beginning to come clear to him that he would not make his objective when he picked up a radio message from the bridge. Realising that all had not gone as it should, and that Frost was in trouble, he decided to abandon any idea of reaching a position in the north of the town and to head directly to help 2nd Battalion on the river.

With the Reconnaissance Squadron pushed back to the DZ, with 3rd Battalion stalled on Utrechtseweg, near the Hartenstein Hotel, and with 1st Battalion scrabbling into Oosterbeek just north of the Hartenstein and still some six miles away, John Frost was alone at the bridge. The Germans, despite the speed of their comprehensive response to the airborne landings, had not been able to block his approach route. His own C Company having moved into the town to its secondary objective, some distance from the bridge, he had detached B Company to deal with some Germans on high ground on the edge of Arnhem and was left at the bridge only with A Company as a coherent infantry force. He would be joined later by the remnants of his B Company, and by C Company of the 3rd Battalion. A considerable portion of his force at the bridge comprised

Brigade Headquarters staff, signallers, Royal Engineers, RASC and RAOC, bringing his total to around 750 men. He had not secured the pontoon bridge which he had found to have been disassembled.

Brigade Headquarters arrived at the bridge area about forty minutes after the bulk of the 2nd Battalion. Corporal Norman Harris RASC was in the Intelligence Section of the Headquarters, with Horace Goodwich. The Brigade chief clerk was Sergeant Ron Batchelor and Corporal Austen Johnson was BRASCO's clerk.

> *I had the job of collecting the ammunition from the wounded. I passed it to the WO1 physical training instructor, who was the brigadier's bodyguard, and he redistributed it.*
>
> Corporal A. Johnson RASC, BRASCO'S Clerk[10], HQ 1st Parachute Brigade

Near the pontoon bridge area the Germans were covering a square, and firing across it, and men were split into small groups to dash over it. The driver of one of the RASC jeeps was wounded, and Corporal Doug Beardmore went back, under fire, and drove the jeep, with its two vital trailers full of ammunition, to safety; and eventually to the RASC platoon position in the local department of public works' office.

> *Soon after our arrival at the bridge we were given a position to hold on the north-east of the perimeter behind the headquarters building and facing the Arnhem prison, and there we remained until the end of the fourth day by which time the whole bridge area was becoming untenable. The trailers we had brought with us from the LZ had been loaded with ammunition, and were invaluable. There was no resupply to the bridge area at any time.*
>
> Captain W. V. Gell RASC

As the RAOC party arrived Captain Manley, with Staff Sergeant Walker, was met by an airborne officer and a Dutch civilian and taken into a well-lit building. They were informed that A Company were in the thick of fighting in the town and they needed all the help they could get. The orders were that they should forget the RAOC reconnaissance role and take an active part in securing the bridge. It was about 7.00 p.m. There were some signallers in the building and they were all put together with the RAOC as a single party. Moving off, they entered one building, full of chairs and with no lights, and experienced great difficulty moving around inside. Clearly unhappy with the situation Manley left the building and they regrouped on the road – to the sound of crashing chairs as people fumbled in the dark. From here they made their way along beside some houses to the archway under the bridge, passing on their left the buildings occupied by John Frost and his battalion headquarters and, next door to it, brigade headquarters. They had to crawl as bullets were flying everywhere and no one could see who was firing at whom. It was at this stage they lost touch with Ron Pugh, and would not see him again for the rest of the battle.

> *I lost the group, and as I was looking for them I bumped into an officer who took me to a school house near the bridge. I spent my time there either on patrol or*

manning the schoolhouse and didn't see the RAOC party again.
Private F. R. G. Pugh RAOC

Reaching the archway under the bridge and about to cross, the RAOC party was scattered by a burst of tracer coming down the road. They regrouped and made their way north a short way to another archway where, waiting for a lull in the firing, they crossed the road to a row of terraced houses and knocked on the door of the one on the corner.

Eventually the door was opened by a Dutchman and we tried to explain that we had to occupy the house and it would be safer for them to leave the house and the area. Shortly afterwards the man fetched his wife and small daughter from the cellar, packed a small suitcase and they left, walking down the middle of the street away from the bridge. My thought was: I hope they don't get shot by the Germans and where on earth could they go.
Private E. V. B. Mordecai RAOC

On arrival 2nd Battalion officers decided where we were to go. We were sent across the road, beyond the bridge, to a short terrace of houses. In front of us was a green area. It was a nice house, and we had to order the occupants out. We never saw them again.
Captain B. V. Manley RAOC

By 8.00 p.m. paratroopers at the bridge were taking stock of their positions, some six to seven hours after landing on the heath. An attempt to cross the bridge had been made by a platoon of A Company, commanded by Lieutenant Jack Grayburn,[11] but it had been beaten back by Germans in strongpoints on the bridge, and on the south bank. John Frost decided to wait until morning before trying again.

The RAOC and Royal Signals group now numbered twelve in all. During the night Major Digby Tatham-Warter, commanding A Company, and famous for carrying his umbrella, appeared outside their building and asked who was there. Once he knew he asked for six men to come and accompany him whilst he checked another building. This they did, and found it to be full of Sappers and Gunners. Tatham-Warter, satisfied, then went about his business, with his umbrella. However, as the party returned to their house they came under heavy machine-gun fire which speeded their return, with no casualties.

We made a sortie in the dark, out of the house towards the bridge, but did not make contact with the enemy. Then, while we were out in the open, we came under heavy machine-gun fire. As I ran across the road back to the houses bullets were flying all round me. In the excitement (terror?) to get under cover, I entered the wrong house and I had to summon up my courage to go outside again and move up three or four doors back to Captain Manley and company.
Private K. J. Heaney RAOC

And Whilst All This Was Going On...

Elsewhere, in Belgium and England, units were getting ready to play their part in the operation. The Seaborne Echelon had been briefed at 10.00 a.m. that morning in the conference room at XXX Corps Rear, followed at 5.30 p.m. by a more detailed briefing by a Lieutenant Colonel Curtis. They were to be at thirty minutes notice to move with effect from midday on 18 September.

In England preparations continued, right up to the last minute, for the departure of the second lift the next morning. Sergeant Bill Chedgey, however, was experiencing cause for concern:

> *I was preparing my gliderborne jeeps for taking off from Harwell when this new young officer arrived to take over the section. He had never seen a glider before, and asked if it were possible to have a look at one. He also brought with him twelve or fifteen men, none of whom had seen a glider, and they went into action with us the next day. Their only training session was to be told to home in on blue smoke. It did them no good, their glider came down in Nijmegen.*
>
> Sergeant W. H. Chedgey RASC

Meanwhile, along the corridor, the spearhead of XXX Corps was prevented from achieving its first night objectives by stiff German resistance. By nightfall the Guards Amoured division had liberated Valkenswaard, six miles south of their objective for the first day: Eindhoven. However, it was here they halted for the night, already behind schedule. The successful demolition by the Germans, that afternoon, of the canal bridge at Son, north of Eindhoven, would put them even further behind.

Everywhere, men settled down for the night, waiting for what the morrow might bring.

1. ADMS: Assistant Director of Medical Services, the senior doctor in a division.
2. Flak: Fliegerabwehrkanone - anti-aircraft guns. Flak was a term used by the Germans and the Allies alike to describe anti-aircraft fire.
3. Q Cell: A supporting office for the AA&QMG, in which his logistics staff worked.
4. Despatcher in this instance refers to the air force NCO in the rear of the aircraft who supervised the exit of the paratroopers. It has nothing to do with RASC air despatch, which involves the ejection of stores and supplies.
5. Char and a wad: A cup of tea and a sticky bun.
6. Author's Note: Until I researched this book I had always accorded with the accepted wisdom that there had been only one casualty from the parachute drop, the result of a partially opened parachute. This death, witnessed by Private Ted Mordecai, shows there to have been at least two. Speculating on the possible reason, a 2" Mortar Bomb, High Explosive, fuzed with the No 151 Fuze, or a 3" Mortar Bomb High Explosive, fuzed with the No 161 Fuze, could well have been the cause. Their successors, the 152 and 162, still in service into the seventies, were fitted with a safety pin in order to obviate the predilection of the 151 and 161 for detonating when least expected.
7. Research was by Mr J Thuring of Heesch. Source 'Roll of Honour' 4th Revised Edition 1999, J A Hey
8. Author's Note: It is not certain if he dropped or landed in a glider.
9. Parachute battalions had no anti-tank capability other than the PIAT. They relied on attached troops from the Royal Artillery.
10. Author's note: I have deduced this as his appointment, but cannot be certain.
11. Jack Grayburn would, eventually, be one of the five Arnhem VCs.

Chapter Five

The Second Day

The Germans Increase the Pressure

Out on the LZs and DZs the night passed relatively quietly. The Germans were busy building up their response to the landings, but it was taking time. In the west, General Hans von Tettau was assembling what troops he could and forming them into units despite having no operational staff with which to work. Nonetheless, with the speed and effectiveness that was a hallmark of the German Army, he was putting together three battlegroups which would give him a force to work with. One of these, and probably the least effective, comprised mostly Dutch SS, and they had one or two clashes during the night with 7th KOSB of 1st Airlanding Brigade who were defending DZ Y in anticipation of the 4th Parachute Brigade landing the following morning.

To their south-east the 2nd Battalion The South Staffordshire Regiment (2nd South Staffords) were guarding LZ S, on which the balance of the 1st Airlanding Brigade would land. There had not been enough tug aircraft to deliver the entire brigade on the first day and they had, in particular, to leave two companies of 2nd South Staffords off the first lift. Further south 1st Border were protecting Renkum Heath, which would provide the LZ for the 4th Parachute Brigade glider element, and the balance of divisional troops. These would include Divisional Rear Headquarters staff, the OFP main airlifted body and 2nd Parachute Platoon's jeep section.

East of the LZs and DZs SS Lieutenant Colonel Spindler, 9th SS Panzer Division's artillery commander, was setting up a blocking line west of Arnhem across the likely line of approach to the town, principally north of the Ede-Arnhem railway line, whilst Krafft's battlegroup, reinforced by elements from Marine and Police regiments, was taking control of the ground north of the Ede-Arnhem road. Between them von Tettau, Krafft and Spindler were forming the sides of a box into which 4th Parachute Brigade would drop later that day.

In Arnhem more and more German troops were moving gradually into position. Those who headed for the bridge came up against John Frost's force and a number of skirmishes ensued. Three trucks tried to cross the bridge from the south, not knowing the north end was held by the British. They were destroyed by the paratroopers, the crews either dying in their doomed vehicles, or being cut down, some of them burning, as they tried to escape on foot.

As daylight broke the British were stood to.[1] South of the bridge SS Captain Graebner, having found nothing at the Nijmegen bridge[2] was seeking to return his reconnaissance battalion to its parent division, the 9th SS. Knowing the north end was now held by his enemy he decided the best option would be to rush the bridge seeking to overrun the defenders. It was a tactic he had used successfully earlier in the war at Noyers Bocage. The trick was to make the rush when least expected; in other words, after the enemy had stood down. All he had on his side were surprise and shock action; and, after all, the opposition comprised only lightly armed infantry. Given the speed of his twenty-two armoured cars and half tracks, all equipped with machine-guns and some with 75mm howitzers, he was quite sure he could do it. His cavalryman's disdain for foot soldiers and his reckless character set the seal for him and his soldiers. At 9.00 am, hoping against hope that their brash and impetuous commander knew what he was doing, the SS troopers mounted their vehicles and prepared to move off.

They would be heading along a two lane road, which limited their frontage. For the first 250 metres they would be out of sight, hidden from the airborne defenders by the rise in the centre of the bridge. They would not be exposed until they reached the crest of the 200 metre span, before being completely at the mercy of the paratroopers on the 250 metre run down the bridge ramp on the other side before reaching the relative safety of Arnhem town centre.

Armoured cars in the lead, and responding to the pumped hand signal of their commander, and the exhortation 'marsch, marsch', they set off, reaching speeds of around twenty-five miles per hour. The first two armoured cars swept through into the town, their cannon and machine guns firing from the moment they crossed the hump of the bridge, then two more, and then another three. Just as it looked as if success might be within their grasp the British woke up to what was happening, in time to be able to concentrate their fire on the much slower half-track personnel carriers. Suddenly, a six-wheeled vehicle hit a British Hawkins Mine[3] and slewed to a halt. Mayhem ensued as the British opened well coordinated fire with intense ferocity.

Private E. V. B. Mordecai RAOC. Like many airborne soldiers he chose to wear the winged cap-badge, rather than that of his parent corps. There appears to have been something of a laissez-faire attitude to this throughout Airborne Forces.
Author's Collection

Shortly after daybreak we heard the sound of engines revving up and looking towards the other side of the bridge to the south we saw a line of open-topped Opel armoured cars coming across the bridge in 'line astern'. These cars were very small, reinforced with steel and carried between four and six occupants. The cars were about ten yards distance from each other and as the first car across reached the top of the ramp there was an explosion as one of our 6-pounder anti-tank guns mounted just below the ramp fired and caught the car in the middle. The other cars following pulled up immediately, offering a perfect target for all of us. Everyone within range immediately opened fire on the cars with Brens, Stens, rifles and grenades. As soon as a German soldier tried to get out of a car he was knocked over. It was just like snap shooting, as soon as anything moved every paratrooper who saw it just opened up. It was a hectic ten or twenty minutes or so and it was soon over. Then we realised it was breakfast time and the most any of us had eaten since leaving England the day before was a few boiled sweets and a few sips of water.'
Private E.V.B. Mordecai RAOC

Memories vary, and the battle probably lasted longer than Ted Mordecai's 'ten or twenty minutes'. Indications are that firing continued, gradually becoming more and more sporadic, until midday. However, whatever the

The Arnhem bridge, and the wreckage of Graebner's abortive attack can clearly be seen. Courtesy Imperial War Museum

timings, the first serious German attempt on the bridge had failed; and Graebner paid for it with his life.

Meanwhile, in the west von Tettau's scratch formation, now known as Division von Tettau, was pressing harder and harder against 1st Airlanding Brigade and advancing with some success. Infiltrating the areas around Heelsum and Renkum they were forcing the defenders back and were beginning to make their presence felt.

During the morning Driver Jack Taylor was one of a group of five from 1st Parachute Platoon, 250 Company, detailed to find some transport. The group also included Lance Corporals Plant and Hurst and Drivers Start and Zanbernini. They entered the village of Heelsum where one of the local women warned them that there were Germans in and around the village and in the woods.[4] They made no contact with them at that point, and went further into the village where they found a school bus which, so Jack thought, had come out from Arnhem on an early morning task. On being told that they required his bus the driver expressed concern that being left-hand drive they would have difficulty handling it and that he was quite happy to help. He was content to drive it so long as they promised, if caught, to swear they had forced him to do it.

> *We had left the DZ loaded up and headed for the dump at the Hartenstein without incident and unloaded the supplies. On the way back, just before Heelsum on an 'S' bend we were fired on by a machine-gun from the woods at a point where the ground rose above us on our left, and also from a position ahead and on the right.*

The Dutchman was killed at that point. We left the bus and took up defensive positions in the garden of a house that was close by where the bus came to a stop. Lance Corporal Plant was fatally hit at this point. We continued to return fire until we ran out of ammunition and the Germans came out of the woods and took us prisoner.

Driver J. A. Taylor RASC

The Second Lift

The second lift was due to leave England at around 7.00 a.m. However, unpredictable weather brought a dense fog on the embarkation airfields and they were delayed. This added to the problems being faced by 1st Airlanding Brigade who would now have to hold the LZs and DZs longer; and it gave the Germans still longer to organise their reaction.

Arriving at the airfield an imposing sight met our eyes. Gliders by the score were lined up along the runway in a double line with the tug aircraft, American two-engined Douglas C-47s, forming an additional line on either side. Most of our equipment had been stowed away on the gliders the previous day and therefore all that remained to be done was to put aboard the few small items of personal kit we were carrying with us – not the least important being three thermos flasks of hot tea for use during the flight and after landing at our destination.

WO1 (Sub-Conductor) G. E. Jenkins RAOC, HQ 1st Airborne Division

Eventually departing at 11.00 am, and with WO1 Jenkins sharing his glider with WO1 F.F. Eastwood, BOWO 1st Airlanding Brigade, the flight was expected to last about four hours. For the first three-quarters of an hour they flew westwards to a rendezvous to form up with the other gliders from other airfields. Course

Hamilcars in serried ranks, awaiting take-off. The tug aircraft, Halifax bombers, are parked to the left and right. Courtesy Museum of Army Flying

was set for Holland at about 11.45 a.m. at an altitude of 2,500 feet , which gave a lovely view of the English countryside. People below could be seen staring up at the combinations as they flew overhead.

> *At about 11.00 a.m. the first tow planes with the gliders left the airfield. After a last, hasty, cup of tea - nicely provided by an RAF NAAFI truck - we went to our seats in the glider, buckled on and waited for our turn. At intervals of forty seconds the planes left. We did not have to wait long. You always have that peculiar feeling when you let loose from the ground and you see mother earth disappearing. Soon we were at a height of 2,500 feet.*
> WO1 (Sub-Conductor) G. E. Jenkins RAOC

The second lift took 2nd Parachute Platoon and 2nd Parachute Platoon Jeep Section from Saltby in Lincolnshire. There were fourteen glider loads, also taking additional elements of 250 Company. The total lift was two parachuting loads and twenty-eight Horsas. There were also the three Hamilcars carrying extra stocks from Tarrant Rushton. Loaded by Captain Jerome and his men from 253 Airborne Composite Company, there were four soldiers in each glider, all from 250 Company.

> *On 18 September 1944 we took off from Tarrant Rushton in a glider. The glider was carrying a jeep and a trailer with ammunition. Except for the glider pilots, the only RASC men in the glider were my friend Driver Johnny Walford and myself. Our landing zone was 'X', close to the Wolfheze railway.*
> Corporal S. P. J. Staple RASC, 2nd Parachute Platoon 250 Airborne Light Company RASC

Crossing the North Sea, and looking down, they could see the white topped waves, and the Air-Sea Rescue launches waiting to pick up the crews and passengers of any downed aircraft. These were most likely to be gliders that had broken their tow, or had to be jettisoned early by the tugs.

> *Ahead of us could be seen a thin line of white on the water which gradually resolved into a foaming wake of one of the craft travelling at speed. Then we spotted the glider floating on the sea with its complement sitting on the wing awaiting rescue - confident that it was a matter of moments away.*
> WO1 (Sub-Conductor) G. E. Jenkins RAOC

At the bridge, in the house occupied by the RAOC party, Ted Mordecai cooked up some of Kevin Heaney's OXO cubes as a drink for everyone. Bernard Manley ordered them to try and get some sleep and Ted, with Mac McCarthy, dropped onto a double feather bed, but sleep would not come. Twenty minutes later there was a mighty explosion and a large cloud of dust and smoke flew through the bedroom door. It was either a mortar or a tank round, but the back of the house had a gaping hole where the wall and roof should have been. Three of the Royal Signals soldiers had gone into the back room to sleep. Two were only stunned,

You always have that peculiar feeling when you let loose from the ground and you see mother earth disappearing. A Stirling bomber takes off towing a Horsa glider. Courtesy Imperial War Museum

but one, who had lain on the bed, was badly hurt. Covered in blood and looking dead, they could not be certain if he was alive. He was taken to another room and put on another bed. Harry Walker gave him morphine from the little syrettes they all carried, just in case it might do some good. Given the intensity of the firing it was decided that the survivors should all move down to the cellar for shelter. There they found some milk, which did nothing for thirst, and a couple of bottles of wine from which they took a few mouthfuls each.

> *My pack was in the back bedroom, and I was disappointed when it was lost. I had not touched the rations inside.*
> Private K. J. Heaney RAOC

As the firing died down, at about 2.00 p.m., they ventured out again and occupied the upstairs rooms once more. For the rest of the day there was some minor activity on the bridge, but for the most part it was quiet. The paratroopers, however, were merciless, and fired on anything that moved.

> *A German prisoner being held in one of the corner houses on the left made a break for it. He was running very fast, his boots sounding noisy on the road. He had covered about forty yards before he was killed by two well aimed tracer bullets.*
> Private K. J. Heaney RAOC

Far away and to the west the second lift began to experience heavier resistance in the air than their predecessors; but the Germans were, by now, expecting them. There was flak as they crossed the Dutch coast, causing the gliders, and presumably the tugs, to buffet as they flew along. It was distinctly uncomfortable for the passengers. Fred Eastwood's glider was hit by shrapnel which came through the skin and struck the metal struts of the glider, but which caused no problems. They flew through it into calmer conditions.

> *Normally I would have felt OK, but not on this day. After a while our glider started to swing and shake in a strange way. We soon realised that we were being shot at by German flak. Suddenly there was a blow, much closer than the others had been. We heard it clatter against the metal framework.*
> WO1 (Sub-Conductor) G. E. Jenkins RAOC

In the glider with the two warrant officers were a jeep and trailer with its driver, a corporal, as well as the two crew from the Glider Pilot Regiment. It was shortly after their first encounter with flak that they suffered a more serious blow, and one which was to have a profound effect on their lives for the next few weeks.

> *We were about twenty minutes flying time from the LZ. Now another battery of flak opened up on us and this time the million to one chance came off. An explosive bullet, or pieces of shrapnel, zipped right into our tow rope, cutting it cleanly and setting us free from the pull of our tug aircraft.*
> WO1 (Sub-Conductor) G. E. Jenkins RAOC

The pilot put the aircraft into a steep spiral dive and made a perfect

WO1 (Sub Conductor) F.F. Eastwood RAOC, BOWO 1st Airlanding Brigade.

landing in very difficult circumstances in a field some distance south-west of Nijmengen. Having got down safely they began to sort themselves out, and gather their kit, but there were others with different ideas. No sooner was the door of the glider opened than they were shaken by the explosion of a mortar bomb that landed nearby. It was a ranging shot, and the second dropped right beneath the tail of the glider, whilst a machine-gun opened up from a copse some 200 yards away. All five occupants of the glider dashed for a ditch leaving behind their food which was in the jeep, located near the tail of the glider, and which was the target for the mortar and the machine-gun. Making their way through ditches for over an hour, they sought to make their escape. It was exhausting, and during this time they lost the corporal[5] and had no idea what happened to him.

On DZ Y it was an opposed landing. At 3.00 p.m. the Dakotas appeared, but despite the best efforts of 7th KOSB the Germans had infiltrated all around the area and were firing up at parachutists as they fell from the sky. Mortar bombs were landing everywhere, and machine-gun fire ripped across the heath, the heather burning freely and sending up dense clouds of smoke which obscured the ground. Even up to the last the Scottish soldiers were making every effort to protect their brethren in the air and as they landed on the ground. However, ghastly as it was, there were lighter moments, one of which is recalled with vicarious pleasure by Lance Corporal Tom Smith of the KOSB:

At 3.00 pm we heard a mighty roar and all hell broke loose. We were ordered to fix bayonets and chase the Germans from the zone so, when the piper began to drone, we did that and they ran like hell. Paras were dropping like snowflakes all around us; then supply, food, ammunition etc came down. A para landed smack on our position. We helped him to his feet, he looked very young and sort of dazed, as if he was wondering what the hell he was doing here. We noted that he wasn't armed or equipped. My officer asked him 'why'. This is what he said: 'I shouldn't be here. I am on a forty-eight hour pass, I volunteered to push the supplies from the Dakotas because I had never flown before.' He was in the RASC. The Dakota was shot down. We equipped him from a dead man. The officer said: 'Your leave has been cancelled, and you are now in the KOSB. Your NCO is Corporal McKay.' I never saw him again, or knew his name or if he survived the battle. We pissed ourselves at the expression on his face.[6]

Lance Corporal T. Smith, Anti-Tank Group, Support Company, 7th Battalion The King's Own Scottish Borderers

Standing in the body of their Dakota the parachute element of 2nd Parachute Platoon, 250 Company, prepared to jump. Only those in the doorway had any idea of what lay below, but nothing was said.

Captain Kavanagh would always be in the door, on the edge and well forward. His runner would always be number two in the stick with his head under the captain's arm, with me and the Bren Gun tucked in hard on his right. We virtually jumped as a threesome so as to stay together.

Driver K. W. Clarke RASC, 2nd Parachute Platoon 250 Airborne Light Company RASC

We landed successfully and rendezvoused with Captain Kavanagh and made our way to the level crossing at Wolfheze. We tried, unsuccessfully, to contact 156 Battalion who were needing our supplies. We had not been furnished with the correct radio frequencies.

Corporal B. Blaxley RASC, 2nd Parachute Platoon, 250 Airborne Light Company RASC

However, not all of the 2nd Parachute Platoon was able to stay together, and men were spread over a wide area. Driver John Prime's experience was not untypical:

I landed in a tree, right at the top of it, and felt very exposed. There was firing going on nearby. I released the kitbag with the Bren and released myself from the harness, and eventually got down. I took the Bren and two pouches of ammunition, but left the rest of the kitbag with the spare canvas wallet of Bren magazines and the Bren cleaning kit and my rations. I shouldn't have, but I was alone in the trees and wanted to get to the DZ. I followed the direction of the firing. I heard others in the trees, but I was looking after number one. We had expected an unopposed landing, and things were going wrong. I got out onto the open heath and made for the blue smoke of our platoon RV. There were several of us by then, running in an extended line, not running very fast really because of our loads; we kept having to stop to take a breather. The German fire was sweeping the whole DZ two or three feet above the ground. We were about a hundred yards across when one of the men was hit. He gave a huge gasp and fell down on his face like a sack of potatoes. We all went to ground again. Tubby Ashman ran over to him (or shuffled, we were like Christmas trees), turned him over and said that he was dead. When we eventually got to the RV one of the lads there had been hit in the face, not seriously, but was in shock with his hands over his face covered with blood. Captain Kavanagh was squaring him up, telling him to pull himself together.

Driver J. Prime RASC, 2nd Parachute Platoon 250 Airborne Light Company RASC

The last element of nine Dakotas became separated from the main formation and delivered their sticks north of the DZ, and some men were dropped about eight miles away. Two of the sticks were from 133 Parachute Field Ambulance, and in a fight with some Germans[7] an RASC driver with the Field Ambulance was killed.

The gliderborne elements also experienced difficulty on the LZs at Renkum.

As we cast off from our tug, our glider pilot was shot in the chest and collapsed over the controls. The glider nose-dived, and the second pilot shouted to me to pull the injured pilot off. I tried to, but the pilot would not leave the controls. As I eventually pulled him back the controls came back as well and the glider levelled off. The pilot then regained consciousness and shook his head and said 'I'm... bringing her in.' He did, and made a lovely landing. With the help of the second pilot we got him out and sat him up against a tree. We then unloaded the jeep and trailer, we just had one trailer behind our jeep, by getting the tail off and went to our destination.

Corporal S. P. J. Staple RASC

Corporal S. P. J. Staple RASC.

Courtesy Airborne Museum 'Hartenstein'

The 250 Company arrivals made their rendezvous, both jeep and parachute elements coming together. They were to spend that first night in a level crossing keeper's house near Wolfheze. The Ordnance Field Park, on the other hand, being gliderborne, had been able to concentrate much more easily.

> *The Ordnance Field Park in three gliders, with the divisional headquarters element including Lieutenant Colonel Mobbs, landed with the Divisional Headquarters and assembled at the planned point in good order, although one glider required the tail to be wrenched off due to the rusting of one of the holding bolts.*[8] *There was considerable rifle and machine-gun fire to welcome our arrival.*
> Major C. C. Chidgey RAOC

Bill Chidgey also took with him in his jeep the rails used to run vehicles out of the glider, not being sure if they were part of the glider's equipment or the jeep's; but they would be useful for all sorts of things such as trench revetment or crossing ditches.

The gliders also brought in with them the balance of Divisional Rear Headquarters. They assembled in time to find that Divisional Main Headquarters was in the process of moving to a new location: the Hartenstein Hotel in Oosterbeek, just beside the Utrechtseweg which bisects the village. They arrived at 5.30 p.m.

> *We formed up and marched up the main road to the Hartenstein. We thought it was just like an exercise. We went past the body of General Kussin. We went straight into the cellar.*
> Sergeant N. G. Griffin RASC

The extent to which infantry battalions brought their own support elements with them varied. Generally speaking their 'A' Echelon would contain immediate reserves of ammunition, fuel, compo and essential spares and little else. Other requirements, including spare clothing and stores of a more general nature,

Loading a Horsa glider through the front side door. Courtesy Imperial War Museum

would be with B Echelon, much further back; and B Echelons for the battalions at Arnhem were with the Seaborne Echelon. However, what was actually contained in the echelons and how the battalion's own logistic support resources were split, depended on the view of the CO and his quartermaster. This included the cooks, both ACC and regimental. At that time a parachute battalion, for example, was established for a sergeant, two corporals and ten private soldiers ACC, but how they were deployed varied significantly.[9] In some cases they did not join in the airlift, but in others they were quite clearly considered very much a part of the airborne element of the battalion. In 156 Parachute Battalion in 4th Parachute Brigade the chief cook commanded what was called the 'administrative platoon' in Headquarter Company, and was expected to do rather more than just cook.

> *Looking back now on those hectic days I find that everything is rather like an interrupted dream. First the rather tense, but pleasant enough, trip across, and a good drop for all, except Private Preece who broke his collar bone.*
> Sergeant J. Lambert ACC, Chief Cook,156 Parachute Battalion

The Operational Situation – The British Make Adjustments

Whilst the second lift had been on its way it had been necessary to make a number of changes in the British plans, given the problems being visited on them by the Germans, to say nothing of the delay in the arrival of reinforcements. A key problem was that General Urquhart was still missing. He had continued forward with 3rd Parachute Battalion that morning, and had followed it as it changed course from its central route down onto the lower road taken by Frost's battalion. In the area of the Rhine Pavilion, near the St Elisabeth Hospital, he had decided to attempt a return to his headquarters, not having been in touch for

The first DAA. The white elipse 1 marks the location of Major Chidgey's OFP in the trees, whilst in elipse 2 can be seen what are probably 250 Company vehicles. The jeeps in the foreground are driving along Utrechtseweg, just in front of the Hartenstein Hotel. Courtesy Imperial War Museum

over twelve hours. He was unsuccessful and due to German activity was forced to take refuge in a small terraced house very near the hospital, together with two other officers. In so doing, he continued to render himself utterly incommunicado, and 1st Airborne Division continued to be leaderless. In seeking to help his divisional commander to escape, commander 1st Parachute Brigade, Gerald Lathbury, was wounded and had to be left with a Dutch family, never to rejoin his brigade. This not only left his brigade leaderless with its headquarters stuck at the bridge, but he had been the nominated successor if anything happened to Urquhart. Now, at this crucial stage, both of them were out of commission.

Following behind 3rd Battalion as it headed into town was 1st Battalion. Lieutenant Colonel Dobie, having decided to head for the bridge, had also moved down to the lower road and was proceeding towards the Rhine Pavilion area. However, he was meeting tougher opposition than those who had gone before him and it would be 4.30 p.m. before he was to reach the area being occupied by Fitch's Battalion. Both battalions would spend the night in the area, neither being aware of the presence of the other.

Not knowing if the General was alive or dead, his staff decided to call on Brigadier 'Pip' Hicks, commanding 1st Airlanding Brigade, to take command of the Division. Reluctantly, he agreed, being the only brigadier available and Urquhart's second choice in the event that Lathbury might not be available – which he wasn't. Hicks made two decisions: to send 2nd South Staffords into town at once to support attempts to reach the bridge; and to order 11th Parachute Battalion from 4th Parachute Brigade to do the same once they had landed. It should be remembered that 2nd South Staffords at this stage only had two companies. The other two were coming in on the second lift and would have to follow on into town once they had arrived. Brigadier Hicks did not choose to send with the two battalions any headquarters elements for command and control. Presumably he assumed Headquarters 1st Parachute Brigade still to be functioning and capable of taking control. It was, of course, fighting for survival at the bridge.

Brigadier John Hackett, at thirty-four a very young and fiery brigadier, was not best pleased to be told that he was losing, within minutes of landing, one third of the infantry he had trained so assiduously to fight as part of his brigade. He acceded, with poor grace, insisting that he should be given 7th KOSB to plug the gap. This was agreed, but 7th KOSB were not made aware of this for some time. Command and control muddles mounted, and were becoming a serious hindrance to the prospects of success.

Having detached 11th Parachute Battalion, John Hackett began his advance on his objective for the next day. It was on high ground north of the Wolfheze railway, and it lay beyond the line where SS Lieutenant Colonel Spindler was already strengthening his blocking position.

> *As platoon commander, advancing along a railway line with my ten ACC boys and the others of the Administrative Platoon, I had orders to start cooking when our positions had been consolidated, and wondered when that would be.*
>
> Sergeant J. Lambert ACC

The Divisional Administrative Area Takes Shape

At 3.30 p.m. HQ RASC, comprising Lieutenant Colonel Michael Packe, his adjutant, Captain J. D. Naylor RASC, and nine soldiers moved to the area of the Hartenstein Hotel. They established their own headquarters and that of the DAA in front of the hotel, in the cellar of a house on the edge of a triangle of grass bounded by Utrechtseweg, which is the main road running west to east past the Hartenstein, and two minor roads. This was done under moderate enemy fire, although no enemy activity was reported except some sniping which would occur later, during the night. A resupply drop was carried out in conjunction with the second lift, but the parachutes dropped largely on the predetermined SDP north of the Wolfheze railway line at LZ L, out of reach of the airborne soldiers. However, some stocks were collected, and two captured German vehicles were put into running order and were used for ferrying ammunition to the DAA and later for delivery of gun ammunition to 1st Airlanding Light Regiment Royal Artillery. This was all undertaken by Captain Jack Cranmer-Byng's platoon, plus one or two lost souls from 2nd Parachute Platoon which had landed that day.

> *When we landed I didn't see Captain Kavanagh. I followed the crowd and we ended up at the Hartenstein. The first person I saw there was Lieutenant Colonel Packe, and near him was Sergeant Watson digging a slit trench and just then we were mortared and all dived for cover.*
>
> Sergeant W. H. Chedgey RASC

The vehicles of the OFP comprised four jeeps, each towing a trailer. One was a GS trailer for bulkier items and the others were 19½-cwt binned trailers. These had a somewhat lower centre of gravity than GS trailers and were used by the RAOC for the fitting of bins. Scalings were worked out after careful discussion with the quartermasters and the MTOs[10] of the infantry battalions. There was a close liaison with the Royal Signals and Royal Engineer units, and the OFP also carried the repair parts for the REME workshop, which had no inherent spares capability of its own.[11]

The small RAOC unit was positioned in the shrubs on the western end of the triangle. This placed Major Bill Chidgey RAOC and Sergeant Bill Chedgey RASC in the DAA, within 100 yards of each other. Neither knew the other, and they were not to meet for some thirty or so years when they were both involved in local politics in Somerset and realised they shared a common experience.

In the evening, at 8.30 p.m., the DAA officially opened for business on the main road facing the Hartenstein. The contents of the DAA came from the balance of the reserve of ammunition from 1st Parachute Brigade, from the limited supply drop with the second lift and from the Hamilcars carrying reserves of ammunition and other stores. Regrettably, only two of the three big gliders could be unloaded before enemy activity prevented further collection of stocks. It appears, however, that one of the two whose contents did reach the DAA was carrying the Ordnance Stores. No packed petrol was available within the DAA.

A convoy of six jeeps, each towing two trailers loaded with ammunition, was organised and stood by ready to go to 1st Parachute Brigade; but it never left. There was no chance at all of reaching the bridge. However, part of the load was subsequently transferred to two Bren carriers which later got through to 2nd South Staffords and 1st Parachute Battalion on the western edge of Arnhem.

> *Travelling in jeeps with the double trailers seemed like a good idea, but they snaked terribly and damaged the tyres. The concept was difficult to make work.*
> Captain P. W. H. Jay RASC, 165 Company[12] RASC (Airborne Light) AFDAG

The Day Draws In

As darkness began to descend the Irish Guards battlegroup leading the XXX Corps advance had reached the Son bridge, having been delayed from the very outset by a mixture of enemy action and exuberant Dutch people. However, the new bridge was not yet complete and they would have to wait before they could proceed. By Montgomery's original timetable they were due at Arnhem the following lunchtime.

Further south the Seaborne Echelon was still at thirty minutes notice to move toward Arnhem, but had still not moved anywhere. In the OFP Don Eyres was concerned that stocks of acetylene were running low, although they had plenty of oxygen. Provision and replenishment of industrial gases were always a problem, and this operation was proving no different.

In England the AFDAG moved to three airfields in East Anglia in preparation for embarkation: Folkingham, Spanhoe and Barkston Heath.

Meanwhile, near the town of 's-Hertogenbosch in Holland, the downed RAOC warrant officers and their pilots, having spent the day in a maize field, set out north-east, in the direction of Arnhem, which they thought to be about forty miles away, in an optimistic frame of mind. However, after some distance they found their way blocked by a canal and, hearing movement everywhere, which they assumed to be Germans because of the curfew, decided to lay up until daylight when they would be able to see. They found a haystack.

> *A word about Dutch haystacks. They are not built in the same way as those seen in England, but were far better suited to our purpose. A central pole stands approximately to a height of thirty feet, and the hay is stacked evenly around. Thatching is not resorted to, but instead a separate thatched frame is suspended on the pole and is adjusted to the fluctuating height of the hay. This roof, having quite considerable space underneath, suited our requirements admirably.*
> WO1 (Sub-Conductor) G. E. Jenkins RAOC

Advancing along the line of the Wolfheze railway line C Company of 156 Parachute Battalion, spearheading the advance of 4th Parachute Brigade, bumped the outposts of Spindler's blocking line. It was very dark in the woods, and the Battalion withdrew to the area of LZ L to await the morning light before proceeding further. As they did so, 7th KOSB was moving into the same area. Still not aware of their new status as part of 4th Parachute Brigade, and having completed their defence of DZ Y, they were moving to their next task: to protect

LZ L in anticipation of the landing of the Polish Brigade's heavy, gliderborne equipment the next morning.

During the night at the bridge the Germans continued to probe Frost's position.

The sun dropped low and it grew dark. Jerry opened up on us again with long range stuff and was answered back by the 6-pounder which did some good work that night, but was eventually put out of action towards midnight. The Germans had evidently spotted it and had put a heavy concentration of mortar bombs on its position and the large house alongside. This house was blazing like an inferno and lit up the surrounding area for the rest of the night and eventually petered out towards dawn. After the barrage it quietened down with just a little spasmodic firing thereafter, but we still couldn't afford to relax or sleep due to German patrols sneaking up on us.

Private E. V. B. Mordecai RAOC

Also during the night the last stocks of ammunition were issued from Bill Gell's platoon. He had nothing left, and the bridge defenders would receive no more.

1. To 'stand to', the 'stand-to', to be 'stood to' all refer to the British practice of waking soldiers thirty minutes before dawn to have them alert with their weapons ready at what was judged the most likely time for a surprise attack. It would normally last until half an hour after first light, hence the duration of a stand-to was one hour.
2. In planning his assault on bridges in the Nijmegen area, General Gavin of the 82nd Airborne Division had reasoned that if he failed to achieve his other objectives any effort on the main Waal Bridge would be wasted, and he left it to the last. Consequently, when Graebner arrived on the evening of the 17th there had been nothing for him to see.
3. Hawkins mine: a small anti-tank mine, very light and more of a grenade. It had only limited effect, and was unlikely actually to damage a tank. However, it would cause difficulty for a wheeled vehicle.
4. Almost certainly troops from Division von Tettau.
5. The name of the corporal is uncertain. The manifest for the glider shows him as Corporal Stevenson RASC, wounded and taken prisoner. Subsequently, Staff Sergeant R. G. Evans, the glider's pilot, records the fifth man as being Corporal Thompson, but does not note his corps. Corporal Thompson RAOC was part of the Ordnance party, but Private Dennis Brown RAOC, of the OFP's Second Seaborne Echelon, who saw them depart from England, is certain Thompson went in Major Chidgey's aircraft. Reliant only on memory for its resolution, the mystery is likely to remain just that – a mystery.
6. The only resupply missions flown on the 18th were thirty-three Stirlings from 295 Sqn RAF from Harwell, with their loads destined for LZ L. All Dakotas that day were used on parachuting missions. There is no doubting the truth of Tom Smith's story, or the day on which it occurred, but the RASC soldier must have leapt from one of the parachuting aircraft.
7. Most probably Dutch SS, part of Division von Tettau.
8. When loading a Horsa glider with a jeep and trailer it was manhandled in through the passenger door on the side of the aircraft at the front. To unload, bolts, which held the tail section onto the body, were removed and the tail section was swung away to one side. The jeep and trailer were then driven straight out the back, down ramps carried in the glider.
9. There is no need to look further than the example of Corporal Menzies whose first, and only, drop is recorded earlier in this book. Not only was there never any intention to take him, but his name does not appear on any record made by officers of 2nd Parachute Battalion, either as surviving, being wounded or being made prisoner-of-war. Officially, he was never there – but then speak to the soldiers with whom he fought.
10. MTO: Motor Transport Officer.
11. It is clear when talking to Major Chidgey that there was huge emphasis placed on recovery and reclamation of stores. It was an RAOC task that was always taught on courses long after the War, but no real practical attention was paid to it in the post-war years; and much was forgotten with the passing of time. The role now lies, in the modern British Army, with the REME Territorial Army.
12. This unit appears under several names, and I have chosen to use the one shown in the official documents recording the composition of the AFDAG.

CHAPTER SIX

Day Three – 1st Airborne Division's Last Attempt to Reinforce the Bridge

A Busy Morning

The first hint of grey appeared on the horizon beyond Arnhem to the east. At 5.00 a.m. there was stand-to for an hour in the DAA. There was some sniping from a built-up area behind HQ RASC, but they were secure with well-dug slit trenches and well-organised defences. However, from a few miles away in the direction of the rising sun they could hear the sounds of an intense firefight. In the small hours the 3rd Parachute Battalion had tried to follow the road from the Rhine Pavilion along to the bridge, a route known as the Onderlangs. They had been beaten back and as they returned in the dark at around 4.00 a.m. they met 1st Parachute Battalion launching their own attack.

The 1st Parachute Battalion's action was part of a coordinated attack organised by Lieutenant Colonel Dobie and the CO of the 2nd South Staffords, with the 11th Parachute Battalion in reserve. The 2nd South Staffords' line of attack paralleled that of Dobie's men, but on the higher road above the Onderlangs. With fire support, mostly small arms, from the remnants of the 3rd Parachute Battalion the attack proceeded. With Germans to their front, on the south bank of the river to their right and along the railway marshalling yards to their left the two battalions advanced into a veritable valley of death.

As the airborne battalions moved forward in the gathering light, the coming of dawn elsewhere across Holland meant different things to different men. At the bridge the night had been almost as bright as day from the flames of burning buildings. Bernard Manley's men were down to half a water bottle of water each, and local water supplies had been shut off, even the toilet cistern was empty. What they had was pooled and a hot drink was made.

Along the corridor the growing light showed that the work to span the canal at Son was almost complete. For the downed RAOC warrant officers it meant waking, lost somewhere south of Nijmegen, damp and cramped, to see what the day might bring.

> *The night was almost over, and as you can imagine we slept not much. We waited anxiously for the dawn to come. At first light we saw we were between trees. In the distance was a small farm with an orchard and some farm land.*
>
> WO 1 (Sub-Conductor) G. E. Jenkins RAOC

As it grew light, Desmond Kavanagh's 2nd Parachute Platoon was given orders to move from the level crossing keeper's house where they had spent the night,

Captain D. T. Kavanagh RASC, Officer Commanding 2nd Parachute Platoon, 250 Light Company.
Author's Collection

via Wolfheze, to the Hartenstein Hotel. On reaching Wolfheze they occupied the post office. Driver Ken Clarke had clear sight of a Focke-Wulf 190, flying so low and so close he could see the pilot in his cockpit, but was refused permission to fire in case he gave away the position. The question in everyone's minds, however, was how it could fly over the area with such apparent impunity when the Allies had command of the air.

We decided to leave half our supplies camouflaged at Wolfheze and set off in the early hours of the 19th in platoon strength. One or two hours later I was instructed by Captain Kavanagh to return to Wolfheze and retrieve these supplies, bringing them to divisional headquarters.
Corporal B. Blaxley RASC

We drove in the direction of the railway line towards the village of Wolfheze. We encountered German machine-gun fire, so we turned around and headed south towards the road which runs through Oosterbeek to Heelsum. When we arrived on this road[1] *we picked up two Dutch Underground men. They told us that the Germans were coming along the banks of the Rhine towards Oosterbeek, in the area of the Bilderberg Hotel as far as I can remember. We handed the two over to the recce officer for interrogation and we went on to the ammo dump.*
Corporal S. P. J. Staple RASC

At 7.00 a.m. XXX Corps cleared Son, and would be with the 82nd Airborne Division's southernmost outpost by 9.30 a.m., at the Grave Bridge a few miles south of Nijmegen. However, further real progress would be denied to them: the 10th SS, together with local garrison troops, were defending Nijmegen in considerable strength; and the Americans had yet to capture the main road bridge over the River Waal – the last bridge before Arnhem.

At 7.30 a.m. General Urquhart was able to escape from the attic in which he had hidden. This was due to the departure of the German vehicle that had been parked, with its crew, all night in the street outside and preventing his earlier departure. Driven by Lieutenant E. E. Clapham, serving with 1st Airlanding Anti-Tank Battery Royal Artillery, he returned to his headquarters, much to the surprise and delight of his staff. He made a number of decisions, key among which was that further attempts to reach the bridge would be useless. Accordingly, he ordered the 11th Parachute Battalion not to take part in the relief attempt currently under way involving 1st Parachute Battalion and 2nd South Staffords, but to attack north and west of Arnhem to join up with 4th Parachute Brigade on its objective. Consequently, just as the two attacking battalions trying to reach the bridge needed their reserve it was denied them. Their attack was abortive, as was that of 11th Battalion seeking to reach Hackett's men. By the end of the morning all three battalions would, like the 3rd Parachute Battalion before them, cease to exist as cohesive fighting units, having suffered massive casualties.

At the bridge there was no respite from intense German activity, and in particular from armoured vehicles. To many it seemed fairly certain that the armour had broken through the outer defences and that they were cut off. However, the defenders were in good shape and taking advantage of every target offered. The RAOC group spotted five Germans trying to set up charges on the bridge and kept them under observation until they were able to knock them all out with one burst from a Bren gun.

From the bedroom window I saw one of our officers with an umbrella in his hand standing in the middle of the road and shouting encouragement to us in the houses. He told us we would not have to hold on much longer and that we would soon be relieved.

Private K. J. Heaney RAOC

Later on, during the early part of the morning, the Germans visited a particularly heavy barrage on the bridge area.

The barrage then stopped and we resumed our positions with me on the left and Staff Sergeant Walker on the right looking out onto the road and embankment opposite. Whilst we were looking out of the window we observed one of our medical orderlies emerge from the archway under the bridge about twenty-five yards to our left. His white armband with a plain red cross on it was clearly visible and he was escorting three German prisoners. Suddenly a shot rang out and he staggered back towards the arch with two of the Germans with him. The third prisoner started to run in our direction hoping to make a break for it. This was fatal as one of our chaps with a Bren Gun in a house near the archway opened fire and hit the German in the legs. He fell on the ground, but still tried to crawl away and was immediately hit with another burst from the Bren. This finished him off, and we could see the tracer bullets going straight through his back and ricocheting off the pavement in front of him.

Private E. V. B. Mordecai RAOC

Shortly afterwards there was a conference in brigade headquarters. Officers in charge of parties in the area of the bridge were told that XXX Corps had been held up by enemy opposition and it would be some time before they arrived. In the meantime, they were to hang on to the bridge for as long as possible. At this stage the pervading feeling was still that they would be relieved in due course, and the paratroopers settled down, determined to fight on until reinforcements arrived.

In the DAA at 10.30 a.m. about forty Messerschmitt 109s and Focke-Wulf 190s attacked. With no anti-aircraft weapons with which to offer a defence, soldiers fired up at the attacking aircraft with machine-guns and rifles. Seeing the threat this enemy activity posed to the planned supply drops, and believing the enemy might already hold the planned SDPs, Michael Packe tried to send a signal altering the pre-arranged supply dropping point.

Re-supply signals used to be put into SLIDEX.[2] We got a couple of supply drops through. Stanley Maxted[3] was there, and passed re-supply information through

the BBC link and then on to 1st Airborne Corps. On one occasion Colonel Preston sent me out with a Very pistol to attract pilots' attention, but the Germans were doing the same thing on the perimeter and it was to no avail.
Sergeant N. G. Griffin RASC

For most of the morning, and just north of the DAA, less than a mile beyond the Ede-Arnhem railway, 156 Parachute Battalion had been involved in a heavy battle with SS troopers on the left flank of Spindler's blocking line. Pitted against well prepared positions, and armoured vehicles equipped with cannon, mortars and howitzers, the lightly equipped infantry had little chance. They were beaten back, with A and B Companies virtually destroyed.

To their north, by a pumping station on the main Ede-Arnhem road, and near a hotel called De Leeren Doedel, 10th Parachute Battalion were also embroiled, this time with Spindler's right flank. The whole battle involving 4th Parachute Brigade was so close by that in the DAA men could not only hear the noise, but feel the vibration and shock of explosions.

At the bridge Ted Mordecai and Harry Walker were on watch again when they saw movement at the top of the embankment to their front. Slowly, two German soldiers emerged from different parts of the high ground, and a little way apart. Quite what they were up to was not certain, and they did not appear to know there were British soldiers about. Agreeing that Walker would take the one on the right, who was behind a tree, and that Mordecai would attend to the other one behind a bush, they raised their Sten guns and fired.

Harry dropped his man almost immediately and mine came down the bank on his hands and knees screaming out with pain and fear. I gave him another short burst and he stopped screaming and rolled down the bank to lie perfectly still at the foot of it.
Private E. V. B. Mordecai RAOC

In the DAA the drills practised on exercise meant that the resupply routines and management of DAA stocks continued despite the difficulties faced by the logisticians. Proof positive of the value of intensive, high quality and imaginative training.

Our part in the battle was to supply the troops with ammunition. Therefore we set up an ammo dump in the woods at the side of the Hartenstein Hotel. Our vehicles did not last for long as they were destroyed by German mortar fire. We dug trenches in the piece of land in front of the Hartenstein, where the memorial now stands. Here we parked our jeeps and trailers. From this point we went out on patrols to drive the Germans out of the houses. Also, we went on patrols to capture a German for interrogation, but we did not succeed in this.
Corporal S. P. J. Staple RASC

The lack of packed fuel was ameliorated when petroleum pumps some 200 yards east of the Hartenstein were taken into use. Units were advised that they could draw up to eight gallons per vehicle using their own jerrycans. Issues were made by the OFP of spare parts for armaments, wireless sets, small arms and vehicles.

I personally enjoyed issuing stores, mostly vehicle and wireless items, without paperwork and without the hassle of normal bureaucratic processes. It was now soldiering time, and the men formed part of the defence force, with patrol and foray duties, in addition to their much reduced Corps role.
Major C. C. Chidgey RAOC

The Day Wears On - A Busy Afternoon

Mortar fire was becoming a frequent nuisance in the DAA. When the first barrage landed in their area, and not yet used to being bombarded, both Major Bill Chidgey and Staff Sergeant Wilson dived for cover under a jeep. Staff Sergeant Wilson's nickname was 'Tubby', indicating that he was not of slim build; and neither was Major Bill a small officer. Hence, whilst they found getting under the vehicle, in extremis, quite easy, getting out was less so. There was considerable mirth and not very much sympathy among the soldiery at the predicament being enjoyed by their elders and betters; and they were less helpful than they might have been in assisting them from beneath the jeeps.

The attempt by 4th Parachute Brigade to break through Spindler's line failed. By mid-morning 156 Parachute Battalion had only C Company remaining as a cohesive sub-unit. To its north, the 10th Parachute Battalion was embroiled in its battle around the pumping station when General Urquhart visited Brigadier Hackett in his headquarters in the woods just north of the railway line. At this stage 7th KOSB was still fulfilling its task of protecting the LZ for the landing of the Polish heavy equipment, and was not involved in the 4th Parachute Brigade battle. Discussing the situation, the two men agreed that a withdrawal south of the railway might be necessary, but when Urquhart left to return to his

Enemy mortar fire was a constant problem, and many vehicles were damaged or destroyed. Courtesy Imperial War Museum

headquarters no such order had been given.

However, later that afternoon Brigadier Hackett became progressively more concerned that he was being pressed from the rear, and the final straw came with the mortaring of his brigade's vehicles at the Wolfheze level crossing. The high embankment of the railway was a real obstacle to movement, even on foot. Feeling he was about to be hemmed in, and with the Wolfheze level crossing his only route round the embankment, Hackett gave the order to withdraw. The two forward battalions proceeded to undertake that most difficult of military operations – a withdrawal in contact with the enemy and in broad daylight. It was just then that the gliders bringing in the Polish heavy equipment began to land on LZ L, right into the middle of a running battle, and with 7th KOSB trying to defend the LZ. It was chaos.

In England bad weather had delayed the departure of the 1st Independent Polish Parachute Brigade main body, despite the fact that its equipment was already in the Netherlands. It was to be a delay until the following day, but it mattered little: virtually all their heavy equipment had been destroyed or captured within thirty minutes of landing.

Resupply by Air – The First Major Attempt

It was about this time, at around 3.00 p.m., that the resupply drop came in onto the pre-arranged supply dropping point just to the north-east of Spindler's blocking line on the Dreijenseweg, despite all the attempts to signal alternatives. In one of the Dakotas was Driver Harry Simmonds, and this was to be his only trip over Holland.

Driver Harry Simmonds RASC, 253 Airborne Composite Company RASC. Author's Collection

The manifest for the drop showed compo in all panniers, but when we got to the airfield we were switched to another aircraft carrying plastic explosive and petrol. Approaching the DZ there was a great bang and a tracer came through the fuselage and jammed in one of the rollers where it burnt itself out. Our crew commander, a dour Yorkshireman, stood in the doorway and shouted: 'Bloody 'ell, there's a hell of a battle going on down there.' Then a tracer bullet came through the open door. 'Bloody cheek, they're shooting at us!'[4]

Driver H.C. Simmonds RASC

The battle they were witnessing was the final stage of the 4th Parachute Brigade action, with the Germans by this time chasing the withdrawing paratroopers. This would have allowed the anti-aircraft guns and other heavy weapons in Spindler's force to bring all their weight to bear on the slow-moving resupply aircraft.

Harry Simmonds was lucky. Despite the attentions of the German flak units, and just about anyone else who could fire a weapon skywards, his aircraft completed its mission and returned safely to base. Others were not so fortunate. Corporal Jack Sales was a crew commander in 253 Company. He cannot remember all the details or dates for his drops. Sticking in his mind, however, was the young despatcher who made the mistake of wearing his parachute whilst despatching, was hooked up by a disappearing pannier and was carried to his death.

> *Norman Enderby was on the same mission as me, on the same day. He had made the drop and was returning to the coast when they were hit. He was married, and his wife was pregnant with triplets. He has no known grave.*
>
> Driver H. C. Simmonds RASC

Norman's aircraft, a Stirling, was hit by flak over enemy-held territory, and crashed in the municipality of Aardenburg, diving nose first into the ground. It was completely compressed, and when the wreckage was recovered in 1945 it was impossible to identify any of the occupants.

Lance Corporal Wilbye Whittaker was the NCO in charge of an air despatch team from 223 Air Despatch Company in a Dakota. As they approached the SDP a member of his crew, Driver H. Davis, was badly wounded through both thighs and bled profusely. He decided very quickly he would have to leave the wounded man in order to despatch his load, but was also faced with the problem of rallying his crew who were badly shaken. This he did so successfully that the drill was carried through without a hitch and all the panniers were despatched in one run. The aircraft subsequently crash-landed in Belgium and the wounded man died. However, Wilbye Whittaker, having been given the opportunity to bale out, had opted to stay with his wounded comrade in the event that he might survive. He returned to England with his crew, so shocked by his experiences that he had developed a bad stammer. He volunteered to go on other sorties, but was denied permission. He was awarded the Distinguished Flying Medal.

> *Approaching the Dutch border Phil Nixon's plane was hit and the starboard engine was out of action. His Dakota, on my port side, lost altitude and was lost to my view as it veered underneath us. I was hoping he would bale out, but he was not a trained parachutist. Either that, or he and the flight crew were adamant in attempting their despatching. Whatever it was, they were forced to make a second pass over the DZ and this allowed Phil to despatch his load just before the 'Dak' exploded. The pilot, Flight Lieutenant Lord, received the VC for his bravery. Whether Phil's bravery was cited for 'sticking to his guns' I'll never know. His wife had recently given birth to Brenda who I believe was six weeks old. I cannot say whether Phil had seen her before he was killed. Fifty years later, at a lunch with the Princess Royal in Wellington Barracks, my eyes met another pair across the room. 'You're Mickey Marshall, aren't you; my Dad's best friend.' She was the spitting image of Phil.*
>
> Lance Corporal C. Marshall RASC, 63 Airborne Composite Company RASC

Corporal Phil Nixon was twenty-nine years old. A keen sportsman, and a physical training instructor, he commanded a crew of three from 63 Airborne Composite Company RASC. Driver James Ricketts had joined the Army from his family's carting and haulage contracting business, and had the ambition to build up the business, once the War was over, by replacing the horses with motor vehicles. Another sportsman, Driver Leonard Harper had played for Harlington

Corporal Phil Nixon RASC, 63 Airborne Composite Company.
Courtesy Eric Pepper

Driver James Ricketts RASC, 63 Airborne Composite Company.
Courtesy Eric Pepper

Driver Leonard Harper RASC, 63 Airborne Composite Company.
Courtesy Eric Pepper

Driver Arthur Rowbot RASC, 63 Airborne Composite Company.
Courtesy Eric Pepper

Rovers Football Club in the Hounslow and District League before being called up in March 1943. He was in 63 Company from the outset. The youngest of the four at age twenty-seven, Driver Arthur Rowbotham had been a coach driver before being called up for military service. All four perished when Dakota KG 374 plunged into the ground near Reijerskamp Farm having made two passes over the DZ in order to drop its entire load, despite having been on fire from before the start of the first pass. Its fate was witnessed by many on the ground:

> *One Dakota was hit by flak, and the starboard wing set on fire. Yet it came on, descending to 900 feet. It seemed that every anti-aircraft gun in the vicinity was sighted on the crippled aircraft. With its starboard engine blazing, it came through to the dropping zone. At the end of the run the Dakota turned and made a second run to drop the remaining supplies. From foxholes and slit trenches and from the restricted spaces to which we were trying to attract the pilots; from blasted buildings and ditches and emplacements of rubble and earth, the eyes of hundreds and probably thousands of careworn soldiers gazed upwards through the battle haze. We were spellbound and speechless, and I dare say there is not a survivor of Arnhem who will ever forget, or want to forget, the courage we were privileged to witness in those terrible eight minutes.*[5]
>
> Major General R. E. Urquhart CB DSO, Commander 1st Airborne Division[6]

There was only one survivor, the navigator – Flight Lieutenant Harry King RAF. His is the final tribute to the soldiers who died:

> *These men were not volunteers*[7] *like aircrew. They received no flying pay, yet were, without doubt, superb in their fulfillment of duty even though KG 374 was burning for the whole period over the dropping zone.*
>
> Flight Lieutenant H.J. King RAF, Navigator KG 374, 271 Squadron RAF, Down Ampney

A Dakota, FZ 626 from RAF Down Ampney, was hit by flak, and crashed on Bakenbergseweg in Arnhem, partially destroying the house at number 262. The casualties were buried in the garden, and were moved to the Arnhem Oosterbeek War Cemetery after the war. Among the dead were two of the air despatchers

Lance Corporal James Grace RASC, 223 Air Despatch Company RASC.
Author's Collection

Driver W.D. Cross RASC, 63 Airborne Composite Company.
Courtesy S. Fenton

Driver G.L. Weston RASC, 63 Airborne Composite Company.
Courtesy D. Mellors

from 223 Air Despatch Company RASC: Lance Corporal James Grace and Driver Richard Newth. The other two, Drivers V Dilworth and W Jenkinson, were made prisoners-of-war.

James Grace had been a pre-war regular soldier in the Royal Horse Artillery and was called back into the Army at the outbreak of war. He was married to Betty and they had three children.

> *When I heard that an operation called Market Garden had started to free the Dutch and bring an end to the war I was feeling quite good about it, but at that time I had no idea how it was going to affect me. Jim came home for a few hours for little Jim's birthday party on the 17th of September. I walked back with him to where he was to get his transport back to Burford. We talked about things; not the war, we had other things to talk about. He said: 'Whatever happens to me take care of the three boys.' Then he kissed me, a thing he had never done before in public - then he was gone.*
>
> Betty Maskell, formerly Betty Grace [7]

There were 162 missions flown, involving ninety-nine Stirlings and sixty-three Dakotas. Twenty air despatchers were killed, three from 223 Air Despatch Company of 48 Column, and seventeen from 49 Column: eleven from 63 Company and six from 253 Company. Fourteen were missing. Of these at least one crew, from 63 Company, comprised four drivers – not an NCO among them. Drivers J. Bowers, W. D. Cross, R Hodgkinson and G. L. Weston all went down when Dakota KG 388 crashed at Zijpendaal, 1,000 yards east of SDP 'V' and on a German cemetery. Their deaths were subsequently confirmed, but they have no known grave. Eleven men were wounded and three were made prisoners of war. Of the 360 who flew forty-eight were casualties.

Collecting What They Could

> *A few canisters which fell off target, and there were only a few, were picked up by the collectors from Michael Packe's RASC units.*[9]
>
> Major General R. E. Urquhart CB CBE

By this time the 1st and 2nd Parachute Platoons of 250 Light Company RASC were both in the DAA. Looking north Michael Packe could see the resupply parachutes dropping, some of them tantalisingly near. Harry Simmonds' load, for example, dropped only a few hundred yards away, just beyond the Oosterbeek Hoog railway bridge, at the bottom end of the Dreijenseweg – among the units forming the left flank of Spindler's blocking line. Packe ordered Captain Desmond Kavanagh to take the 2nd Platoon and retrieve what he could.

> *Captain Kavanagh said there were two jobs, one lot to go to recce the DZ to look for supplies, and one lot with shells to the bridge. He disappeared with three jeeps. The team that went for the bridge took one jeep with two trailers and got as far as the St Elisabeth Hospital. Here we were stopped by an officer who asked what we were doing. On hearing he told us we should go back, we wouldn't get 300 yards.*
>
> Driver R. G. Pearce RASC, 2nd Parachute Platoon 250 Airborne Light Company RASC

Collecting an F Type container. Courtesy Imperial War Museum

> *Captain Kavanagh detailed me to prepare my section for immediate departure to pick up these newly dropped supplies. On this occasion I decided to take only one trailer per jeep; this would provide extra mobility. I left one man, Driver Stevens, to guard the remaining trailers. Captain Kavanagh occupied Jeep Number One, driven by Driver Thomas. I followed in Jeep Number*

A few canisters which fell off target...were picked up by the collectors from Michael Packe's RASC units. A pannier containing 75mm ammunition at 8 Stationsweg Oosterbeek. Courtesy Airborne Museum 'Hartenstein'

Two driven, I believe, by Driver Doherty. The remaining jeeps took up position behind me, supervised by Lance Corporal J. Syme. Sergeant McDowell was with the Platoon Scout Section who spread themselves out among the convoy.
Corporal B. Blaxley RASC

Paddy Kavanagh raced up Stationsweg heading towards the supply dropping zones, passing as he did so a burning Bren carrier with the crew all dead around it. Given this gruesome sight, and the noise from the battle that had been going on most of the day just beyond the bridge they were approaching, some caution might have been appropriate. Kavanagh, however, was not a cautious officer and he led his jeeps, at speed, straight across the bridge. In those days the bridge was very much more of a 'hump-backed' construction than is the case with the current structure. Their view of the ground beyond it was, consequently, limited. Corporal Burnham Blaxley at least tried to take some precautions by deploying a machine-gun for covering fire, but with little effect.

Suddenly, without prior consultation, Captain Kavanagh streaked off, turning left onto the main road to Oosterbeek Station.[10] *The road was narrow with hedges on both sides, but it suddenly opened up with a road bridge over a cutting. On the right hand side was a reconnaissance vehicle with the crew laying dead all around it. Captain Kavanagh made a brief pause. I now allocated the Bren Gunner with his Number Two to dismount and give us covering fire over the bridge. We then proceeded quickly over the open ground into an ambush which had been well prepared and dug in. I dived from the jeep into a hedge and then into a garden where two of our men, both severely wounded, were already taking cover. They were Percy Batsford and Wilfred Bennet, who later died of his wounds and is buried in an unknown grave.*
Corporal B. Blaxley RASC

It was just beyond the bridge that the attack took place. The first jeep suffered a direct hit, its bonnet flew up and smoke poured from the engine compartment. It came so suddenly that the following jeeps and trailers, given their considerable speed, all telescoped into each other. Those not thrown out jumped out and took cover at the side of the road. There was a house on the right from

Although tantalisingly near, much of what was dropped fell among the enemy, who were delighted to receive the unexpected bonus.
Courtesy Bundesarchiv, Bild 101 I/2KBK 772/4

Corporal Burnham Blaxley RASC, 2nd Parachute Platoon, 250 Light Company.
Author's Collection

which the Germans were firing and lobbing grenades over the hedge. Captain Kavanagh, from the lead jeep, had dived to the left, as had Driver Ken Clarke, travelling in the trailer of the second jeep, and a number of others. The Platoon commander called for a Bren gun, and Ken Clarke brought his up alongside him.

He exchanged his Sten for my Bren and said: 'When I stand up you all run back over the bridge.' This he did, standing in the road and obviously diverting attention to himself.
Driver K. W. Clarke RASC

Men do strange things in the heat of battle. Having taken Ken Clarke's Bren Gun, Kavanagh had his pouches full of Sten magazines with their 9mm ammunition. Clarke now had a Sten gun with his pouches stuffed with Bren magazines containing .303 ammunition. In making the change Paddy Kavanagh had limited both men's firepower to only the twenty-eight or thirty rounds they each had in the magazine on their weapon.

Ken Clarke knew that Germans were occupying the houses opposite, since he could see them. It had been from the third house along that a grenade had been thrown and a shot fired that killed one of his best friends, Corporal Wiggins. Driver Clarke asked permission to throw a smoke grenade into the house, but Kavanagh refused, and his last instruction was: 'No, just run for it.' As he ran towards the embankment leading to the railway Clarke was ordered by Sergeant McDowell to stand on the corner and give covering fire with the Sten gun. This he did for long enough for the others to get away.

The Captain shouted at us to retreat and he ran at the machine-guns firing. We never saw him again.Three of us threw ourselves onto the barbed wire and the others ran across our bodies and pulled us off. We got into a row of houses and were arguing which way was best to go, because the Germans were all over the place. Across the road a door opened and this huge chap, skinny as a rake, appeared with a little girl. He could not speak English, but she could, and said she would lead us out. She went down the road and beckoned us one by one.
Corporal D. Cutting RASC, 2nd Parachute Platoon, 250 Airborne Light Company RASC

I defended myself and my wounded until, whilst changing my magazine, I was ordered to put down my weapon and stand up. Looking over my shoulder I saw a German lieutenant speaking excellent English and aiming a long barrelled Luger directly at me. I had no choice but to obey. I was instructed to find a jeep that worked which, eventually, I did and put my two wounded in it. The German officer put his wounded in alongside and, accompanied by the officer, I drove the jeep back behind German lines. It was then I saw the German armoured vehicles and self-propelled guns and realised there was no hope whatsoever of any recovery being made with our inadequate resources. We were sitting ducks.
Corporal B. Blaxley RASC

I followed last of all. Sadly, Captain Kavanagh was killed along with other members of our party, and this has always stuck in my mind as my most vivid and dreadful memory of the campaign. Captain Kavanagh's gallantry was a lasting memorial and an inspiration to all who knew him. In my opinion this officer deserved a decoration.
Driver K. W. Clarke RASC

Kavanagh was one of the best.[11]
Driver R. G. Pearce RASC

The Platoon's survivors slid down the railway embankment and gathered on the station platform in order to gain a couple of minutes relief out of sight of the Germans. Scrambling up the other side, they headed back on foot to the DAA. As he walked through the neat, well ordered Dutch houses with their manicured gardens and beautiful late summer displays of flowers, Ken Clarke was struck by the looks of horror on the faces of the occupants of the houses, concerned at reprisals they knew would come their way for supporting the British. Clearly, all was not going according to plan.

My father, William, was a linguist. He listened to the German radio and heard their reports of Arnhem. Ken had been home a few weekends before, and we knew he was on standby for something. I knew he was there.
Christine Bradshaw, subsequently Mrs Kenneth Clarke

Other attempts to collect some supplies met with very limited success, and interference from German fighter aircraft which ranged unmolested across the divisional area.

The site of Paddy Kavanagh's ambush looking south to where the jeeps approached from the DAA. The bodies of dead RASC paratroopers can clearly be seen either side of the road. The jeeps had been cleared by the time a German soldier took this photograph.
Courtesy Bundesarchiv, Bild 101 I/2KBK 771/18

> *One of the Intelligence Section, looking up at the sky, said, very quietly, 'FW 190s' and started walking to a tunnel. True enough, the 'planes circled round and peeled off to strafe us. They hit the house and barn setting them on fire - the cannon shells hitting the ground and trees a few yards in front of where we were hiding. They also started to strafe the RASC boys who were trying to collect supplies that had been dropped a short time previously.*
>
> Lance Corporal J. L. Hughes RASC

There were also some attempts to obtain supplies locally, but these only brought forth a sack of flour and a pig. Both were handed over to the ADMS for the dressing stations.[12] Mortaring and small arms fire continued to cause casualties in the DAA. Concern now rising that all was not going well, and having, effectively, lost the first day's resupply by air to the Germans, all units were warned about conserving ammunition, supplies and petroleum. Future issues of compo would now be on the basis of one third of a ration per man per day and units were advised that limited quantities of ammunition were available from the DAA.

Meanwhile...

During the afternoon the survivors of the failed attempts to reach the bridge were withdrawing along the lower road that had been Frost's route into town just two days earlier. Once beyond the Oosterbeek Laag railway bridge they would form together to defend the southern end of the eastern side of the thumb-shaped perimeter forming around part of Oosterbeek with its base on the Rhine.

The 4th Parachute Brigade made its way south over the railway line and would settle for the night in the woods in the general area of Wolfheze. It was, however, much depleted, with its two parachute battalions down to not much more than company strength. They were joined by 7th KOSB which had fared a little better, but which by then had lost its A Company and had taken casualties elsewhere.

With all the activity around Oosterbeek, the fighting at the bridge continued unabated. The RAOC party were ordered to evacuate their house, which was becoming untenable. Bernard Manley sent Private Kevin Heaney across to the house occupied by Captain Eric MacKay, his Royal Engineers and part of C Company 3rd Parachute Battalion. His task was to ask if the RAOC could take shelter with them.

Moving across the rubble, Kevin Heaney, more worried at being shot by his own than the Germans, gained the Sapper position. Returning with a positive message to Captain Manley the whole party made their way across. However, after about three hours they were told to make their way to the bridge, trying to avoid German tanks as they did so. Moving in under the bridge supports they found that the building next to it protruded out into the road and this provided some cover from the direct attention of neighbouring Germans.

In England 963 AUCL moved to Barkestone Heath aerodrome, where it waited for further orders. On the corridor there was a short-notice cancellation of any move by the Seaborne Echelon due to congestion.

Having spent a fruitless day in their haystack, which, surrounded by trees, had not proved to be the observation platform they had hoped for, the two RAOC warrant officers, still accompanied by the two glider pilots, were feeling decidedly uncomfortable. Needing water they approached a local cottage which they knew to be occupied, but their knock brought forth no response. The occupants assumed they were German and would not answer. However, they helped themselves to water from the well in the yard.

> *Our only means of obtaining water was by attaching one of our helmets to the rope and lowering it into the water. First we filled our water bottles, and then satisfied our thirst – the owner of the helmet having the misfortune to replace it on his head whilst it was yet half full of water – thinking it to be empty.*
> WO1 (Sub-Conductor) G. E. Jenkins RAOC

Knowing that 1st Airborne Division was a spent force, and hoping against hope for relief from the south, the men at the bridge were not to know that the advance units of XXX Corps were stuck in Nijmegen fighting with the Americans of the 82nd Airborne Division against stiff opposition. Wilhelm Bittrich knew that the key to defeating the 1st Airborne Division was to prevent its reinforcement, and holding the Nijmegen bridge was the means of achieving it. If he got his way the bridge over the Waal would never fall, even if he had to blow it up in order to prevent an Allied crossing. There was to be no relief for the defenders of the Arnhem road bridge.

1. Utrechtseweg
2. SLIDEX was a simple method of encoding signals, still in use in the British Army into the seventies
3. Stanley Maxted was a BBC reporter.
4. Harry Simmonds' aircraft dropped its load in the field between the Dreijenseweg, along which Spindler had his blocking line, and today's Air Despatch Memorial near the Arnhem-Oosterbeek War Cemetery. Facing the memorial the aircraft would have been coming straight towards it from the west.
5. Flight Lieutenant David Lord was awarded the Victoria Cross for his courage in delivering KG 374's load over the DZ. There is no record of any citation for a member of the air despatch crew.
6. From 'Arnhem' by Urquhart, Cassel, London 1958
7. Being 63 Company soldiers they were, of course, volunteers for airborne duties, of which air despatching was one. Flt Lt King, in paying his compliment, was not to know this.
8. Betty was not to know for some time that James was missing, presumed killed, and she suffered terribly as a result of the uncertainty. She eventually re-married twelve years later. In 1989, aged 72, she was informed that James' grave had been identified in the Arnhem-Oosterbeek War Cemetery following detailed research by two Dutch civilians: Jan Hey and Lex Röell. Widowed now a second time, she returns every year to the grave and will continue to do so as long as she is able.
9. From 'Arnhem' by Urquhart, Cassel, London 1958
10. Oosterbeek Hoog station at the top of Stationsweg.
11. Lieutenant Richard Adams, commanding C Platoon in 250 Company's Seaborne Echelon, would go on in later life to write his masterpiece: Watership Down. Many of the characters and events contained in it are based around the men of 250 Airborne Light Company RASC and the battle of which they were a part in Oosterbeek. The character Bigwig is based directly on Desmond Kavanagh.
12. Dressing stations are created from a part of the Field Ambulance, and form that part of the medical evacuation chain where the casualty first encounters a surgeon. The rest of the Field Ambulance comprised collecting sections, whose task was to recover casualties from the regimental aid posts back to the dressing station.

Chapter Seven

Day Four – And Still No Relief

Battle Rages – Everywhere

Major General James Gavin, commanding the United States 82nd Airborne Division, was a troubled man. His division had taken their early objectives from the very outset of the battle, allowing XXX Corps to make its way into the southern suburbs of Nijmegen. However, they had been beset by Germans probing from the east which had drained their strength, and the defence in Nijmegen of the Waal river bridge was proving too tough a nut for his lightly armed paratroopers to crack. Even with the support of the Guards Armoured Division, the streets of Nijmegen were turning into a graveyard. Since their arrival the Americans had suffered 300 dead, 700 wounded and several hundred missing or cut off, and as the morning wore on he discovered that his overdue third lift would again be delayed due to poor weather in England. He was running out of fighting power, he had to find another way of taking the bridge.

He was not to know that Model's plan was to hold the River Waal with what he had in place, in preparation for a counter-attack by 10th SS Division. Part of this delaying tactic was to be a series of spoiling attacks from the Reichswald, with a pronged attack involving three battle groups which was to be coordinated by the Corps Feldt. The Germans were due to cross their start line at 6.30 a.m. just as Gavin was begining to believe that the anticipated threat of armoured attack from the east had been misread by his intelligence staff.

As the Germans south of Nijmegen were beginning to come to terms with their forthcoming assault, their comrades facing the British in Arnhem and Oosterbeek were already at work on a damp, drizzly Wednesday morning. The 5.00 a.m. stand-to in the DAA brought with it heavy mortaring and some probing infantry attacks, whilst at the bridge the fireworks started soon after daybreak. In the woods just south of the Wolfheze railway crossing the beleagured Brigadier Hackett was contemplating how best to get the remnants of his brigade in to the defensive perimeter forming around Oosterbeek. He decided to move south, through the woods to join the main Utrechtseweg, before turning left and heading east towards the Hartenstein Hotel.

At the Arnhem bridge John Frost's small force had dwindled from the 750 or so he had commanded on that first night to some ninety men still capable of fighting effectively. All around the tightening perimeter men fought with a strength and determination far beyond that which might be expected from soldiers who had not eaten properly or slept at all for two and a half days, who had received neither reinforcement nor replenishment, and who had been under virtually constant bombardment. By now they knew the chances of relief were slim, yet still they fought on.

The particular challenge facing the RAOC party involved some Oerlikon[1] ammunition stored in one of the pillars on the bridge, and the twin Oerlikon cannon mounted on the bridge. The intention of the local commander was to capture the guns, but the first two of his men trying to climb the stairway to gain access to the blockhouses were shot. Consequently, it was decided to barricade the rails running alongside the steps in order to provide a covered route. Staff Sergeant Walker and Privates McCarthy, Heaney and Mordecai were given the task, using wooden sleepers. It was hard and heavy work, but they were two thirds of the way up the steps when, suddenly and urgently, they were called down. One of the officers had spotted movement down the road. The Germans fired an 88mm shell which hit the stairway, and then kept up a steady fire. Ted Mordecai was hit in the shoulder by a piece of shrapnel which, mercifully, had spent its force and he was unhurt.

The building on the western side of the arch which had sheltered Bernard Manley and his men was a hindrance to the Germans and it did not take them long to reduce it to rubble. The paratroopers soon came under fire from both east and west: from mortar fire, Mark IV tanks and light machine-guns. A decision to move under another arch did little to remedy matters as Tiger[2] tanks began to move in.

At one point we had to line up with fixed bayonets as it was expected that the Germans were going to make a bayonet charge. I felt very vulnerable with the short bayonet on my Sten Gun. It was at this point that McCarthy asked me if I would like some bacon and eggs, reminding me that we had eaten nothing since Sunday. McCarthy looked quite cheerful, and I tried to look the same, but inwardly I was pretty scared.
Private K. J. Heaney RAOC

Whilst all this was going on, and far to the south, the Seaborne Echelon had moved off from its overnight location and was five miles north of the Dutch border. For ease of control it had been split into three groups, confusingly called 'columns' although they bore no relationship to an RASC column. In the lead, in

3 Company on The Corridor, time for some personal dministration. Courtesy Imperial War Museum

Soldiers of 250 Company Seaborne Echelon on sentry duty as the unit waits near Eindhoven. Courtesy Imperial War Museum

Although the waiting, for some, is less onerous – 93 Company takes a relaxed approach. Courtesy Imperial War Museum

the first column, was the RASC with ammunition. Behind them the second column contained divisional RASC whilst the third comprised divisional troops, including the balance of the OFP. By 9.00 a.m. they were across the Escaut Canal. However, nine miles south of Eindhoven they had to stop whilst 43rd Wessex

The officers of 250 Light Company while away their time. Major J.R. Halls RASC is lying on the bank reading the Daily Express. *Major John Gifford, the OC, is wearing the glasses and smoking, with Lieutenant E.T. Evans RASC sitting to his left on the beer crate. The names of the other two officers are not known.* Courtesy Imperial War Museum

Division passed by them seeking to get up the road to reinforce the Guards Armoured Division and help break through and beyond Nijmegen.

In the Nijmegen area the German attacks from the Reichswald by Corps Feldt commenced late, but were well under way by about 9.30 a.m. They were to last throughout the day, and proved to be a constant thorn in Gavin's side as he sought to complete the final and, arguably, most important part of his mission: to capture a crossing over the Waal. Without it the paratroopers in Arnhem were doomed; with it, there might just be a chance.

The idea was beginning to form that an assault river crossing may be the only way of breaking the German stranglehold on the approaches to the bridge. There were actually two bridges over the Waal: the road bridge and a parallel railway bridge some 500 metres downstream, to the west. Even further west, on the south bank, and a few hundred yards from the railway bridge, was a power station. In front of it was a launching point for small boats and an area where tanks might give covering fire to a force seeking to cross. There would, however, be no concealment from German forces on the north bank, well dug in on the dyke. Casualties would be high, the chance of success limited and the implications of failure something the General did not wish to contemplate.

The assault was planned for 2.30 p.m., with British assault boats due for delivery by 1.00 p.m. Major Julian Cook and H and I Companies of the 504th US Parachute Infantry Regiment were to undertake the crossing.

In Oosterbeek: Replenishment and Re-supply Carry On

By mid-morning life in the DAA was becoming difficult. Exposed as they were in open ground in front of the Hartenstein Hotel the men of 250 Airborne Light Company and the OFP were almost constantly under fire. Movement of any sort was becoming very dangerous.

Sergeant N. G. 'Bill' Griffin RASC.
Author's Collection

Colonel Preston told me he wished to see Colonel Packe, and asked me to go and get him. I asked Norman Davidson to come with me. 'Not likely' was the immediate reaction, but he came anyway. We crossed the main road, and saw a house with a dim light which was a cellar. I stuck my head in and said 'Colonel Packe?'. I was lucky not to get shot. I told him he was wanted, and with a very unhappy Colonel Packe we padded back across the road.

Sergeant N. G. Griffin RASC

The OFP continued to make issues, but they were hampered by enemy activity, with snipers presenting a particular problem. Eventually, they were going to have to move, along with the RASC company, to a spot where, as far as possible, they were out of the direct line of sight of the enemy.

The divisional Ammunition Examiner, Staff Sergeant

Lieutenant Colonel P. H. H. M. Preston, South Lancashire Regiment, AA&QMG 1st Airborne Division.
Courtesy Imperial War Museum

Brown, was a member of Lieutenant Colonel Mobbs' staff, but for the operation was attached to the OFP; and he was one of the busiest of the Ordnance party. Ammunition dropped from the air often requires inspection in order to ensure it is going to work as it should, and would not be dangerous to our own troops if fired. His services were also required to deal with unexploded bombs and shells and to inspect captured enemy ammunition. One day, and there is no record of which day, he went out on a task and never returned. He has no known grave.

> *It was Wednesday when it became apparent that life was going to be difficult – there was a breakthrough just forward of the OFP area. Some glider pilots came through in order to re-group and take up a position ahead, and in the afternoon that day the unit became an integral part of the perimeter defence with increased patrol duties. Sergeant Bennet was wounded on a patrol, but returned to duty that day. From then on we were part of the events that have been well recorded in numerous books as temporary residents in 'The Devil's Cauldron'. The aspect of the whole scene which, at the time, seemed normal was the resilience of each individual to every change of emotion, in the mixed cacophony of noise, thirst, hunger and physical disturbance; but amidst this jumble a caring for individuals near you was dominant – perhaps there was no time but now!*
>
> Major C. C. Chidgey RAOC

The DAA eventually moved behind the Hartenstein, into the wooded gardens and the units dug in, mostly in the area of the tennis courts, which were being used as the divisional prisoner of war cage.

> *I remember how mixed they were as men, some were as tired as we were, but some of the SS were very arrogant and abusive. There was a female prisoner among them and she wished to use the toilet, but no one was willing to escort her. I don't know how she managed in the end, but we did hear some time later that she was found dead.*[3]
>
> Driver K. W. Clarke RASC

CRASC's headquarters became a deep slit trench with overhead cover between the 3" mortar and the small arms ammunition stacks, and was exactly thirty-three paces from the AQ office; much easier for Bill Griffin to get him next time.

This photograph of a Royal Signals officer on a stretcher shows, behind the five men, the panniers stacked in the DAA behind the Hartenstein Hotel. On the bottom left of the picture can be seen part of the balustrade on the back steps, from where it was taken. Courtesy Imperial War Museum

Drive for Arnhem - Just Keep Going

With all this activity going on in the 1st Airborne Division area, it is important to remember the desperate attempts being made further south to bring relief; and not all was going according to plan. The boats due at 1.00 p.m., in preparation for the assault river crossing over the Waal in Nijmegen at 2.30 p.m., were late. Major General Gavin had laid on a strike by rocket firing Typhoons to support the attack in order to keep the Germans' heads down so as to increase the chance of success. The Typhoons were on time, but the boats did not appear until 2.40 p.m.; hence the value of the air strike was largely wasted as the Germans had precious minutes in which to recover.

Never having seen the flimsy, canvas and plywood craft before it was with great trepidation that the Americans, with three British Royal Engineers in each boat as crew, made their way to the river's edge and launched their flimsy craft. Their only cover now was provided by smoke from Irish Guards' tanks, and then some direct fire support from the same vehicles; their only recourse was boldness and daring; their greatest attribute was courage and determination.

Another Aerial Resupply Attempt

As the 504th Parachute Infantry were paddling furiously across the Waal under intense enemy pressure and with a dangerously high casualty rate, the move of the DAA was taking place in Oosterbeek. At the same time, the desperate fight to hold on to the Arnhem bridge carried on with no sign of slackening; and, with all this happening, the daily resupply lift arrived from the United Kingdom - unaffected by the localised fog which had postponed the Polish parachute drop by yet another day.[4] Ninety-nine Stirlings and sixty-three Dakotas flew and the result could be declared a partial success in that some 2,000 rations were collected, which was sufficient to maintain an issue rate of one third of a ration per man per day, and to provide some relief for the hospitals. There were also 330 rounds of 75mm ammunition and 140 rounds for the 6-pounder gathered up and held in the new DAA in the trees behind the Hartenstein.

Losses among the aircraft were again high, although the fifteen missing were a small improvement on the previous day's eighteen. The fate of Lance Corporal Rextrew and Driver Leach of 253 Company was not untypical. Their Stirling, piloted by Flying Officer Matheson from 190 Squadron at Fairford, was shot down and crashed near Oosterbeek, killing everyone on board. It was one of five aircraft from Fairford that did not return, and it was the Stirlings, with a total of eleven losses, that were the hardest hit.

Lance Corporal Fredrick Rextrew RASC, 253 Airborne Composite Company RASC.
Courtesy S. Fenton

> *I had never flown in a Stirling, but I knew what I had to do. Aged nineteen, my number two was aged about thirty. 'Little Thomas', we had two of these; the other was 'Big Thomas'. Taff was quite content to let me take charge. In a Stirling the person in charge had to be plugged into the intercom. The view*

*outside is quite limited so it was head down on your 'chute and dream of home. Our dress was denims, PT shoes, an airborne smock,[5] a Mae West and a revolver with twelve rounds. We had four panniers and twenty-four containers. The containers were the bomb aimer's job and nothing to do with us. The navigator/wireless operator came back to open up the floor aperture. It was very dangerous to attempt to get back to his seat with this hole open. Until then I had only vaguely heard any firing. I gazed down at the ground and I remember distinctly seeing a motorcyclist weaving along; then, suddenly, it was tracers and I could actually see the ack-ack gun firing. Then came a very long burst from our rear gunner. By now it was all flame and noise. I seemed to be in a dream. An inner voice was telling me to stay calm, and that I should stand perfectly upright and rigid. I thought I would make a small target, and then if I was hit how far up my legs would it go. I could not move; I was plugged in. I remember looking across at the wireless operator. It was as if there was no one there, no expression, no trace of fear; just as if he was like me, in a trance. But I reckon that gave me some confidence. I suddenly became aware of a voice shouting obscenities in my ears: 'Chuck the ******* bastards out.' It was then I saw all the containers' chutes opening as they were jettisoned. About that time, Thomas, who had been curled up in a ball on the other side of the panniers, jumped up. I remember stupidly shouting to him that the shit was coming up through the floor and not sideways. Like greased lightning out went our four panniers. He then rushed forward to get our 'chutes, and handed me mine. As he did so he opened it. I was horrorstruck, and had visions of baling out hanging onto Taff's harness. It was then Taff pointed to the right and I saw two stopped propellers. I became aware of a list to starboard and smoke coming along at knee height and going out of the hole. The flight engineer had his arms buried somewhere under the floorboards as he, I think, managed to keep the two engines going. I gave thanks to God for four engines. I don't remember very much of the journey home, but I do remember the RAF stores corporal giving me a bollocking over my opened 'chute. He got back as good as he gave.*

Driver R. A. Clancy RASC, 63 Airborne Composite Company RASC

We had tried to get messages back by every means to prevent the airmen from dropping their loads in the scheduled places which were in German hands. We had sent co-ordinates of the places they should try to put the stuff down. Hopefully, as the Dakotas came on, we watched for the first sign that the pilots were aware, by order or by observation, of the situation. Again, the ground signals were laid and lit, and the troops held out parachute silks. But the aircraft kept to the planned dropping points and the Germans again found themselves receiving gifts from their enemies. Only the overs reached us. Some crews, overshooting, came round in face of most appalling flak. Some aircraft were on fire. Hundreds of us saw one man in the doorway of a blazing Dakota refusing to release a pannier until he had found the exact spot, though the machine was a flaming torch now and he had no hope of escape.

Major General R. E. Urquhart CB DSO[6]

'Again, the ground signals were laid and lit, and the troops held out parachute silks.' Paratroopers desperately try to change the aircraft dropping points. Courtesy Imperial War Museum

Twenty-seven air despatchers were missing at the end of the day, with nine known to have been killed. Their efforts were appreciated beyond measure, and the courage exhibited by the air despatch crews has remained a lasting memory for those who took part in the battle. However, the efforts of those in the base issuing the stores were, sometimes, less well received.

> *We received some weapons as part of the resupply drops. However, they were greased for long term storage and we could do nothing with them. The stores people in the base seemed to have no idea of the needs and problems of the soldier in the field.*
> Major C. C. Chidgey RAOC

The Oosterbeek Perimeter Begins to Consolidate

During the day the remnants of 4th Parachute Brigade, seeking to make their way into the defensive perimeter now firming up around Oosterbeek, were split up due to enemy action. Essentially, 10th Parachute Battalion made its own way into the area, whilst brigade headquarters with 156 Parachute Battalion, having bumped into enemy on Utrechtseweg, had withdrawn into a large depression in the ground in the woods to the west of Valkenburglaan, just a few hundred yards from the north-west tip of the area being defended by the Division. There they remained, fighting for survival until the position became untenable and they had to make a dash late in the afternoon into the relative safety of the Oosterbeek perimeter. Once in, the remnants of 4th Parachute Brigade were tasked with the defence of the eastern edge of the position, occupying buildings, digging in to gardens and taking on their enemy at extraordinarily close ranges. Straight away they began to inflict and to take casualties.

Corporal Creasy, one of my lads, with a snap shot killed a Jerry attempting to cross the road; and a corporal and two of the other boys were killed by a mortar when withdrawing from a blazing building soon afterwards.
Sergeant J. Lambert ACC

Corporal J. Sorsby ACC was also wounded that day. Attached to 1st Airborne Division signals, he was taken to a dressing station and subsequently became a prisoner-of-war.

7th KOSB made their way independently and occupied an area at the northern tip of the perimeter, although they were by now much reduced having taken casualties and lost another company taken prisoner.

Resistance at the Bridge Is Overwhelmed

As the day wore on the atmosphere and the tension at the bridge in Arnhem had grown unbearable. The mood swung between hope and despair. Lack of news from the rest of the Division and XXX Corps was bad for morale and the word began to spread that it would soon be necessary to make a run for it. Rumours began to abound: that the wounded would have to be left behind, or that they would have to be shot before the survivors left.

The RAOC were ordered to occupy another house nearby on the western side of the bridge. Because of the weight of fire coming their way they decided to split into small groups, or move singly, in order to minimise risk. It was here they lost their cohesion.

I was in a building looking out onto the main street down which we had moved on the first night. I saw a stream of tracers emerging from some bushes on the embankment opposite to the one we had covered earlier. This tracer fire was directed at our chaps under the bridge so I stopped and taking steady aim with my Sten let go a full magazine spraying the bushes back and forth. The firing stopped, and after observing for a couple of minutes with no answering fire I assumed that I had put the gun out of action.
Private E. V. B. Mordecai RAOC

Ted Mordecai was now out of touch with his friends. In searching for them he ended up on a pile of hot bricks, feeling 'cooked', and then saw he was near the building occupied by brigade headquarters. He decided to make for it, risking the 200 yard dash. Making his way towards it he was fired at and dived for cover into the mortar pits dug on a triangle of grass just in front of the Battalion Headquarters. Eventually reaching his destination in one piece, he was given a drink of wine and, having explained the position under the ramparts, was told to rest. He had barely had a few minutes when the cry went up seeking anyone who knew anything about Bren guns. He was shown a machine-gunner with a corporal as his number two, complaining that the gun did not work. After a few checks he discovered that the magazine had been over-filled, preventing cartridges from feeding into the chamber. Ted was asked by the officer to take over the gun, and could not very well object. With the same corporal as his number two, he became the last Bren gunner in the last bastion at the bridge.

Off to the left of his position was a German machine gun firing into the building, but Ted could not see it. He asked others to spot it, and it was located by a sharp-eyed paratrooper who saw it in a bush half way up the embankment, the one Ted had shot at earlier with his Sten. Taking on his new target he and the enemy gunner embarked on a short duel.

He was good and his aim was excellent as every time I pushed the barrel of the Bren out of the window he let fly and bullets spattered off the outside wall. His angle of fire was probably such that he couldn't get a burst through the window. However, by ducking below the window edge and putting the Bren on the right hand side of the window I managed to silence him.
Private E. V. B. Mordecai RAOC

Just then the headquarters was mortared and there was a hit on the corner of the room which killed or wounded four men and left the Bren under a pile of rubble, with Ted Mordecai covered in filth and concussed. Deciding his present position was untenable he evacuated to the garden behind the building where some trenches had been dug.

The 88s were blasting away quite regularly now. I was trying to clean the Bren which I had recovered from the debris when someone offered me a tin of pilchards. I opened them with my jackknife and was just about to eat the first when a shell landed nearby. Once again I was covered in earth, and when I looked for the pilchards the tin was empty and covered in dirt. I was annoyed because I hadn't had anything to eat for hours; and I had to set to cleaning the Bren again.
Private E. V. B. Mordecai RAOC

Having recovered his composure and cleaned his gun, Ted found himself part of a group that carried on fighting through the day, scurrying between buildings and gardens, trying to avoid the patterns of gun and mortar fire coming their way.

Jerry started shelling again and once more we dashed back and forth across the street as each alternate shell landed. This couldn't go on for long and it was on one of these runs that Jerry changed his order of fire and dropped two in succession on the same place. Four of us had just dashed through the hole in the wall into the orchard and just as we arrived so did a shell. It exploded right in front of us and the three chaps in front of me went flying in the air. I saw the explosion and ducked my head to one side as the blast reached me. It lifted me off my feet and knocked me flat out, and when I came round I couldn't see anything.
Private E. V. B. Mordecai RAOC

Ted, able to see out of one eye only, eventually found a trench into which he fell, onto the man lying at the bottom. He was to stay there all night, whilst the shelling continued unabated; and there was no reply at all as he tried to contact any British soldiers in the area.

They were either lying low, or there weren't any left.
Private E. V. B. Mordecai RAOC

As Ted had left from under the bridge so had Kevin Heaney; and trying to stay in touch with his friend he too had found himself alone. His first obstacle was a six foot wall, and men were being shot as they jumped or climbed over. Kevin Heaney, watching men hit in the head or chest, likened it to a shooting gallery with live men as the targets. Eventually he managed to get into a garden, when a hand grenade exploded about a yard away. A young soldier crouched behind him received a severe wound in his throat and began to call for his mother.

Dispositions of RASC and RAOC units and men at the Arnhem bridge. This aerial photograph, taken on 18 September 1944, clearly shows the wrecked vehicles from Graebner's abortive attempt to cross from the south. Locations and routes are:

1. The building with the chairs
A. The RAOC route on the first night
2. The first RAOC building, 17-19 Sept
3. The second RAOC building, 19 Sept for 3 hours
B. The route to the RAOC position under the bridge
4. The RAOC position under the bridge, 19 and 20 Sept
C. Ted Mordecai's withdrawal route
5. The mortar pits.
6. Brigade HQ, Mordecai's last stand
7. The RASC platoon location
8. Corporal Roberts' Aid Post
9. Kevin Heaney's capture

Courtesy Public Record

Heaney applied a field dressing to the wound. Scrambling out of the garden he entered the hallway of a house, where he found himself with four other men. Germans, some fifty yards away, were firing directly into the building. There was nowhere left to go. Heaney put his hand inside his jacket, tore off his white singlet and passed it to the man nearest the Germans. He waved it, and the Germans shouted back. Assuming this to be an invitation to come out they did so, with Kevin as number five in a group of six.

As we came out the Germans started firing and the four men in front of me were shot, including the lad who had been wounded in the neck. The remaining chap and I dived back for cover, deciding that the Germans were not taking any prisoners. I have since decided that we were giving ourselves up to a German platoon who were still being fired on by some of our troops who were in a better position than ourselves.

Private K. J. Heaney RAOC

Subsequently, as the Germans moved in to help some British soldiers who were trapped, Heaney and the other soldier he was with yelled for help and a large German with a machine gun appeared and signalled the two of them to get behind German lines. Their battle was over.

Ron Pugh, never having found his friends since becoming detached on the Sunday evening, was wounded that afternoon.

'I was in a window during the afternoon firing at some Germans when I was hit. The bullet entered my upper left arm and smashed it very badly. I was dragged into the cellar, where I remained until the surrender. My wound was treated by Captain Logan, but there was no morphine and only a sip of water. After that the treatment was horrible. I went to the St Elisabeth and then on to a hospital in Apeldoorn where they put a tube through my arm. After three or four days a German nurse removed the sling, with no subtlety, and it hurt like hell. I went without food for days and the transport to Fallingbostel was awful. There was no dressing change for days at a time, sometimes weeks. I could feel the wound tugging away, and didn't want to look at it. A French medical orderly eventually

Private Ron Pugh RAOC, 1st Airborne Division OFP Forward Parachute Detachment. Author's Collection

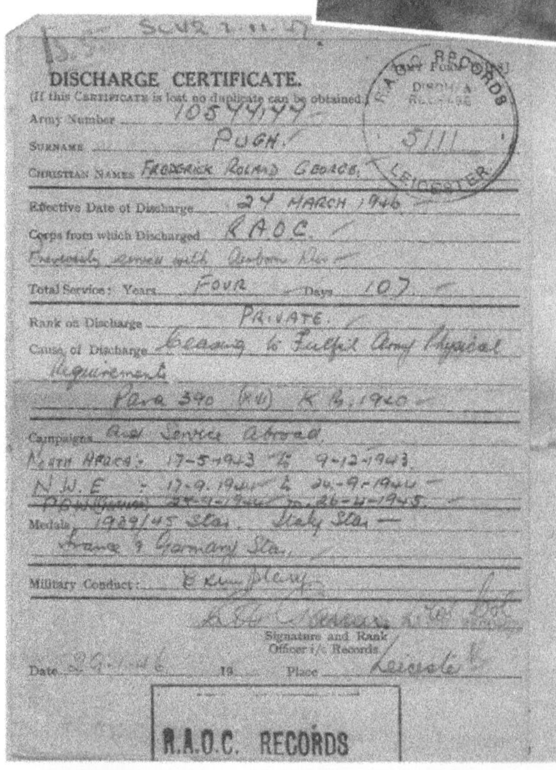

DISCHARGE CERTIFICATE.
(If this CERTIFICATE is lost no duplicate can be obtained.)
Surname PUGH.
Christian Names FREDERICK ROLAND GEORGE.
Effective Date of Discharge 24 MARCH 1946
Corps from which Discharged RAOC.
Total Service: Years FOUR Days 107.
Rank on Discharge PRIVATE.
Cause of Discharge Ceasing to Fulfil Army Physical Requirements
Campaigns and Service Abroad
Medals 1939/45 Star. Italy Star — France & Germany Star.
Military Conduct:
Signature and Rank Officer i/c Records
Date 19 Place Leicester
R.A.O.C. RECORDS

Ron Pugh's post-war discharge certificate, noting that he ceased to 'Fulfil Army Physical Requirements'. It didn't stop him going on to score 150 goals for Winchester Town football club. Author's Collection

> *took off the dressing in the prison camp, and as he did so I heard him say 'ooh la la' as handfuls of maggots fell onto the floor. But they'd eaten all the dead flesh and the wound was clean. Other blokes with similar wounds died of blood poisoning.*
>
> Private F. R. G. Pugh RAOC

Staff Sergeant Harry Walker never left the immediate area of the bridge supports by the river. He remembers a Royal Engineer officer going out to do something to the charges the Sappers had laid earlier. Crawling on his belly, the officer was relying on Harry and a corporal to cover him. However, having completed whatever it was he wanted to do, and on withdrawing, he stepped right into their line of fire and was shot in the legs. They both went forward to help the officer, assisted by another two soldiers. Between the four of them they managed to get him back and hand him on to some form of medical treatment - albeit very limited at that stage. Shortly after this there was a mortar barrage, which resulted in Harry Walker being rendered unconscious. He remembered nothing more until he woke in the dark, cold, stiff and alone.

> *I remember waking with awful pains in my back. I couldn't straighten up. That bloody lumbago!*
>
> Staff Sergeant H. W. Walker RAOC

Bernard Manley had also remained at the roadside where it passed beneath the bridge, beside the river.

> *I tried to hole up in the hope of getting away. I was only very slightly wounded, although my ear drums were shattered. Then there were six German infantry around me and by then I had no ammunition. There was nothing I could do.*
>
> Captain B. V. Manley RAOC

Private McCarthy RAOC was wounded and taken prisoner. However, there are no details of what befell him.[7]

It was during the course of the afternoon, at about 1.30 p.m., that John Frost had been wounded in the legs by a mortar blast. Unable to carry on, he had nominated Major Freddie Gough to replace him as commander of the force at the bridge.

In the building occupied by the RASC things took a turn for the worse. Up until 20 September their position had been protected to some extent by its proximity to the wall of the prison near which it was located. However, now it came under direct fire and was hit, with a large hole being made in the wall. The defenders assumed they would suffer an infantry attack, seeking to exploit the damage and confusion. However, the Germans were content to wear down the airborne soldiers and to minimise their own casualties. Consequently, they were subjected to more shellfire.

> *The first shot hit the corner of the roof. It didn't explode because the only resistance it had was the slates on the roof, but it left a hole nearly two yards across. The lads underneath it were showered with debris; I wouldn't like to repeat what they said. The shell exploded against the brickwork at the other end of the*

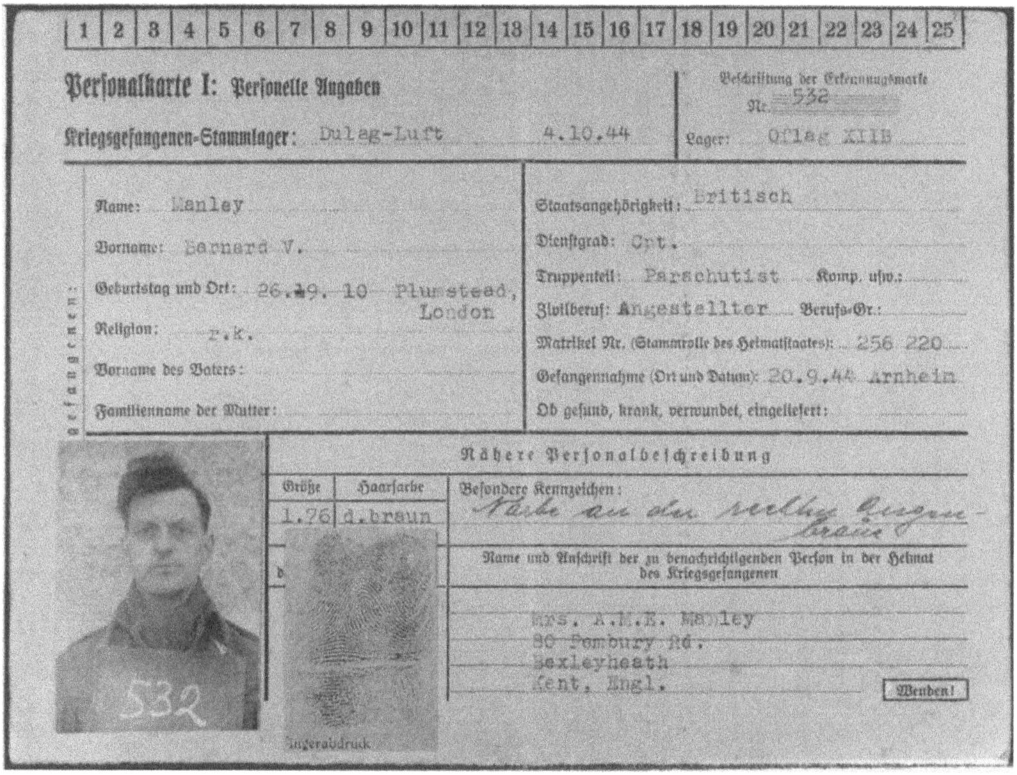

1	2	3	4	5	6	7	8	9	10	11	12	13	14	15	16	17	18	19	20	21	22	23	24	25

Personalkarte I: Personelle Angaben

Kriegsgefangenen-Stammlager: Dulag-Luft 4.10.44

Beschriftung der Erkennungsmarke Nr. 532
Lager: Oflag XIIB

Gefangenen

Name: Manley
Vorname: Bernard V.
Geburtstag und Ort: 26.19. 10 Plumstead, London
Religion: r.k.
Vorname des Vaters:
Familienname der Mutter:

Staatsangehörigkeit: Britisch
Dienstgrad: Cpt.
Truppenteil: Parachutist Komp. usw.:
Zivilberuf: Angestellter Berufs-Gr.:
Matrikel Nr. (Stammrolle des Heimatstaates): 256 220
Gefangennahme (Ort und Datum): 20.9.44 Arnheim
Ob gesund, krank, verwundet, eingeliefert:

Nähere Personalbeschreibung

Größe	Haarfarbe	Besondere Kennzeichen:
1.76	d.braun	Narbe an der rechten Augen-braue

Name und Anschrift der zu benachrichtigenden Person in der Heimat des Kriegsgefangenen

Mrs. A.M.E. Manley
80 Pembury Rd.
Bexleyheath
Kent, Engl.

Wenden!

Fingerabdruck

Bernard Manley's prisoner-of-war record card. Author's Collection

> *long room. We were all down on the floor. A lot of shrapnel was flying about, and I think one man was killed and one wounded. We decided to get out, down to the ground floor, when the second shell exploded against the front wall of the room we had been in; we would all have been killed if we had been there.*
>
> Driver J. Wild RASC

The brigade headquarters building had also benefited from being partially protected by other buildings, but now it was alight, and the wounded in the cellars were at risk. The RASC building was, at that stage, the only nearby building not on fire and it became the chosen destination. However, realising that the evacuation could not proceed fast enough a truce, lasting two hours, was agreed with the Germans for evacuation of wounded. The truce having commenced the able-bodied men from Brigade Headquarters were sent off by Major Gough, northward into the town. Corporal Dennis Freebury was one of them:

> *Major Gough, with his arm in a sling and his silver hair, in his shirtsleeves – a swashbuckling character - gave us a pep talk. It was a bit like Hollywood. He said: 'I want you to go out, do your best and see if you can get back to our own forces – and just remember that you belong to the finest division in the British Army.'*

Nobody cheered or anything like that, but it made one feel good.
Corporal D. F. Freebury RASC, HQ 1st Parachute Brigade

Major Gough waved goodbye and wished us good luck. I went over a wall, down an alleyway across a square and into a garden. I found a pear tree with pears in the garden, and I saw a rabbit hutch with a tame Angora rabbit still in it. I released the rabbit and dug a trench behind the hutch, using the structure as overhead cover. I shared it with a REME sergeant. I took the bolt out of my rifle and buried it - I had no ammunition. I had a nap, and suddenly there was a banging on the hutch door and a huge German was there. Why do they always look eight feet tall when you are down a hole? Anyway, he said: 'Come out Tommy, I know you are in there.' We stood, thinking we were the only ones in the garden and all around us about twelve other blokes appeared from various other holes.
Corporal A. Johnson RASC

Tomorrow, Maybe Tomorrow They'll Come

As darkness descended the Americans finally secured the northern end of both the railway and road bridges across the Waal river in Nijmegen. It had been a superhuman effort, which had cost them dear, but they had fought with the desperation borne of a need to give their airborne comrades, just eleven miles to the north, some hope of relief. Their joy as Sergeant Peter Robinson of the Grenadier Guards led his troop of Sherman tanks across the road bridge knew no bounds. Their anger when the British armour stopped just a few hundred yards north of the river was beyond measure. With the infantry of the 43rd Wessex Division snarled up in the town and on the congested road to the south it was considered simply too dangerous to move against an unknown enemy who might be dug in and with little or no possibility of manoeuvring armour off the narrow roads in the area.

As they halted, the defence of the bridge in Arnhem collapsed and although the paratroopers in the town would fight on until the next day the Germans could now move armour south; and they wasted no time in so doing. The opportunity for the Allies to rush something to the bridge may just have been there, briefly, but the chance was now lost – as were the men left in Arnhem.

1. Oerlikon: A Swiss arms manufacturer, and the guns in question were light anti-aircraft weapons which could also be used effectively against ground targets.
2. If correctly identified by Ted Mordecai these tanks were probably the two Tigers belonging to Kampfgruppe (Battlegroup) Knaust.
3. Irene Reimann was freed by the Germans on 26 September, and returned to Germany.
4. The localised fog which held the Poles on their launching airfields did not affect the bases further south from which the resupply flights were departing.
5. This order of dress, especially the PT shoes, appears to have been peculiar to 63 Airborne Composite Company.
6. From 'Arnhem', Urquhart, Cassel, London 1958
7. Private McCarthy is the only one of the six RAOC at the bridge with whom it has not been possible, since the war, to make contact.

Chapter Eight

Day Five – The Last Hours at the Bridge

In the Dark and the Early Morning

It was a feature of the fighting at Arnhem, confirmed by many survivors, that the Germans did not seem to like fighting by night. As darkness fell their activity dropped off markedly, and they could often be heard in their positions talking really quite loudly as if to draw comfort from the sound of voices. Consequently, there was relative quiet during the night in Arnhem and Oosterbeek, with the Germans now able to use the bridge to move their forces to Nijmegen.

On the corridor, however, the luxury of relative quiet was denied the Seaborne Echelon. They were faced with a night move, which was to prove very difficult with the densities of traffic they were experiencing on the congested road. There were no lights, and the volume of traffic was huge, especially around Eindhoven. Their circumstances were not helped by German artillery fire which added further to the confusion. Almost inevitably they became disorganised, and the Command, Medical and RASC ammunition elements were separated from the rest. It would be some time before they would meet up again.

At the bridge in Arnhem the coming of dawn was greeted with the move of yet more German armour, silhouetted against the gathering light as it moved south towards the small bridgehead being formed by XXX Corps on the northern end of the Nijmegen bridge. Exhausted paratroopers peered through bloodshot eyes, seeking a way out of their predicament, either by escape or by surrender. These were the only choices, for they had no hope of recovering the access to the bridge.

> *The house we were holding was on fire and subject to constant German activity at the end. I was then ordered to attempt to break out with ten men and try to reach the divisional position some seven miles away. After a short interval Lieutenant Daniels led the remainder of the unit with the same objective. We could not get very far. The Germans were too thick on the ground and as we had been on the go for four days without much food or water we were in need of a rest. We tried to hole up in a bombed out building, but we were probed out by the Germans not long after first light.*
> Captain W. V. Gell RASC

Major David Clarke RASC, CRASC's second-in-command, had been wounded. He was ordered by Freddie Gough to give himself up with the rest of the casualties to the first Germans who appeared. Clarke refused, pointing out that a man of Gough's strength could carry him to safety. Gough disagreed, and sought to make his own escape. Major Clarke was eventually taken prisoner.

For Ted Mordecai, lying in his trench with his dead companion, the night had been long, painful and uncomfortable. He had no ammunition, no food and no

Corporal Roberts RASC, the medical orderly with C Coy 3rd Parachute Battalion, having been taken prisoner at the Arnhem bridge. Courtesy L.W. Wright

water; and no sight in his right eye. Deciding that he really could not go on any longer he watched carefully as others gave themselves up. Once he was sure the paratroopers were not being molested or shot he took a white towel from his small pack and, taking a deep breath, walked up the street with his arms in the air and the towel showing clearly. He found that the men to whom he gave himself up were Hungarian satellite troops. They gave him a sip of wine and placed him with a group of airborne soldiers, most of whom were wounded.

In the DAA the stand-to took place, as usual, at 5.00 a.m. However, it was not until 7.00 a.m. that the morning's mortar barrage began. Referred to by many as the 'morning hate' it was to go on for some considerable time.

Jerry started mortaring early. He seemed to be working on a plan...until approximately 1200 hours, then stopped – for dinner. Naturally we took the opportunity to grab our meal too.
Lance Corporal J. L. Hughes RASC

During the barrage Michael Packe's headquarters received a direct strike, and one RASC and one RAOC soldier were hit. The RAOC casualty was Corporal Freddie Grantham, who was seriously wounded and died some two hours later.[1]

I saw Freddie Grantham killed. He was standing in a doorway of a house when the mortar exploded.[2]
Private S. G. Harsley RAOC

Corporal Grantham had rejoined Airborne Forces, having being previously invalided out of the OFP and returned to his original unit. This was an anathema to any airborne soldier worth his salt, and Freddie had worked hard to overcome

Members of the OFP. Corporal Grantham (1) was killed at Arnhem, Sergeant Plowman (2) escaped. Both men were private soldiers when this was taken. Author's Collection

his injury, returning to the OFP just a month earlier. Slim, tall and dark, he was a very good storeman, and a very fit soldier; and Major Chidgey liked him enormously. It was he who helped Lieutenant Colonel Gerry Mobbs to bury Freddie Grantham in a field just west of the Hartenstein Hotel.

I knew Freddie Grantham and his wife Emily very well. They were a lovely couple. There were no children.

Sergeant R. Collins RAOC, 1st Airborne Division Ordnance Field Park, 1st Seaborne Echelon

The mortar fire was heavy throughout the day, and adversely affected attempts by RASC and RAOC soldiers to transfer as much stock as they could to the new DAA forming in the trees behind the Hartenstein Hotel. In particular the RAOC tried to retrieve twenty of their thirty panniers from the Hamilcar, but lost three vehicles in making the vain attempt. They were now largely devoid of stock, with their trailers also having been destroyed in the bombardments. From now on they would operate mainly in an infantry role.

Resupply By Air – The Worst Day Of All

On 21 September the Royal Air Force suffered its worst casualties of the entire operation. The aircraft sustained heavy damage from flak and enemy fighters. RAF fighter escort support had been noticeably patchy up to now, but on the 21st it was practically non-existent. Most of the American fighters based in England were supporting a major bombing raid into Germany and almost half of the RAF fighters were grounded by bad weather. The result was that a large force of German fighters was able to wreak havoc among the 63 Stirlings and 63 Dakotas which took part in the day's operations; of the 126 aircraft, 31 failed to return.

Resupply from the air, an easy target for the German flak gunners. Courtesy Imperial War Museum

Twenty-one air despatchers were reported killed and a further sixty-four were reported as missing in action. Worst hit was 223 Air Despatch Company from 48 Air Despatch Column, with thirty-eight killed or missing on this one day.

Lance Corporal Harribin of 223 Company flew with 48 Sqn RAF from Down Ampney. His crew included Lance Corporals Moorcroft and Pilson and Driver Everett. The aircraft was shot down by German fighters at around 5.30 p.m., crashing on Volkel airfield. The order had been given to abandon the aircraft, but with German fighters still about Harrabin, the last to jump, decided to try a delayed drop as several men the day before were known to have been shot up after baling out. He'd never made a parachute jump before and he tried to judge his height by waiting until trees and hedges looked fairly distinct before pulling the ripcord. On landing his first act was to feel in his pockets to see if he had dropped any money. Lance Corporal Pilson was killed in the air, as were the pilot and his co-pilot – confirming Lance Corporal Harribin's fears. Even worse, arguably, was the shooting of the wireless operator as he hung, helpless, in his parachute harness from a tree. Another of the aircraft crew, and two of the air despatchers, joined up with a Stirling crew from Fairford and hitch-hiked from Grave to Eindhoven. Eventually picked up by XXX Corps they made their way by staff car to safety in Brussels.

The only officer to be killed undertaking air despatch operations was Lieutenant Herbert Edwards. Aged twenty-seven, he was also in a 48 Squadron RAF Dakota with Lance Corporal Eric Roscoe and Drivers Jack Taylor and Ben Welham. In an appalling twist of fate, their aircraft was hit from above by the load falling from another Dakota which caused the loss of a wing. The aeroplane crashed just north of Driel on the southern bank of the Rhine, about level with the line of the western edge of 1st Airborne Division's perimeter. All the occupants were killed.

Pilot Officer Peel, who belly landed his Stirling at Dennenkamp, was congratulating himself on a success with all his crew alive when he discovered his two air despatchers had bailed out, but at too low a height for their parachutes to be effective, and were dead. They were Driver W. G. Thompson, who has no known grave, and Driver J. F. Johnston, both from 253 Airborne Composite Company RASC. Flying Officer Peel wrote, in 1986, that a friend, flying beside him, had seen him go down, and had remarked that two bodies had fallen from the aircraft just before it crashed. There had been no sign of parachutes. The wireless operator, having been nearest the two air despatchers, remembered that all he could see in the fuselage was smoke and flame, and ammunition was exploding. In his view the two men had little option: either to jump to their deaths or burn alive in the aircraft.

A Stirling from 196 Squadron based at Keevil was shot down by German fighter aircraft and crashed among houses west of Oosterbeek. The crew and passengers were buried beside the crash site, and disinterred after the war for burial in the Arnhem-Oosterbeek Cemetery. An air despatcher of 63 Company was one of those, one Lance Corporal Stanley Law; and his colleague, also given a named grave, was Driver W. H. Brook. However, Driver Brook was subsequently found to have survived the war and 'his' grave is now shown as being that of an unknown soldier.

A number of aircraft came down south of the Rhine. Although, in some cases, it was the result of flak damage over the SDPs, many were brought down by German fighters. The enemy, it seems, had unrestricted use of the air to wreak havoc on returning resupply aircraft. It was during one of these attacks that the violent evasive action taken by the pilot of a Dakota of 233 Squadron RAF near Ravenstein caused Lance Corporal Ronald Clements of 800 Air Despatch Company to be flung from the aircraft without a parachute. Subsequently, the aircraft landed safely at Brussels.

Many of the survivors from downed aircraft went on to have yet further adventures; some more pleasant than others. Corporal Conquest and his crew from 223 Air Despatch Company, for example, landed among the Poles from where they were directed to a British headquarters. En route they found themselves among some Dutch girls who chose to accompany them, and who spent the whole of the journey anxiously enquiring if they were married. Subsequently, they were treated to dinner by 'a general', followed by a good night's sleep.

Driver Backler, also of 223 Air Despatch Company, was, so it is believed, on a 271 Squadron RAF Dakota piloted by Flying Officer Finlay which crash-landed near Helmond. The aircraft was attacked by fighters and set on fire. When his turn to bale out came it was too late.

Sergeant Charles Ruston RASC.
Courtesy Airborne Museum 'Hartenstein'

> *I tried to get to the door to jump, but couldn't get near the opening because the rubber dinghies were burning in the doorway. I did the only thing left and rolled myself out onto the roller runway along which we usually push out the supplies. I went out head first and fell several hundred feet before I pulled the ripcord. I landed all right, a bit dazed, to be surrounded by Belgians who seemed very surprised to see me.*
> Driver Backler RASC, 223 Air Despatch Company RASC

> *After all the panniers had been dropped I received the order to bale out. I jettisoned my flak suit*[3] *and put my para pack in position, noting which side the ripcord was and proceeded to the door where the despatchers stood adjusting their 'chutes. We went out in good order and there was no panic. I remember turning over once before the canopy filled and there was no unpleasant jerk.*
> Sergeant C. Ruston RASC, Air Despatcher

Lance Corporal Jones of 799 Air Despatch Company flying in a 437 Squadron RCAF Dakota from RAF Blakehill Farm was a little less fortunate. Only he and the navigator got out after being attacked by an enemy fighter over the dropping zone. The other members of the air despatch crew, Corporal A. E. Hall and Drivers H. Woodward and F. G. W. Yeo all died. Jones was severely wounded and on reaching the ground his parachute caught up in some branches and he was thrown heavily against a tree. When he regained consciousness he found himself in a wheelbarrow being pushed by a Dutchman who was led to a hospital by two

American soldiers – undignified, but at least he was alive.

Corporal Sproston of 253 Airborne Composite Company was one of the two air despatchers in a Stirling. On approaching the SDP the aircraft was hit by flak and caught fire. Corporal Sproston was given orders to despatch the load, and even though the aircraft was ablaze with the rear gunner's ammunition exploding in the fuselage, he continued to despatch his load of high explosives, waiting deliberately to ensure that it was done at the right moment. Having got rid of the danger from the load the pilot was then able to crash-land the aircraft without loss of life.

Subsequently, whilst being driven in an Allied vehicle to Brussels, the convoy they were in was attacked by four enemy Tiger tanks and a number of vehicles were knocked out. A small party from the convoy took up position in a house and Corporal Sproston was put in charge of a forward observation post. Under heavy enemy fire he directed with great effect the fire of a Bofors 40mm gun. His courage, tenacity and the example he set were to earn him a Military Medal.

Flight Lieutenant Jimmy Edwards, the famous post-war comedian, was a member of 271 Squadron RAF from Down Ampney. He was just opening his sandwiches on the return journey when his aircraft was hit by a Focke-Wulf 190 and the engines caught fire. Edwards told everyone to bale out, but having done so was advised that three of his air despatchers were too seriously wounded to evacuate the aircraft. Consequently, he stayed on board and crash-landed his Dakota near Oploo, and although it was a successful forced landing he suffered some unpleasant burns. Regrettably, his efforts on behalf of his air despatch crew were to no avail. Lance Corporal George Chisholme and Drivers Lionel Abbott and Roy Abbott, all from 223 Air Despatch Company, died. Lance Corporal Deridisi survived and with all but two of the aircrew, who were captured, returned to base.

> *We were attacked soon after leaving the dropping zone by a Focke-Wulf which came up from underneath us, and as we had nothing to hit back with it wasn't long before the 'plane was completely out of control and on fire. We received the order to bale out. It was my first parachute jump and, believe me, there's really nothing in it. Our only fear was that we would be shot at while gliding down. We knew this had happened to several other chaps. We also knew that there were Germans in the woods underneath us and we seemed to glide down far too slowly. We'd hardly touched the ground when two members of the Dutch Underground Movement rushed out of the woods, unbuckled our parachutes and hurried us off to a Dutch monastery about three miles away. The priests there fed us, and showed us where we could spend the night in safety. They told us that the schoolroom attached to the monastery had been used by the Germans as a billet. A party of nine of us RAF and RASC, set off in the morning for Brussels. We hitch-hiked all the way, and we reached Brussels after about ten hours. I'm mighty thankful to say that we had no casualties in the crew; and it was good to realise that one can still survive being shot down in flames with comparatively little discomfort.*
>
> Driver Lane RASC, An Air Despatcher

The events in the air were clearly visible to those on the ground, especially the men within the divisional perimeter straining their necks as they looked skywards in the hope that some of the parachutes would fall their way. The sight that greeted them was awful with the brightness and colour highlighting the tragedy they were witnessing. Parachutes fell, coloured like bunting on a village fairground. Each of the parachutes had a colour code, identifying its contents to potential recipients: red was for ammunition, white for medical stores, green was for rations and blue for petroleum products. Yellow meant communications equipment, whilst black was for mail.[4] Like brightly coloured flags they fluttered to the ground as the panniers and containers they were supporting landed and lay, bright against the green of the trees, the brown of the heather or the grey streets of Oosterbeek. Around the aircraft as they flew steadily on were the bright bursts of flak, the high explosive showing red and orange in the midst of the black smoke from the detonating shells. Tracer arced lazily into the sky from a seemingly infinite number of guns, whilst the awful cacophony of noise from firing weapons and bursting flak shells beat incessantly at the eardrums of the helpless, frustrated, angry onlookers.

> *It was with excited hopefulness and almost painful admiration that those on the ground watched these aircraft day by day, and for some reason always at the same hour, flying in to drop their loads. Through a continuous curtain of fire they flew on unwaveringly and very slowly, and so low that it seemed wonderful that more of them were not destroyed – to drop their loads which floated down mostly behind enemy lines. Many were hit and set on fire, but continued to despatch their panniers until they fell from view.*
>
> Unknown British Officer

A pannier in front of the Hartenstein Hotel being opened by CQMS Holderness and a glider pilot – John McGough. Courtesy Imperial War Museum

Supplies being collected in Van Lehnehopweg. Courtesy Imperial War Museum

The last day of flying for 63 Airborne Composite Company RASC was 21 September. They were withdrawn from the operation, in preparation for the support of 6th Airborne Division for subsequent operations. During MARKET GARDEN they lost seventeen men killed, and an additional two from 398 Airborne Composite Company RASC attached to the Company from 6th Airborne Division: Lance Corporal John Waring and Driver Ernest Heckford were both killed on 20 September.

The result of the RAF and Air Despatch effort on Thursday, 21 September was that 400 rounds of 75mm and 170 rounds of 6-pounder ammunition were collected and placed in the DAA. During the four days since resupply drops commenced on 18 September a total of twenty-four rounds of 17-pounder ammunition had also been collected.

At Last, Some Help Is On The Way

With the bridge in their hands the Germans were able to concentrate exclusively on the rest of Urquhart's Division, and seek to break its tenuous hold on the north bank of the Rhine, thereby cutting it off from any real chance of rescue or reinforcement. For his part, Urquhart had some 3,000 men of his original 10,000 fighting for survival in the small, crowded 'thumb', with its base on the river.

Went to div in the afternoon to try and get some ammunition etc. We needed

Vickers Machine Gun ammo urgently. Also wanted two or three Bren guns. Were rather surprised to find that we could have a couple. Some had just come in on the supply drop. Whilst waiting at div we were in the ammunition dump, such as it was, when a shell came in and ricocheted off the ground in front of us – about two yards from a small stack of 6-pounder shells. Our luck was still holding. Back up to the position again, by what we then began to call the 'death walk'.[5] *George was with me on all these wanderings. Found up at the position that Jerry was closing in and had the houses covered with snipers and Spandaus. The position, incidentally, was two or three houses covering an essential crossroads. At the same time as we took up the Brens we took up maps and ammo – also four reinforcements. They were very pleased to have them – manpower was becoming acute. Altogether we made four trips – but George by this time was feeling rather bad. His back wasn't too good. I made one more trip after that on my own. Took five men of the Battalion back to their position. The mortaring etc had been too much for them - and so they had been 'resting' well back. They weren't very keen at going back either.*

Lance Corporal J. L. Hughes RASC

The house in Oosterbeek...held for two days under incessant fire before it finally collapsed over our heads, and during this time finding the Dutch bakery next door, and the bakers... carrying on until actually ordered down to the cellars...severe casualties suffered by the chicken-run in the back yard, and the following day...a full day's cooking with the chicken as the high spot.

Sergeant J. Lambert ACC

Throughout it all the need for logistic support remained undiminished. Essentially, it was a transportation task, with gun ammunition being run from the DAA down to the Royal Artillery gun positions near the Oosterbeek Laag Church on the south-eastern corner of the salient. Their work was inhibited by mortar attacks on the DAA which caused explosions and fires, which were only extinguished with difficulty.

Many of the 250 Company drivers, under cover of the Red Cross, were engaged in carrying casualties to the enemy-occupied hospital or fetching water from an enemy-controlled well. On one occasion a driver, one Dixie Dean, whilst undertaking one of these tasks, met a German tank, but was allowed to go on his way unmolested having first been asked for an undertaking not to disclose the tank's position.

During the afternoon, on the western edge of the perimeter, the British suffered a considerable reverse. Division von Tettau, advancing along the same road that had been followed by Frost just five days earlier, bumped a company position held by the Border Regiment on a feature known as the Westerbouwing. A piece of high ground dominating the southern edge of the Oosterbeek 'Thumb', it was a tactically vital feature, which the Border Regiment had sought to hold with its B Company. After a hard fight the British were pushed back, and formed another defensive line down the hill on the flat land at the bottom left-hand corner of Urquhart's position. There they were to remain, denying for the rest of the battle any attempt by von Tettau's men to breach the line at that point. Fortunately for them, von Tettau failed to appreciate the significance of the hill he had taken, and the airborne soldiers were never really to feel the full potential of the fire that could have been launched against them.

Then two things happened that were to work to the advantage of the beleaguered British force. Lieutenant Colonel Robert Loder-Symonds, the Commander Royal Artillery, was put in radio contact with 64 Medium Regiment RA in Nijmegen by Captain McMillan of 1 Forward Observation Unit who managed to make the link from Oosterbeek. Once it had been confirmed that Loder-Symonds was who he said he was the Gunners from XXX Corps began to provide artillery support from eleven miles south of Arnhem. Described by Urquhart as the most accurate and effective gunnery he had ever seen, the heavy shells of the batteries of 4.5", 5.5", 155mm and 3.7"[7] guns had huge impact on the enemy. Their effect was further enhanced whenever 64 Medium Regiment employed the 25-pounders of the Field Regiments of 43rd Wessex Division to thicken up their barrages.

As if this were not enough, the onset of evening saw the arrival of the 1st Independent Polish Parachute Brigade. They were two days late, and only about half their aircraft made it all the way to a new DZ, further to the west of the bridge near the village of Driel and opposite the base of the 1st Airborne Division position on the north bank of the Rhine in Oosterbeek. The rest of the aircraft carrying the Poles turned back, for a variety of reasons. However, to the desperately tired German soldiers they were a most unwelcome sight, a clear indication of their own strategic weakness and of the power of the American-led alliance that was advancing on their country. To the scratch units, the Landwehr soldiers and the Dutch SS the sight of fresh airborne soldiers, able to fight as hard as the ones they had been dealing with these past five days, was almost too much.

Not only did the Poles' arrival have a detrimental effect on many individual German soldiers, but it forced General Bittrich to detach units from his assault on the Oosterbeek perimeter in order to deal with this new threat, thereby releasing some of the pressure on the hard-pressed British. Just as he had gained the bridge, and thereby the freedom to devote all his attention to the remaining paratroopers, the reinforcements forced him to reconsider his options.

Nonetheless, the Germans continued to make life inside the perimeter unpleasant.

> *...I was potting away and I saw a Jerry come to a top room window. I immediately potted him – got him – but was a fraction too late. He'd thrown a grenade. The grenade burst a couple of yards away from me, but it was one of the usual Jerry type – made of tin – it didn't do much material damage. A few bits of shrapnel in my wrist, left knee and buttock – but the blast shook me. By that time though, the house had really been done up - and so we took our leave.*[8] *We'd had a couple of chaps hit pretty badly in the chest with light machine gun fire – so I took them down to the Div RAP.*[9] *A field dressing was put on my knee – and so was ok. We then returned to the headquarters.*
>
> Lance Corporal J. L. Hughes RASC

The stand-to took place, as usual, at 7.00 p.m., and through the night there was continual shelling and mortaring. Lance Corporal Hughes was, like most others, feeling the strain.

> *On the whole the situation was becoming worse. There was no water – we had to put tins out in the rain for water for tea – if you had any tea, sugar or milk. There was very little food; today was the last day we were given an organised issue. Now it was up to each group to fend for themselves. Jerry was mortaring pretty heavily all the time, but fortunately he didn't put any large-scale attacks in. Otherwise we would have been overwhelmed. The self-propelled guns and tanks were doing pretty well what they pleased.*
>
> Lance Corporal J. L. Hughes RASC

> *After days without food you reached the stage where you really did not want to eat.*
>
> Major C.C. Chidgey RAOC

At some stage in the battle, and the time is not known, the BRASCO of the 1st Airlanding Brigade, Captain L. A. C. Lockyer RASC, was badly wounded in the leg by a mortar blast. From the description it probably occurred on or around 21 September. The British medical officer examining him in the Main Dressing Station was clear that it would require amputation, but it was a procedure beyond his means. Captain Lockyer was, eventually, transferred to the St Elisabeth Hospital in Arnhem where the operation was performed successfully.

Happenings Further South.

Just before 8.00 p.m. the Seaborne Echelon was ordered to follow the tail end of 43rd Wessex Division through Eindhoven, Veghel and Uden. Their journey

The OFP Seaborne Echelon parked by the road south of Eindhoven. The tactical sign '89' can be clearly seen on the vehicles. Author's Collection

passed without incident, other than some damage to a motorcycle. However, they were still split from the confusion of the previous night, and C Column, containing the OFP, was still beside the road south of Eindhoven.

Still in their haystack, the two RAOC warrant officers, together with the pilot and co-pilot of their glider, were having a lean time of it; and were having to forage for food, principally apples and pears, by night in order not to give themselves away. To get in and out of their haystack they had been using a pole in order to climb up and down the side. During the day it had been knocked down by a horse, replaced by a farm worker and then knocked down again; this time to be left. This presented problems for the scavenger, since the pole could not be replaced without drawing attention to their presence in the haystack.

> *The drop to the ground was accomplished without difficulty by our fruit merchant. Getting back in, however, was a different matter, and as one of the horses in the field was standing by the haystack we 'upstairs' strongly advised our plunderer to climb on its back and the rest should be easy. The first part of our advice was easy, but then complications set in. Our man had succeeded in standing on the horse's back when the horse decided that it had been long enough in one spot and moved away, still with one British soldier standing motionless on its back. In the end, however, he got back.*
>
> WO1 (Sub-Conductor) G. E. Jenkins RAOC

1. Corporal Freddie Grantham is the only one of the four RAOC soldiers killed at Arnhem with a known grave, and he is buried in the Arnhem Oosterbeek War Cemetery. The date of death on his headstone is incorrect in showing the 25th of September - there are clear records showing he died on the 21st. Author's Note: I am seeking to remedy this.
2. This probably places Corporal Grantham at the first CRASC headquarters, which was in a building on the north-eastern edge of the first DAA.
3. Air despatchers wore a flak jacket under their smocks.
4. No mail was dropped at Arnhem, but there is a record of one black parachute being used to drop crystals for telecommunications equipment. There are no written records setting out the colour code, and there has to be some doubt if it was actually applied in full.
5. From the sketch map in his diary, Lance Corporal Hughes was operating in the 10th Parachute Battalion area, and the 'Death Walk' lay along the southern edge of the Schoonoord Dressing Station to the finger of houses being held by elements of the Battalion.
6. At the corner of Paul Krugerstraat and Mariaweg.
7. The 3.7" Gun was an anti-aircraft gun; in fact, the British version of the 88mm used by the Germans in both the anti-aircraft and anti-tank roles. Its use in the surface to surface role was unusual.
8. From the description this incident occurred in Stationsweg, half way between the Oosterbeek crossroads and the railway bridge at Oosterbeek Hoog.
9. RAP: Regimental Aid Post, usually staffed by a doctor and some medical staff drawn from the parent regiment. Only minor wounds were treated, with immediate first aid given to other casualties in preparation for evacuation to a Dressing Station.

Chapter Nine

The Cauldron Boils – The Sixth and Seventh Days

22 September 1944 - Der Hexenkessel

German soldiers would refer to a pocket of enemy resistance as a 'Kessel', meaning, in military parlance, an 'encircled area'. The word also translates directly to the English as 'kettle'. However, those involved at Arnhem embellished the expression, referring to the British salient on the Rhine as 'der Hexenkessel': the Witches' Cauldron. The defence offered by the paratroopers against anything they could throw at them caused the Germans continual anxiety, significant casualties and the terrible realisation that this was a fight that would see many more killed and maimed before it was over. Furthermore, they were beset by problems caused by inadequately trained and experienced soldiers being rushed to plug gaps, with little thought of the consequences. One German officer sent 1,600 recruits back to Germany on the basis that to use them against the British would have been tantamount to infanticide.

By the morning of 22 September attacks from the north-east by Spindler's battlegroup had made little progress, and along Utrechtseweg, approaching from Arnhem in the east, the 9th SS were constantly held by strong resistance. Changes in German tactics, operating with small penetration parties focused on specific areas, had begun to have some success, although the casualty rate had been very high and potentially unsustainable. However, the landing of the Poles had caused a major distraction, and meant that Urquhart's men might enjoy some small relief from the undivided attention of their aggressors. For their part, the Germans had spent the night of 21 September putting in place a blocking line south of Arnhem to prevent incursions towards the bridge whilst they planned what else they might do to meet this new threat from the sky at the same time as they pressed against the existing one in Oosterbeek.

Oblivious to this, the first part of the Seaborne Echelon moved through the night up the corridor. However, they were ordered off the road to make way for 43rd Wessex Division which was being moved up the corridor with the intention that they should assist the paratroopers in Oosterbeek. Column A was split by an anti-aircraft unit that was moving up the road, and further delay was imposed when the tanks of Kampfgruppe Walther cut the road about a mile north-east of Uden. By now it was obvious to everyone that they would not make Arnhem in time to help their colleagues, and that they were most likely faced with the prospect of resurrecting what they could from an operation that had gone seriously awry.

They were, however, able to offer a positive gesture of support to the American soldiers who had done so much, and suffered so much, in order to move the British up the corridor. Because of enemy activity and the constant cutting of the road between Veghel and Grave, the American logistic support system was unable to reach their northern units. Short of artillery ammunition, and with both the British and the Americans using the 75mm howitzer, it was a simple thing for the British to issue 500 of the 2,000 rounds they were carrying in order to help their allies in 82nd US Airborne Division.

North of the Rhine the stand-to in the DAA took place, as it had every day of the battle, at 5.00 a.m. Later that morning, the RASC were invited to form a platoon to operate in the infantry role in order to thicken up the defences on the eastern perimeter, under the command of 4th Parachute Brigade. With the opportunity to undertake their normal tasks of collection and distribution of stocks almost non-existent, and having been trained as brigade headquarters' defence platoons in their alternate role, they were a perfect choice for the task. Captain Jack Cranmer-Byng brought together the remnants of 1st and 2nd Parachute Platoons of 250 Airborne Light Company RASC and took over a sector in and around Jägerskamp, just to the north of Lonsdale Force which was based around the Oosterbeek Laag Church at the south-east tip of the divisional area. They were to operate as infantry for the rest of the battle. CRASC's adjutant and the HQ RASC detachment took up a defensive position in depth, in the area occupied by the 1st Airlanding Brigade so as to act as reserve for Cranmer-Byng's party; and they too remained in this role for the rest of the operation. Altogether the whole grouping was about seventy strong, and included Sergeant Colin Bennet and four men seconded by Major Chidgey from the OFP.

Captain Jack Cranmer-Byng RASC.
Courtesy F. Huibers

Meanwhile, the rest of the OFP continued to make issues from whatever limited stocks it possessed, and from what the RAOC were able to salvage. They were helped a little by some limited supplies from the very small amounts received from the resupply flights. The unit was positioned just on the south side of the tennis courts from the Hartenstein Hotel, taking advantage of the woods for overhead cover. However, they were heavily mortared, and the bombs detonating in the trees as well as on the ground caused acute discomfort. Nonetheless, where possible, and where stocks existed, they kept working, principally with the issue of batteries and weapons.

During the day some of the ammunition in the DAA caught fire as a result of mortar bombardments. One stack of 6-pounder ammunition exploded from a direct hit, and the risks to those fighting the blazes was considerable. Nonetheless, the flames were extinguished and the normal work of selection and distribution continued, with issues being made to both 4th Parachute Brigade and 1st Airlanding Brigade, using a Bren carrier as the means of delivery – yet another example of how the training given to the RASC in the use of a wide range of equipment paid dividends. The losses from stock caused by the fire were, however, a serious blow, especially since so little replenishment was actually getting through. There were particular problems with shortages of PIAT, mortar and Sten gun ammunition, and a message had been sent requesting a special drop of these natures.

However, there was to be no attempt that day to deliver stocks by air to 1st Airborne Division. Some resupply aircraft had left England en route for Arnhem, with eighteen aircraft crewed by 48 Air Despatch Column having departed at 8.00 a.m. However, the mission was abandoned whilst they were in the air, and they were diverted to Brussels.

I joined 799 Air Despatch Company in June 1944. In September 1944 I was put into a crew of four. I was aged eighteen and a half at the time. We loaded our lorry at a supply depot with pannier baskets, driving through the night around 20 September to an airfield where we were held up because of bad flying weather. On the 22nd we took off and landed in Brussels with Captain Payne and Lieutenant Croucher.
Driver S. Brooking RASC, 799 Air Despatch Company RASC

Left on the ground in England were the seventy-three Stirlings and fifty Dakotas prepared by 49 Air Despatch Column for that day's re-supply drop. A signal from headquarters Airborne Forces advised that there was to be no take off, and that aircraft were to remain loaded whilst further instructions were awaited.[1]

During the day the corridor suffered badly from attacks by the Germans, seeking to cut the tenuous umbilical that sustained and reinforced the northern units. If they had ever entertained any ideas of rushing 43rd Wessex Division through in an attempt to recover the Arnhem bridge these attacks caused the Allies to dismiss them from their minds. All day artillery and tank fire rained on the road and the key bridges, whilst soldiers battled against infantry and armoured attacks. The Germans paid heavily, unable to fight to their full potential due to shortages of artillery ammunition and the ad hoc nature of many of the units; and many of their good commanders were killed in the actions that took place. Nonetheless, they caused significant problems to the British and the Americans, and served to divert resources from potential operations in the Arnhem area.

For those on the ground in Oosterbeek the problems of obtaining and preparing food worsened. By now rations had been exhausted and water was scarce. Some tinned food was found in cellars and a tin bath was discovered full of water. In addition, a number of tame rabbits went into the pot, and once a small goat was reckless enough to run across the lawn of one of the houses and was promptly brought down. From sources such as these some cooks managed to create two meals of a sort each day and one brew of tea. It wasn't much, but to starving, dehydrated men it was manna from heaven, and greatly appreciated.

By now eight German battlegroups were employed against the British Airborne Division, attacking from the west, the north and the east. The tactics were becoming clear: batter by day with infantry and armour and then batter again by night with artillery and mortars. In time, so the logic went, the British would be ground into submission. Everywhere, as the mortaring, artillery fire, direct tank fire and sniping continued, the casualties mounted. In the Hartenstein Hotel for example, Corporal D. W. E. Holden, an RASC clerk in the intelligence branch of Divisional Headquarters, was wounded by mortar fire and was evacuated to a dressing station.

A few of the boys had been hit pretty badly during the day – for Jerry was using air-bursts, and also his mortars were hitting branches of the trees and exploding. Thus, the shrapnel was raining down on the lads who were in slit trenches underneath.
Lance Corporal J. L. Hughes RASC

It wasn't simply injuries, wounds and deaths that drained away the manpower. Men were also taken prisoner as the Germans tightened their grip and made positions untenable

We were part of the brigade defences under Captain Cranmer-Byng. I was in 16 Jägerskamp with three others, and next door in 18 there were about twelve of us. It had been very quiet for some time, and the rest said there was no point in staying so they went back to the Hartenstein. We decided to stay in our house, those were our orders. Suddenly, there were a load of Germans coming up the street. I shouted to the Lance Corporal who rushed out to tackle them and was shot in the doorway. They surrounded the house, and fired a Panzerfaust into the house. I was with John Prime, who had learned some German in Italy. Surrounded and with no chance of escape or of doing anything productive we had no choice but to surrender, and so he called out in German. They came to the foot of the stairs and called us down.
Driver R. G. Pearce RASC

The 21st Independent Parachute Company were in the area occupied by Hackett's men. Major 'Boy' Wilson, commanding the Company, was in a house next door to the Schoonoord dressing station on the main Oosterbeek crossroads when a German commander sent him a message to say that if the parachutists did not immediately leave their position he would destroy it with his tanks. Wilson replied, saying he would comply provided the Germans promised not to enter the hospital some thirty yards away. At the same time he was issuing instructions to Private Frank Dixon ACC to slip out by the back door and try to engage the German tanks. Despite preferring pots and pans to PIATs, Frank Dixon's first shot hit one of the tanks and set off some of the ammunition inside it, destroying the vehicle. The Germans withdrew and the hospital remained in British hands.

Ken Clarke was part of Cranmer-Byng's ad hoc force, and was one of a small party commanded by Corporal Doubleday. As darkness approached they were moving cautiously towards a position they had been ordered to occupy. Carefully, they approached the large house at 52 Pietersbergseweg, described by Ken as being more like a mansion. There was no one in the house and to gain entry they had to force the front door. As they did so, the bell, an old fashioned one on a spring, rang and everyone dropped flat expecting a German trap. Feeling slightly foolish, they rose to their feet and dusted themselves down, the latter being a pretty pointless exercise given the state they were in. Taking up their defensive positions inside the house they stayed there for the rest of the night.

Darkness fell, and at 7.00 p.m. the men in Oosterbeek stood to.

'Jerry used his propaganda – broadcasting over loud-speakers such things as:

Private Frank Dixon ACC taking on the German tank. This is a clip from the film 'Theirs is the Glory', made by veterans of the battle shortly after the war. Courtesy *After the Battle* Magazine Film Company

Frank Dixon reports the success of his mission to Bo[y] Wilson, before returning to the preparation of lunch. Courtesy *After the Battle* Magazine Film Company

'Churchill's forsaken you; think of your wives, mothers and sweethearts; if you don't surrender we are going to wipe you out', etc etc. Naturally the answer we made to that - which Jerry unfortunately couldn't hear - was not in the best of tastes or languages. This propaganda effort was made at dusk - and after they followed it with a selection of songs. The favourite one of these was 'This is a Lovely Way to Spend an Evening' – and they followed it up with a mortar barrage.
Lance Corporal J. L. Hughes RASC

As night fell the men of the Seaborne Echelon on the corridor were waiting to see what fate had in store for them. Column A was well settled in its wood near Nijmegen.

That night we in 250 Company were all waiting for the order to join the advance to Arnhem and the bridge. As we waited John Gifford characteristically sat his officers down for a four of bridge. I'm afraid I didn't play very well. 'But Dick, we could have made four spades.' (Bang!) 'Sorry, sir.' (Bang!). The order never came!
Lieutenant R. G. Adams RASC

Driver Ken Clarke, 2n Parachute Platoon 25 Airborne Light Company RASC.
Author's Collection

The OFP, in Column C, was still south of Eindhoven as the light vanished. The German attacks during the day had been concentrated on the bridge at Veghel. If taken this would be a hard block for the Allies to shift. The effect was a massive traffic jam to the south, and it was not until 1.00 a.m. the OFP was finally given the order to move off; but only as far as Eindhoven. Trying to get to their friends in trouble, the men of the Seaborne Echelon waited frustrated in traffic jams, by roadsides and in woods. Those in the Nijmegen area could hear the heavy mortar and artillery fire being visited on the soldiers in Oosterbeek that night, could see the flashes lighting the horizon, and could only wonder in an agony of ignorance what was happening to the men from their units who were so tantalisingly close and yet so completely beyond their reach.

Meanwhile, during the night Lieutenant Colonels Mackenzie and Myers from Divisional Headquarters crossed to the southern bank of the Rhine to go to headquarters 1st Airborne Corps at Nijmegen. Later on during the night about fifty Poles managed a crossing to reinforce the perimeter, using rubber boats. Lieutenant David Storrs of the Royal Engineers rowed across the river twenty-three times each way to ferry across one Pole each trip, and this after days with no sleep or food. He was awarded a Military Cross for his endeavour, but died, tragically, in a motorcycle accident following his return to the United Kingdom.

23 September 1944

After one of the worst nights for mortar and artillery fire, the defenders in Oosterbeek awoke to their 5.00 a.m. stand-to. Further south those in the Seaborne Echelon adopted a more leisurely approach, rising at 6.30 a.m. They, however, were not plagued with incessant artillery fire, and there was a persistent sniper who was giving the RASC in Oosterbeek a particularly difficult time from the area of a well in their locality. Looking up through bleary bloodshot eyes from their trenches the men inside the perimeter were also treated to the sight of enemy aircraft flying over the divisional area.

In their house in Pietersbergseweg, Corporal Doubleday's party used the coming of daylight to search their house. They found the dining room with the table beautifully laid, apparently in preparation for a lunch or dinner party which had clearly never taken place. It looked utterly incongruous in the midst of the chaos. The water supply had been cut off, and they had not eaten for some time, but in the cellar there were bottled cherries and beans and upstairs there was a bath full of water. There was broken glass in the bottom of the bath, residue from the shattered windows, but they could skim enough water for their needs to go with the fruit and beans. However, just as they were coming to terms with their surroundings they realised that the Germans knew British soldiers were hiding in the area and very soon shell after shell was being fired into the house.

> *In one of the bedrooms I was in there was a tiled fireplace and as the shells hurtled through the window the green tiles from it shattered in all directions.*
> Driver K. W. Clarke RASC

Deciding it was too hectic where they were, Corporal Doubleday formed the opinion that they should move on, and gave orders accordingly. Taking their lives in their hands, the group managed to run out of their mansion and escape to another house down the road. Here they found a table laden with apples recently gathered from a nearby orchard, from which they snatched a scratch meal.

> *While we were here I remember seeing a German run up the garden path and throw a grenade up to the bedroom window, but fortunately for us his aim was a little feeble and it dropped back on top of him.*
> Driver K. W. Clarke RASC

Moving on yet again, and still trying to make their way to Benedendorpsweg, the lower road which now, effectively, formed the base of Urquhart's 'Thumb', Doubleday's party occupied a number of houses. One in particular stood on a point, described as having roads leading off in many directions,[2] and in which there were about six to eight RASC soldiers. Ken Clarke appointed himself chief cook, and went round the men in the building collecting porridge tablets. Pooling what water they had, together with methylated spirit tablets which were issued for cooking, he created breakfast on the floor in a back room. It was during this process that a German ME 109 strafed the house, removing the roof tiles.

> *I started to make the porridge and take it round to the men, first going up to the attic to Driver Waring, who was complaining about the missing roof, when we heard the sound of a tank approaching. Corporal Doubleday gave the order to prime the PIAT, but there was no time to use it. The tank fired a shell which landed in the bedroom, and I think Driver Hatton was killed here when a second shell landed downstairs. Corporal Doubleday gave the order to leave the house.*
> Driver K. W. Clarke RASC

Corporal Doubleday was a good and conscientious NCO. He made certain his men had the best chance to escape to the new house before he himself followed. As they went the men were fired on by the German tank, and Ken Clarke retains a very clear memory of the heat as one of the shells passed very near the seat of his trousers. Corporal Doubleday then made his attempt to cross the open space when a shell landed in the road, just outside the house they were leaving. It blew off both his legs, and he died. With no equipment Ken Clarke ran across a field with some others, and with the tank following. Making his way deep into the woods that lay between the Hartenstein Hotel and the river he found a dugout with some South Staffordshire men and a 6-pounder anti-tank gun. There were two other 250 Company men there, one of whom was Driver Carter, and Ken settled down with them.

Sergeant W. M. 'Bill' Chedgey RASC.
Author's Collection

Sergeant Bill Chedgey, the Jeep Section Sergeant from 2nd Parachute Platoon of 250 Company, was also part of Jack Cranmer-Byng's force, and he was in the same area as Corporal Doubleday. From upstairs in one of the buildings he saw a German patrol, and tapping his Bren gunner on the shoulder he directed him onto his target. A few well aimed bursts killed a number of the enemy, whilst others were wounded and the balance fled. Bill, realising that he was now a target and expecting the Germans to bring up a tank or a self-propelled artillery piece, led his men out of the house and went back towards Cranmer-Byng's headquarters. The use of a self-propelled gun or tank against buildings had become a standard tactic to drive the defenders out into the open. Once they were clear of the protection offered by the buildings the paratroopers would then be hunted down by the Germans using mortar fire. However, on this occasion Bill and his men were able to escape unscathed and made it back to the headquarters, where they were able to rest.

During the afternoon the resupply drop, postponed from 22 September, arrived over the area. It faced very heavy opposition.

> *We took off not knowing the DZ. I remember the red light coming on and the first stick of panniers were by the door when the green light came on. The first stick went well, but the Dakota banked and the second stick fell over. The plane made another circuit with the corporal giving a running commentary on what he saw with a Dakota going down in flames. After the last pannier was away the plane climbed steeply and I ended up in the tail end, in the toilet, where I was quite sick.*
> Driver S. Brooking RASC

Seventy-three Stirlings and fifty-five Dakotas took off from England, and Stuart Brooking's aircraft was one of eighteen that flew from Brussels. Twelve aircraft failed to return, and ten air despatchers were recorded as killed, with fifteen missing in action and four wounded. It was the last day on which the RAF and their RASC crews would have to face the wrath of the Germans in the skies over Oosterbeek

On the ground there were only a few serviceable jeeps and trailers which could be used, and only a small proportion of supplies could be collected. Gathering what they could those RASC not involved with Cranmer-Byng's work on perimeter defence distributed the precious supplies, either to units with outstanding priority requests, or into storage in the DAA. This included 160 rounds of 75mm ammunition for the Airlanding Light Regiment's howitzers and eighty rounds for the 6-pounders. It was, however, barely enough, and by now stocks of PIAT, mortar and Sten ammunition, which were in great demand and had been in very short supply for some time, were almost non-existent.[3]

It seemed that the mortaring and shelling increased following a resupply drop. Partly it was because there was a greater opportunity for catching men in the open, thereby increasing the chance of inflicting casualties; and partly it was to curb any attempt to collect containers and panniers. It was also designed to deter men from coming into the open to fight the fires which broke out, yet again, in the DAA and which placed at risk the ammunition stacks. In this the Germans were unsuccessful, and once more the fires were beaten back and the precious stocks of ammunition saved. As well as ammunition a few, a very few, rations were received, almost all of which were handed over to the dressing stations.

Any prospects the OFP detachment might have had of continuing any form of business were eliminated when, in the heavy mortaring and shelling, one of its two[4] remaining jeeps and trailers was destroyed by shellfire. Additionally, having sustained relatively few casualties during the battle, the OFP had its strength reduced in losing a man with a straightforward medical problem: Private Pooley was admitted to a dressing station with kidney trouble, a seemingly incongruous complaint in the midst of so much death and destruction.

The level of German activity, bad as it was, would have been far worse had it not been for the arrival of RAF support for the troops on the ground in the shape of rocket-firing Typhoons. Improved weather conditions had, so it was said, permitted these interventions, previously unseen in Oosterbeek. The reasons for lack of air support earlier in the battle have since provided considerable debate. Key among them was the refusal to allow ATAF fighter aircraft to mingle with transports, and since the time of the transports' arrival was never certain the fighters were not available when required. Also, fighters could not see enemy targets in the woods, and although they had an air-support team on the ground to direct them, the communications links were difficult, and the noise of flak made messages virtually indecipherable. However, none of this was in the minds of the men defending the perimeter as they watched with some satisfaction the damage being wreaked from the sky.

> *As the majority of us had never heard a 'Tiffy' before, it gave us all a shock for a minute – as they fired their rockets immediately above our heads into the German mortar positions in the woods before us. From the room I was in I could see the rockets strike in the woods. And boy, did it quieten those mortars down.*
>
> Lance Corporal J. L. Hughes RASC

During the day the logisticians both north and south of the Rhine were busy trying to find ways of bettering their own circumstances, and seeking improved ways of providing as effective a service as possible to those who depended on them. In Oosterbeek, in the very confined space held by the 1st Airborne Division, this was very difficult indeed. One attempt was made to try to find a more suitable place for the DAA; somewhere where it might be less exposed to mortar fire, and provide a supply dropping point which reduced the risk of panniers and containers falling among the enemy. Michael Packe, together with the DAQMG,[5] Major E. R. Hodges, undertook a reconnaissance of the area towards the river. However, the roads and tracks were blocked by debris and branches, which precluded not only

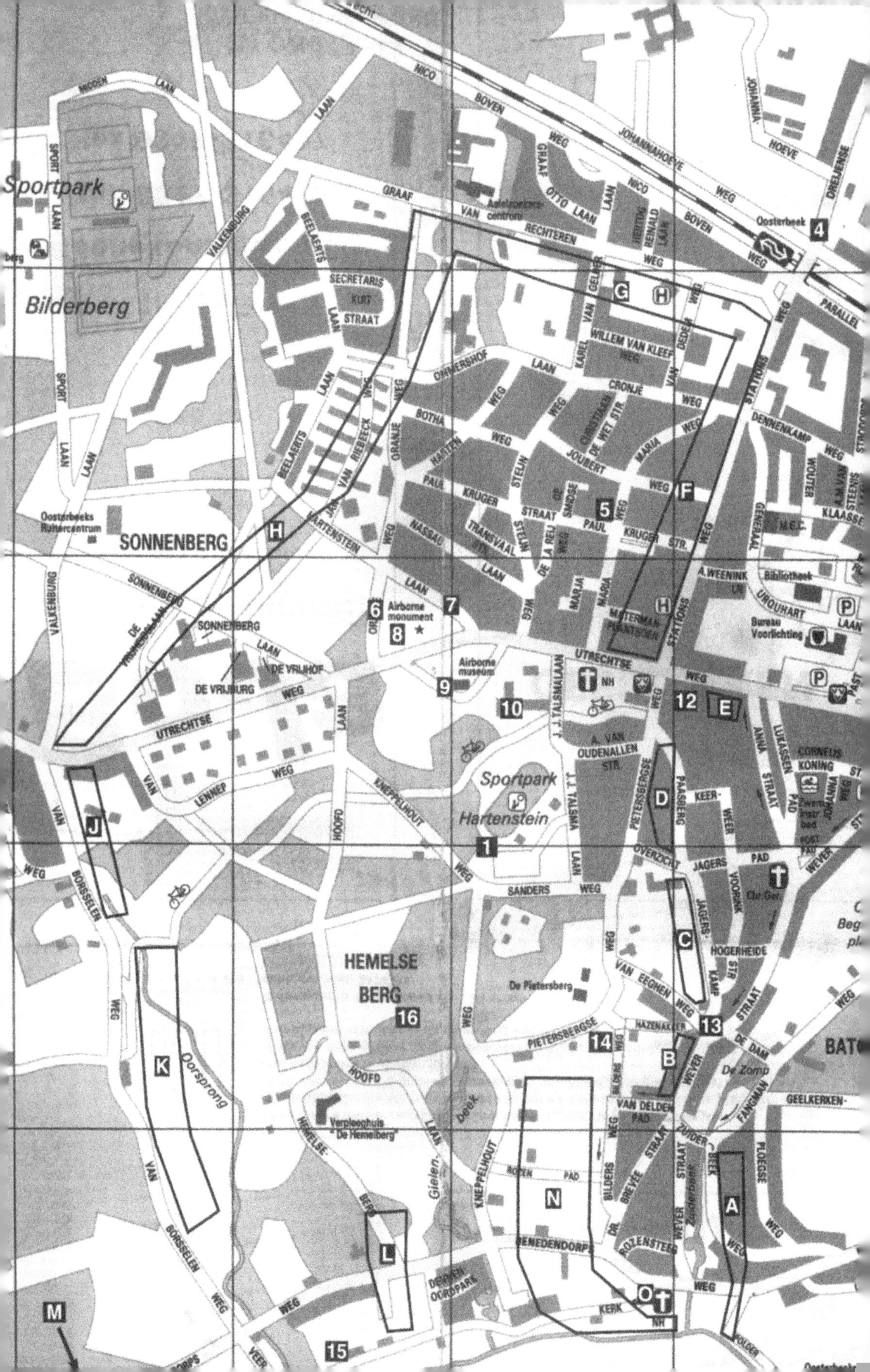

Sportpark
Bilderberg
SONNENBERG
Oosterbeeks Ruitercentrum
HEMELSE BERG
Verpleeghuis "De Hemelberg"
Sportpark Hartenstein
Airborne monument
Airborne museum
De Pietersberg
MATERMAN PLANTSOEN
Bibliotheek
Bureau Voorlichting
Oosterbeek
De Zomp
UTRECHTSE WEG
STATIONSWEG
GRAAF VAN RECHTEREN
NICO BOVEN JOHANNAHOEVE WEG
DE VRIJBURG
DE VRIJHOF
VAN BORSSELEN WEG
BENEDENDORPSWEG
KERKPAD
WEVERSTRAAT
PIETERSBERGSEWEG
VAN EEGHENWEG
KNEPPELHOUTWEG
HOOFDLAAN
SANDERSWEG
DORSPRONG
A B C D E F G H J K L M N O
1 4 5 6 7 8 9 10 12 13 14 15 16

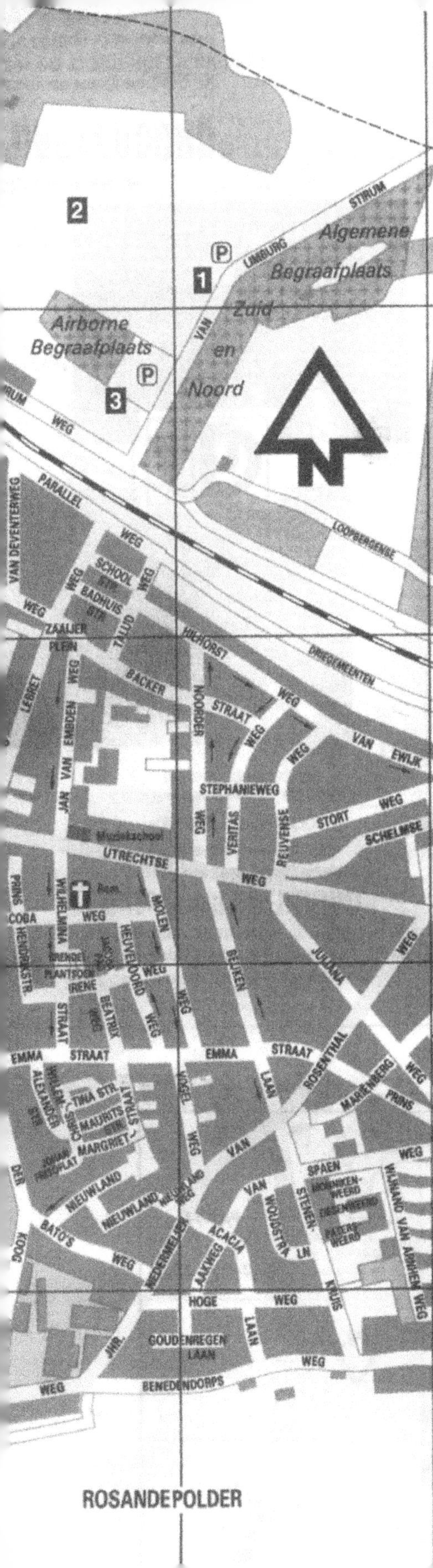

Oosterbeek, Then and Now

KEY: A modern map of Oosterbeek is being used in order to enable visitors more easily to identify sites and locations when visiting the area.

1. Post-war Air Despatch Memorial.
2. Rough area in which Harry Simmonds' load landed.
3. Post war Arnhem-Oosterbeek CWGC Cemetery.
4. Site of Captain Desmond Kavanagh's ambush.
5. The bakery beside which Sgt Lambert ACC was located.
6. OFP first location, with ADOS and staff.
7. 250 Coy first location with CRASC and staff.
8. This triangle was the DAA.
9. HQ 1st Airborne Division - The Hartenstein Hotel. Now the post-war Airborne Museum.
10. Site of 2nd DAA from Wednesday, CRASC was here.
11. OFP second location from Wednesday.
12. LCpl Hughes' 'Death Walk'.
13. Cpl Doubleday killed in this area.
14. 52 Pietersbergseweg - Ken Clarke.
15. Gas works, Private Harsley RAOC. The works are no longer there.
16. Driver Clarke's last position, with the 6-pounder.

KEY: Perimeter Locations, shown blocked with letter identification.

- **A.** Lonsdale Force – from Thursday.
- **B.** G Squadron Glider Pilot Regiment.
- **C.** RASC Platoon, with OFP det, from early Friday, Driver Pearce taken prisoner at No. 16 on Friday.
- **D.** 2 Platoon Independent Coy, from early Friday.
- **E.** 10th Bn, subsequently Independent Coy.
- **F.** Various units at various times, including D Sqn Glider Pilots, 156 Battalion and Recce Squadron.
- **G.** Northern edge, Independent Company and 4 Para Sqn RE early on, with KOSB.
- **H.** Western edge, Glider Pilots, A Company 1st Border and RE.
- **J.** C Company 1st Border.
- **K.** D Company 1st Border.
- **L.** Breeseforce, based around B Coy 1st Border which had been knocked off the Westerbouwing on Thursday.
- **M.** Westerbouwing.
- **N.** 1st AL Light Regiment RA, all 3 batteries.
- **O.** Oosterbeek Laag Church.

a sensible search of the area, but also any chance of moving stocks from the existing DAA location with the very limited transport they had left.

South of the Waal river, Major John Gifford accompanied the DDST of 1st Airborne Corps on a visit to a captured supply depot at Oss, some fifteen miles west of Nijmegen. They were seeking to supplement their stocks of rations using captured produce. What they found were some stocks that would be of value, but overall they were out of balance. For example, there was no food to provide bulk in the diet, such as potatoes or biscuits; and there were no essential items like sugar, milk or tea. However, local arrangements were made with Dutch bakers to bake 12,000 kilograms of bread a day using captured German flour, whilst milk for hospitals was arranged through the Food Controller in Nijmegen. Payment was made in kind, using captured flour and meat which were of far greater value to the local population than money when there was nothing to buy.

Major R. Tompkins RASC, Officer Commanding 93 Airborne Composite Company RASC. Courtesy Imperial War Museum

Column A of the Seaborne Echelon, having finally made it across the Grave Bridge, arrived at about 6.30 p.m. in its concentration area southeast of Nijmegen. The headquarters was established in the Hotel Erica in Berg en Dal.

There was some cheering news that afternoon for Major Tompkins in 93 Company. At 4.00 p.m. Drivers Speller and Clarke reported in to the unit. They told him that, together with eight other members of the Company, they had taken off in the second lift from Harwell at 12.15 p.m. on 18 September. Their glider had been hit by flak and had made a forced landing at Molenbroek. They had salvaged their jeep and with the assistance of two Dutch patriots had reached the Americans before making their way to the unit. They had, however, lost touch with the other eight and had no idea where they were. Numbers were further enhanced that afternoon with the arrival of Driver Jones, who had force-landed in a glider at 's-Hertogenbosch on 17 September and had found his way, alone, through enemy lines to rejoin the unit.

Later that afternoon, at about 5.00 p.m., two 3-ton vehicles of 93 Company loaded with 75mm high explosive rounds, 6-pounder and 17-pounder ammunition, and compo, led by Captain Millar and Sergeant Smith, were told to proceed with a major of the Royal Artillery to Driel. The intention was to ferry the load across the Rhine for use by 1st Airborne Division. However, the vehicles were unable to get through due to heavy enemy fire in the area just south of the Rhine. They took cover at Valburg, where they were held up by a battle being fought some three miles to their north-east, at Elst. In splitting the Seaborne Echelon into columns, 93 Company had also been split, part going with Column A, and the rest in Column B. It was the Column A element that Captain Millar's team belonged to. The balance of the unit in Column B had spent the previous night trying to move north and join the rest of their unit. They had, however, been held up by the fighting and had been returned south to Eindhoven where, parked up, they awaited instructions to move; instructions which eventually came at 7.00 p.m. that evening.

As night fell the defenders of Oosterbeek settled down for another night of unpleasantness as the Germans, with no Typhoons to worry about in the dark, took up their ritual pounding of the divisional area with gusto. Sergeant Bill

Chedgey, however, was taking the opportunity for some well-earned rest and found himself able to sleep a little; something he had not done for three days. He was not best pleased, therefore, when he was woken after only a couple of hours to be told by Lieutenant Grice that he would have to go back into the area he had just left. He was even less pleased to hear that he would have to reoccupy the same house for he was certain he would be targeted. Using the dark to conceal movement, and feeling angry and frustrated, Bill, with a party of men, followed Grice back to the house they had left earlier that day.

During the night some 200 Poles managed to cross to the north bank, landing just after midnight. Lieutenant Colonel Mackenzie accompanied them to brief Urquhart on his discussions at the 1st Airborne Corps Headquarters.

The Germans were also using the cover of darkness to conceal their movements, and, in particular, to bring in reinforcements that were to make a significant difference to their capability. In the railway sidings in Zevenaar and Elten they were unloading the forty-five Mark VI King Tigers of Schwere Panzerabteilung 506.[6] Two of its companies, comprising thirty tanks, headed off to join 10th SS Panzer Division in woods near Elst for use against the Allies south of the Rhine. The remaining company, with fifteen tanks, went to join Spindler's battlegroup on the eastern side of the British area in Oosterbeek.

Private Dennis Brown RAOC, 1st Airborne Division OFP, 2nd Seaborne Echelon.
Author's Collection

Meanwhile, back in England the final remaining members of 1st Airborne Division were preparing to leave. These were the rear parties, not deployed on the airborne operation. They had been left behind to clear up and resolve any final outstanding issues following the departure of the main force. Theirs was not a glamorous task, but it was necessary; and they formed the 2nd Seaborne Echelon. Knowing that all was not well with their friends in the Netherlands, they left their barracks and headed south to be taken across the Channel.

> *I was at the very tip of the Seaborne Echelon (any further docking would have meant my total disappearance). There were four of us, the others being Lieutenant Duncan Bell, Sergeant Jack Colley and Private Reg Pottingshead, and we had the job of clearing up at Grantham after the main sea party had left. We embarked to join them on Saturday 23 September, embarking at 2.20 p.m. on the liberty ship* Sam Vern.
>
> Private D. Brown RAOC, 1st Airborne Division Ordnance Field Park, 2nd Seaborne Echelon

1. The reason for the postponement was not stated, and appears not to be recorded.
2. The junction of Weverstraat and Jägerskamp.
3. In 1945 alone, more than a million cartridges were found, and they continue to be found up to the present, all over the place.
4. This figure is taken from the OFP War Diary. With the three jeeps reported destroyed in an earlier incident, this would make a total of five RAOC jeeps, and only four actually arrived north of the Rhine. The War Diary for the OFP in Oosterbeek was made out after the event by Captain Gratrix, presumably from eye-witness accounts from the escapees. It is, therefore, quite likely to be flawed. Either the OFP obtained another vehicle after landing, or, and this is more likely, Captain Gratrix assumed the headquarters glider with Jenkins and Eastwood had got to Arnhem and he included their jeep in his calculations.
5. Deputy Assistant Quartermaster General, an appointment usually held by a major.
6. Schwere Panzerabteilung: literally translated – a Heavy Tank Unit, in this case, with three companies, it can be considered to be a battalion equivalent.

Chapter Ten

The Final Hours

A Withdrawal – It Has to be a Withdrawal

As the dawn broke in the sky to the east, bringing daylight to 24 September, they stood to and stared out of their trenches and their hiding places. Tired, cold and hungry, they awaited what might come their way following the shelling and the mortaring as the bombardments began to intensify. It was obvious they couldn't hold on much longer. In the minds of some may have been the hope that reinforcements might be a possibility, but most realised that the cause was probably lost and that an alternative would have to be found. Surrender, generally speaking, was not one of the options, but they had been there a week now and something needed to be done.

That 'something' was the subject of a great deal of discussion south of the Rhine. The talking had commenced when Generals Horrocks and Sosabowski met at Driel. With two options, either to reinforce or to withdraw 1st Airborne Division, Horrocks was a troubled man. His view was that reinforcement was the solution, and he considered that a battalion should be put across the river, and then be further reinforced with a brigade. However, with no conclusion reached, and the need anyway to involve others in the debate, the two men moved off, separately, to a meeting, to be held in Valburg, and which would include Lieutenant General Browning, and Major General Thomas, the commander of 43rd Wessex Division.

It was in Valburg, quite unknown to the generals about to congregate there, that Captain Millar's small party from 93 Company had spent an uncomfortable night. At 7.00 a.m. they moved off to Driel where they offloaded ammunition for the Poles in the village. This was to take them some four hours, during which time they remained under constant fire from mortars, shells and enemy aircraft. Eventually, their task complete, and leaving one 3-tonner full of compo with the Poles, they headed off back to their unit location, with shells dropping around the four 3-tonners in their small convoy for the first mile of the trip. Eventually, and safely, they returned at 1.00 p.m. with no casualties.

Whilst this was going on, the meeting of the four generals was reaching conclusions about the resolution of the 1st Airborne Division problem. One of Major General Thomas' battalions would cross to reinforce 1st Airborne Division, together with a Polish battalion, with both crossings commencing at 10.00 p.m. Sosabowski was unhappy: not only had one of his battalions been taken away without consultation, but also the proposed crossing point was opposite the Westerbouwing, thirty-two metres high, steep and strongly held by the Germans. In his view it would be suicide, and the force was insufficiently strong, even if it were successful in its endeavour, to influence matters on the north bank. Nonetheless despite his protests, the plan was to go ahead, and preparations were set in train, in particular for the delivery of boats to the river bank from further back down the corridor.

Meanwhile, Life in Oosterbeek Continues Unchanged

North of the river, Ken Clarke was feeling hungry. In fact, he was so hungry the normal pangs associated with lack of food had been anaesthetised. However, the search for food revealed a rabbit in a hutch, a seemingly impossible find given the length of time they had been there, and the number of hungry men about the place. But they were exposed to more than just the sight of live rabbits.

> *It seems horrible to me now that we took it, but at the time we were so hungry the fact of where it had come from did not matter. We all enjoyed the rabbit stew. There was a farmhouse nearby and we saw many dead laid out in rows in one of the barns. It was a shocking sight.*
>
> Driver K. W. Clarke RASC

Sergeant Bill Chedgey was also unhappy. Led by the officer who had woken him the night before, he and his men had gone back to the building they had occupied the previous day. What followed, however, was a period, almost the whole day, of virtually complete inactivity. This alarmed Bill, and he said so, believing it to be the lull before a storm and that to remain in the position was foolish. As the day wore on, and the sense of foreboding deepened, Lieutenant Grice returned to Cranmer-Byng's headquarters for orders, and just after he left a self-propelled gun arrived – the storm was about to materialise. Sergeant Chedgey dashed upstairs into the front bedroom for a look, and as he did so the gun fired two rounds into the house. Bill was blown over, tumbling over and over as he fell down the stairs, to end up at the bottom with a broken femur. In great pain, he was left with very few options. Clearly the house was no longer a tenable position, for they had nothing with which to defeat the powerful armoured vehicle pitted against them. It could quite simply stand off and blow the building, with them in it, to pieces.

He ordered his men to withdraw, and watched as they raced back across the fields. Some were killed as the German mortars tracked them down, whilst others managed to escape to some relative form of safety in the woods beyond the houses. Discarding his two phosphorus grenades and his two Mills grenades, Bill awaited capture as he lay in pain in the hallway of the house. Soon the barrel of a Schmeisser sub-machine gun was poked into his stomach, and in German he was asked by one of four youngsters where his comrades were. Speaking a little German, he responded that they had gone. Unsure about what to do with their captive, the sixteen-to eighteen-year-old Germans were faced with an injured sergeant. In their world, his equivalent, a 'Feldwebel', was God, and Bill was treated accordingly. Before long they had constructed a stretcher, had made the sergeant as comfortable as they could and carted him off to hospital.

The German pressure everywhere was increasing, but the battered and weary paratroopers fought on tenaciously, everyone involved and everyone playing their part. Bill Chedgey had been unable to do much about his self-propelled gun, but just a few yards away, further down Weverstraat by the junior school, a King Tiger blew up as a British mortar exploded on the air vent of the petrol tank. Others were immobilised by Gammon Bombs and PIATs at close range, and the Germans found their heavy armour to be less effective than they might have hoped in the narrow streets where they could hardly traverse their guns; and especially when their infantry was lacking or not up to the mark.

With the focus on survival there really was no logistic activity at all in the divisional area that day. Resupply flights from the United Kingdom were cancelled as cloud and rain from a small depression over the southern North Sea grounded MARKET GARDEN missions. That said, at midday there was a supply drop south-west of Grave, involving seventeen Dakotas dropping 251 panniers of food and ammunition, together with thirteen bundles of bedding. A few panniers fell in the River Maas, and some came down north of the DZ. However, 237 of the despatched loads were collected and their contents put to stock.

There was constant heavy shelling of the whole perimeter area, which lasted most of the day, and which destroyed the last RAOC jeep.[1] As if that were not enough, Private Wright RAOC was wounded in the arm by a shell splinter and had to be evacuated to an aid station. There was, however, some good news for Major Chidgey with the welcome return of Sergeant Bennet and his four men. They had lost contact with Cranmer-Byng in all the confusion, and had decided the best thing to do was to report back to their parent unit.

The activity of the RASC was also virtually completely curtailed. Almost all their jeeps were out of action, and the DAA was empty except for 17-pounder ammunition, 2″ mortar smoke bombs and petrol.

The routine 7.00 p.m. stand-to brought to an end a long, dangerous, wearisome period of daylight, during which survival had been paramount in the minds of just about everyone. Certainly, there was no technical work left that any of the logisticians could sensibly do. But as they settled down for another night of misery inflicted by German artillery and mortar batteries, there were moves afoot to try and bring them some relief.

An Attempt at Reinforcement – In Vain

It seems likely that the driving force behind the decision to attempt a reinforcement might have been Lieutenant General Horrocks. Possibly, it might have worked, although the effort required to recover the situation north of the Rhine would have been gargantuan. It was not, however, something that would ever be tested, for the Germans had cut the corridor just south of Nijmegen. The battle there had been raging for most of the day, and all along the area between Nijmegen and Veghel Allied armoured and soft-skinned vehicles burned brightly, black oily smoke rising from white-hot hulks as the evidence of the German refusal to be beaten lay everywhere. It would be forty-eight hours before the corridor would be fully usable, and this would spell the end for MARKET GARDEN. Any prospect of delivering forces in sufficient strength to bounce a crossing in support of 1st Airborne Division was gone, and whatever his hopes might be, Horrocks would have to face his second option: withdrawal.

Despite this, the crossing planned for that night went ahead, probably because it had gained a momentum all of its own and it was too late to halt it. It was not, however, a great success. Fires on the north bank lit up the crossing points, and German machine-gun activity was intense. Having started to cross at 10.00 p.m. the attempt was called off at 2.15 a.m. on 25 September. There had been 315 men of the Dorset Regiment involved in the attempt, of whom thirteen were killed, some 200 were taken prisoner and the rest ended up in disarray among the battered units of the Airborne Division. Only seventy-five would return safely, back south across the Rhine. It was a futile effort, poorly conceived, and lacking the drive necessary from the highest echelons of 43rd Division for it to be a success. Sosabowski took no pleasure in having been proved right.

The Last Day Dawns

At 5.00 a.m. on the morning of 25 September the paratroopers stood to for the sixteenth time since landing over a week earlier, not knowing that Lieutenant Colonel Myers had accompanied the Dorsets across the river and was on his way to the Hartenstein Hotel. He brought with him three letters, only one of which was relevant: it was from Major General Thomas of the 43rd Wessex Division, pointing out that the commander of 2nd British Army, of which XXX Corps was a part, had ruled that there would be no attempt to reinforce the bridgehead. Withdrawal could, therefore, take place whenever Thomas and Urquhart judged it expedient.

Given his situation, with the previous night's crossing having brought no relief, his men and units now very weak and intelligence reports indicating a potential major German attack from the east, Urquhart was left with little choice. Two hours after Myers' arrival, at 8.00 a.m., he contacted Thomas, saying that he wished to go that night.

Urquhart held his planning conference for their departure at 10.30 a.m. that morning, and from then on everything focused on a successful evacuation. The concept was for a classic withdrawal, with perimeter defences progressively withdrawing, and the crossing commencing at 10.00 p.m. Heavy concentrations of artillery were to mask the move, and the men were to follow taped routes marked out by glider pilots and Royal Engineers. Glider pilots would act as guides where they could. Padres and medical staff were to remain behind, and wounded men were to maintain activity for so long as they could in order to delude the Germans while the rest made their escape.

Even as they prepared, however, the defenders were beset by yet further attacks, particularly in the area near the Oosterbeek church held by Lonsdale Force. Here, German armoured battlegroups gave the airborne men a very hard time indeed, their discomfort being heightened by the most appalling weather. Sheets of rain made worse by a driving wind made life very uncomfortable.

The preparations for withdrawal also affected those south of the Rhine, getting ready to receive the evacuees. The importance of this task was felt most keenly by the men of the Seaborne Echelon whose airborne comrades and friends were in such danger. They, above all others, wished to do all they could, and at 1.00 p.m. 93 Company received the order to offload all their ammunition in preparation for moving up to the 'Arnhem area' to pick up 'airborne personnel'. They also sent ten 3-tonners to 3 Casualty Clearing Station to pick up stretchers for the evacuation of airborne soldiers, 4,500 rations and 2,000 men's worth of 'medical comforts'.

A supply drop was expected in the Seaborne Echelon area, but was cancelled. Instead, 250 Airborne Light Company was reorganised to help with the evacuation from Arnhem. Further south the OFP Seaborne Echelon was still in Eindhoven, thanks to the continual cutting of the corridor. Meanwhile, the 2nd Seaborne Echelon was still afloat, stood off Arromanches, uncertain about what was to happen.

In 93 Company, as the offload commenced and the other company vehicles set about their allotted tasks, Sergeant Smith returned to Driel with a single 3-tonner full of ammunition for the Poles. A mile north-east of Valburg the road was very soft and in a bad state, the result of damage caused by the passage of tanks. At 2.30 p.m., about two miles south of Driel, the vehicle skidded into a ditch, but was retrieved with the aid of a DUKW[2] and carried on its journey to Driel.

About a mile south of Driel the road gave way under the near-side wheels of the truck, causing it to slide once more into a ditch. Efforts were made with the help of two tanks to recover it, but without success. It was offloaded, the ammunition being carried over a bridge and stacked under a tree. Sergeant Smith then commandeered the first empty vehicle to pass, which happened to be another DUKW, and the ammunition eventually arrived with 1st Independent Polish Parachute Brigade at 4.10 p.m. The Poles, however, refused to accept ammunition in their area in daylight as they were under constant shellfire, although they did agree to sign for it. His duty to the Poles complete, Sergeant Smith then returned to the DUKW company headquarters with the amphibious vehicle full of the Poles' ammunition and arranged with an RASC officer for it to be taken forward when the opportunity presented itself. He then headed back to 93 Company where he reported the location of his ditched vehicle, which was recovered by the Company's Workshop Platoon the next morning. Sergeant Smith's action that day, whilst not significant in the great scheme of things, stands out as a shining example of diligence in the face of adversity, and of adherence to the basic creed of the military logistician at every level: to sustain, against all odds, the fighting elements who depend on those providing logistic support.

The Evacuation Begins

The weather that night was foul. Gusting winds and heavy rain made movement a misery, but had the beneficial effect of masking the sounds of movement. The massive artillery bombardment alerted the Germans that something was going on, but unsure if it was a reinforcement, an evacuation, or even something else, their response was confused. All this worked to the advantage of the withdrawing division, and at 8.00 p.m. the RAOC party received their order to move to the river.

The tape-marked route petered out after a few yards. I was on the left flank, Gerry Mobbs in the centre and Staff Sergeant Wilson on the right flank with Sergeant Bennett bringing up the rear. Entering a small copse we met opposing fire and decided we should bear left away from it. After some fifty yards or so we ran into immense heavy machine gun fire. I told Sergeant Bennet to withdraw those he could and make his way further left to the river whilst we would help by delaying the enemy. After about half an hour, during which time we were pinned down, the three forward sections eased their way to the left with the intent of following the rear section down to the river. This was not to be as the enemy had closed the gap. Trying to contact Colonel Mobbs through a link man, Sergeant Andrews, on my right I heard a thump and a gasp which told me Andrews had been hit and, by his silence, was killed instantly. There were other sounds of casualties in our group. I felt two hits, one in each shoulder and a searing pain in my back. I passed out. When I came to I found I was unable to move my legs, but there had been plenty of noise and disturbance around for our own artillery had been giving covering fire for the withdrawal and shells had landed on our position. The next morning at daylight Colonel Mobbs and I decided there was no way out. He was severely wounded, I couldn't move and the men had suffered casualties. We jettisoned the firing mechanisms of our weapons and accepted the inevitable.[3]

Major C. C. Chidgey RAOC

Sergeant Reg Plowman RAOC. Author's Collection

Sergeant Andrews, who has no known grave, was described by Major Chidgey as having been rather elderly, and at thirty-eight years of age was certainly not the youngest man at Arnhem. He had been Mentioned in Despatches as a civilian during the Blitz before joining the Army and entering airborne forces.

Sergeant Bennet, and the others who had escaped the ambush on the RAOC party, reached the river by 4.00 a.m., by which time the 2nd Army boats had gone. Consequently they had to use some of the derelict boats beached on the

Private Victor Gibson (1), WOI Gordon Jenkins (2), Sgt Colin Bennet (3). Courtesy Airborne Museum

north bank, and they were not alone since many other evacuees had arrived late. Sergeant Plowman and Corporal Longley each gained a place on a boat, but Staff Sergeant Wilson offered his up to a wounded man. Being a non-swimmer he thereby consigned himself to becoming a prisoner of war.

> *Tubby Wilson being taken prisoner created a staff sergeant vacancy in the unit, and got me promoted.*
> Sergeant R. Collins RAOC

Sergeant Colin Bennet RAOC, having reached the south bank of the Rhine, still carrying his weapon.
Courtesy Imperial War Museum.

Sergeant Colin Bennett decided to try his luck as a swimmer and made it across to the other side. However, as the three survivors of the RAOC party made their way back to British lines they were not to know that another member of the Ordnance Field Park was crossing further downstream. Private Sidney Harsley had become detached from the main body as they moved out from their positions by the tennis courts in the grounds of the Hartenstein Hotel and had found himself with a group of men; and to this day has no idea who they were.

> *I never went with the RAOC party. I was on my own and saw people moving away from the area and so I followed. I ended up near a gas works where there was an upturned dinghy. There were three or four other blokes there. We turned it the right way up and using our rifles as paddles made our way across the river.* [4]
> Private S. G. Harsley RAOC

The order for HQ RASC to move came at 9.00 p.m., and at 10.15 p.m. they commenced their journey to the river. They ran into an ambush by an enemy machine-gunner, but, suffering no casualties, made a detour around this and other enemy positions until the river was reached. By the time they left there were only two RASC jeeps in working order, and all that was left in the DAA was still the 17-pounder ammunition, the 2″ mortar smoke bombs and the petrol.

> *We bound our feet in blankets to muffle the sound of us marching and destroyed everything that was valuable. We made our way in the pitch black and rain holding onto each other's straps.*[5] *It was fine until a German patrol opened up on us and we scattered. I had a tiny compass and headed south. Ten guys joined me. We were ambushed again, one was hit. We all carried a morphine injection, so we gave him that and left him. We had to. We were told not to stop for anything, to head for the water.*
> Corporal D. Cutting RASC

Corporal Dennis Cutting RASC.
Author's Collection

Johnny Walford.
Courtesy R. M. Gerritsen

As the days went by our area got smaller and on the ninth day we got the order to pull back to the Rhine. I got across that night and was lucky to get to Nijmegen. My mate, Johnny Walford, unfortunately was killed on the piece of land in front of the Hartenstein and he was never found again.
Corporal S. P. J. Staple RASC

We were gathered together and told about the taping of the route to the river. I had the great joy of smearing Colonel Preston's face with lamp black from the Tilley lamp.[6] *We were told that if a man was wounded he was to be left behind. It was my twenty-first birthday, and I thought 'today I'm going to die'. I never thought I'd see my twenty-first birthday out. Three of the divisional headquarters clerks got out: Me, Corporal Daniel Lewis and Lance Corporal Norman Davis. I got out in a Canadian boat. We couldn't start the engine and it was drifting down the river before we eventually got it going. Having got over I headed for a Dorset soup kitchen. Heading back from the river in a DUKW it slipped on a dyke and we all ended up in the ditch, but the driver got it out and drove us to Nijmegen.*
Sergeant N.G. Griffin RASC

Ken Clarke reached the river by about 10.00 p.m. having moved there under his own steam. He lay on the soaking grass and fell into an exhausted sleep, and it was 4.00 a.m. before a voice woke him and he climbed into a boat, to be delivered onto the south bank.

I recollect crossing enemy lines with the Colour Sergeant to get the password for withdrawal into the divisional perimeter, and then the incredible calm of our eventual withdrawal across the river to find tea on the other side. Then finally back to England ahead of the main body to fix up 'grub' on arrival with only two of my para cooks left. Quite a business, this Army cooking!
Sergeant J. Lambert ACC

1. According to the War Diary, this adds further to the discrepancy over RAOC vehicle numbers.
2. DUKW: A two and a half ton, 6X6 amphibious vehicle. D–1942; U – Amphibious; K – 6x6 Drive; W – Tandem
3. There remains a mystery over the fate of the fourth of the RAOC soldiers to be killed at Arnhem. Major Chidgey has a clear memory of Private Victor Gibson having been hit on the withdrawal, and of giving him morphine to quell the pain. It was his long-held belief that Private Gibson had subsequently died in a prison camp, and this is how his death is recorded in the official RAOC history of the 21st Army Group operations in Europe. He has no known grave and the Commonwealth War Graves Commission records his death on the Groesbeek Memorial as 18 September, the day he landed, yet there is no traceable record anywhere to show that as the date of his death, or who reported it. Neither is there any record of him ever having been a prisoner of war. Regrettably, his passing must remain, for the time being at least, one of the unsolved mysteries of the Battle of Arnhem.
4. In his book, *With Spanners Descending*, Joe Roberts of the REME describes his own crossing of the Rhine, and it is almost certain that he and Sidney Harsley used the same dinghy. Neither remembers the other.
5. The 'straps' were a form of gusset which buttoned under the paratrooper's smock, and when left loose became, effectively, a tail onto which the man behind could hold.
6. Tilley lamp: a pressurised paraffin lamp.

CHAPTER ELEVEN

The Aftermath

The RASC

With all that was happening to recover what was left of 1st Airborne Division, the units in the Seaborne Echelon were, on 26 September, engaged in a wide range of tasks, mostly in support of the evacuation, or associated with it.

The move of the 1st Independent Polish Parachute Brigade away from the south bank of the Rhine was assisted by 250 Light Company. Meanwhile, 93 Company issued the remainder of its 75mm ammunition to 82nd US Airborne Division, together with 2,104 rounds of 6-pounder. Subsequently, thirty 3-tonners were sent to one of the bridges south of Nijmegen to assist in the transportation of 1st Independent Polish Parachute Brigade to Grave. That day the Company was joined by Lieutenant Lyon from the UK, with fifty-three soldiers, forty jeeps with trailers and five motorcycles. They took a little harassment from the enemy, with a mortar bomb landing near the petrol point they had opened, and a truck hitting an anti-personnel mine and being burned out. Thankfully, there were no casualties. They also lost a vehicle in a shell hole, with another hitting a tree in the dark.

The AFDAG

This was also the day on which the AFDAG had the opportunity to play its part. Taking off at 11.25 a.m. from three airfields in England, they arrived at Grave at 1.52 p.m. after a relatively uneventful journey.

> *The flight started in a gale and as England slowly swayed past details of the briefing came to mind. 'In the event of a 'plane getting hit the crew will bale out, airborne personnel will take their chance.' The skies over the North Sea proved boisterous and it was easy to sympathise with the unknown men who waved from a rubber dinghy 700 feet below. To them the passing of such a mighty armada must have been symbolic – a big brother who had been knocked down by a bully. Towards the Belgian coast a British submarine nosed forward to its duty. It was difficult to imagine that the thing which looked like a huge cigar was in reality a dangerous fighting machine.*
>
> Major S. Clapp PC

Landing at Oud Keent airfield were 209 aircraft, with the AFDAG personnel in the leading aeroplanes, ready to work as soon as they arrived.

> *A sudden tilt, a rush of air, a slide across the sky and the landing was accomplished. Planes lined two abreast on a small, wet green space surrounded by canals. There was no runway, no landing sock; just wet grass and a few glider pilots waving silk squares to give wind direction.*
>
> Major S. Clapp PC

Cramped as it was, the small airfield had to be cleared as swiftly as possible, and the aircraft turned round and sent back to England. Moving to their various tasks the units dispersed, with 155 Detailed Issues Depot RASC going straight to Nijmegen to take over supplies dumped in the town market. These they sorted and restacked ready for issue. Meanwhile, the Pioneers of 277 Company set to with a will to turn aircraft round as fast as they could.

> *Over 200 aircraft were landed without incident, the Pioneers doing a grand job, unloading the whole formation in under three hours. Only a bare five per-cent of the Pioneers were airsick, and their enthusiasm was tremendous.*
> Major F. B. Wooding PC

The aircraft were unloaded and freed to return to England, taking with them American glider pilots from 82nd US Airborne Division. With the whole operation complete in just three hours and fifty minutes, at a rate of fifty-five aircraft per hour on a single strip, it was a magnificent achievement. Following this, the Pioneers formed patrols, set guards, dug themselves in and prepared a hasty meal before settling down for the night, satisfied with a job very well done, and wishing they could do more for those in trouble further to the north.

The officers of 165 Company RASC (Airborne Light). Back row: *2Lt (Stanley) Wilson (HQ Subaltern), Lt (Douggie) Hay, (2502 Comp Pl), Lt (Tony) Alison (2504 Lt Tpt Pl), Lt (Stan) Waggett (2503 Comp Pl), Lt (Alf) Briggs (2501 Lt Comp Pl).* Middle row: *(Jimmy) Mitchell (HQ Capt), (Tom) Ison (2504 Lt Tpt Pl), (Roger) Dubois (HQ Capt), (John) Hopps (2501), (Ivor) Renwick (2502), (Douggie) Craig (Admin Capt).* Seated: *Capt (George) Le Flay (2503), Major (Jimmy) Reid (RAOC), Major (Roy) Stephens (OC), Capt (Phillip) Jay (21C), Capt (Bob) Tanner (HQ Capt).* Author's Collection

It could have been so different had luck and the weather been on the side of our fighting men. For those who were in the operation it was thrilling to think that they of all the Pioneer Corps had been chosen for the job. At least, even if they did not get the chance to help the men of Arnhem, they did make history by being the first Pegasus Pioneers.
Major S. Clapp PC

By 8.00 p.m. all AFDAG units were dug in and the defences were laid out around the airfield, with the headquarters set up in a Jesuit monastry. Lieutenant Ivor Renwick RASC had some difficulty standing up in his tent, and sought to remedy the problem by digging a four-foot deep hole and placing the tent over it. However, his limited engineering skills meant that he did not get the drainage right and before long his bright idea was a pond under canvas – and it took him a very long time to get his kit dry. His brother officers were not sympathetic.

Private Leo Burns was a member of 2501 Platoon of 165 Company. He was one of four soldiers, commanded by a sergeant, who had been detached to the Seaborne Echelon. The role was unclear, but Leo presumed they were to be some sort of advance party to help prepare for the arrival of the main body of the Company, at Deelen. However, since the sergeant never told them what was going on they spent their time with the Seaborne Echelon undertaking odd jobs and operating in complete ignorance. Leo and his colleagues never actually saw 165 Company again until after the War, for they found themselves mixed in with XXX Corps, fighting the Germans during the Battle of the Bulge in the Ardennes in the winter of 1944, crossing the North German Plain and finishing up in Belsen in May 1945. And it seems that no one missed them.

The 26th of September was really the AFDAG's only day of activity. Very shortly it would be broken up, with 165 Company heading back to England, without Leo Burns and his friends, and most of the other units being dispersed to work with XXX Corps, apart from the Postal Unit which returned to 1st Airborne Division. Short lived as it was, it had performed a valuable task in setting up the Grave airhead, and everyone who was a part of it would always remember their brief association with Britain's airborne forces.

277 Coy were rightly proud of their red berets, which, by special permission, they were allowed to keep after being re-issued with khaki berets.
Major F. B. Wooding PC

Meanwhile, the 2nd Seaborne Echelon, still hovering off the coast of Normandy, moved nearer the Mulberry Harbour; but it was never to land.

On the 27th rumours were rife of the Division's annihilation, and during the day we were visited by a lieutenant of the Border Regiment asking for volunteers to try to reach Arnhem. On the 29th we were told we were heading home, never having disembarked.
Private D. Brown RAOC

Airborne Logistics – Success or Failure

The concept was good, so good that it survives to the present day. Highly motivated, well trained soldiers from the Royal Logistic Corps still provide the same high standard of support to Britain's airborne forces. Imbued with the same ethos as all airborne soldiers, trained on the same course and wearing the same embellishments they are, as were their forebears, indistinguishable from their comrades in the teeth arms.

The use of a forward detachment, designed to sustain a force for a short period, usually between forty-eight hours and five days, is still part of modern airborne logistic capability. Advances in technology mean that more can now be dropped from the air, and modern aircraft deliver vehicles and large equipments onto roughly made runways, rather than lifting so much by glider. However, the principles have stood the test of time, and remain the same; and therein lies the testament to their effectiveness. There was nothing wrong with the overall concept for airborne logistic support or with the plan for logistic support at Arnhem. As the situation changed, worsening all the time, the logistic system on the ground adapted to meet every need it could, delivering all that it had wherever it could. Given better communications and an ability better to direct the air drops there is no doubt that the system should have been able to meet all the Division's needs. This is borne out in the Divisional Commander's post-operational report.

And Finally

As to summing up events, and to counting the cost, words are hard to find, and would, in any event, be inadequate. Two officers and 62 soldiers from 250 Light Company returned from north of the Rhine, but of the 10 RASC officers and 243 RASC soldiers who took part in the airborne operation only 5 officers and 83 soldiers came back; and this does not include the men in field ambulances, those in clerical appointments or people like Corporal Roberts, the medical orderly with 3rd Parachute Battalion. There were air despatchers who, in many cases, were not properly registered on the aircraft manifest whose fate would not be known for some time to come – and in some cases never.

Some survivors of 250 Light Company awaiting repatriation from Brussels. Ken Clarke is in the centre of the front row, wearing a cap comforter. Courtesy K. W. Clarke

In a very crowded railway shed at Zutphen, where prisoners were being held, one little old fellow stuck out like a sore thumb, dressed in denims and plimsolls.[1] *I asked him what he was doing there, whereupon he launched into a diatribe about what he was going to do to the British Army. 'I should be on bleedin' leave,' he said, 'but they said get on that aeroplane, so I did, next thing I know the bleedin' thing is on fire, and I was told to jump out, so I did, but I shouldn't be 'ere, I should be on leave, and its nothin' for you to bleedin' laugh at.' And that is the story he was telling to anyone who would listen. He was, in fact, RASC and was on a 'plane dropping supplies at Arnhem, when he should have been on leave, nothing was going to convince him that he was a POW.*

Dave Brooks, 2nd Parachute Battalion[2]

As to the part played by the air despatchers, had the operation continued for only three more days the last trained RASC air despatch crews would have been used up. Of a total of 900 trained officers and men, 264 were shot down, some 600 sorties having been flown employing 450 despatchers. Most undertook two sorties and some three.

The formation sign of the Air Despatch Group was a yellow Dakota aircraft on a blue background. It was designed by Headquarters 48 Air Despatch Column in the first days of its existence and application was made for the sign to be granted status as an official formation sign approved by the Army Council. Although it could not be worn at that stage, it was used on all notice boards and other unit signs. When permission to use the symbol was eventually granted it was, in the words of the War Office minute, 'for the good work done by the Air Despatch Group over Arnhem'. It is believed that this was the first formation sign granted officially to an operational RASC formation, and because of the circumstances in which it was granted it was a matter of great pride to all ranks. It is worn today by 47 Air Despatch Squadron RLC.

But it does not stop those men from 63 and 253 Companies wearing, instead, their Pegasus and their red berets – with pride and with honour.

The OFP Seaborne Echelon moved from Eindhoven at 3.30 p.m. on 26 September, arriving in their wood in the Seaborne Echelon area at 3.00 a.m. on the 27th. It was here they received news that four of their number had got out, but they did not know the fate of the others, seventeen of whom were prisoners-of-war and four of whom had been killed. Sergeant Plowman RAOC, one of the escapees, saw the OFP in Nijmegen.

We saw Reg Plowman walking through Nijmegen, so we picked him up and gave him a lift back to England.

Sergeant R. Collins RAOC.

Those RAOC soldiers who could not be accounted for included the two warrant officers, still on the run in the Dutch countryside. Weakened by a week on a diet of apples and pears they eventually approached a Dutch family, assuming the worst and that they would be handed over to the Germans. They were, however, pleasantly surprised. They were taken in by the people of the village of Den Dungen and were hidden in an underground chamber – part of the village sewerage system. They were not alone, a number of American airmen also being in the care of the village. They were finally released when the village was

The group of Allied escapees collected by the Dutch in Den Dungen included British and Americans. WOI Eastwood appears to be on the left and WOI Jenkins is third from the left. Author's Collection

Captain C. R. Harkness RASC, BRASCO 4th Parachute Brigade, having escaped. Courtesy Jasper Booty

liberated late in October, the Germans having left. Once the chance came to release their charges into the open air, the Dutch wasted no time, and they were all invited to join in the celebrations which went on for a very long while. It is hard to imagine the thoughts in the minds of a group of hard-bitten Canadian infantrymen as they approached, in the dark, thinking they were liberating the village, to reach a tavern from which was emanating a great deal of noise, only to peer through the windows and watch an RAOC Sub-Conductor giving a victory speech, standing on a table with a glass in his hand - and somewhat the worse for wear.

Regarding the ACC, we have no real news of their fate, other than the short account of Sergeant Lambert, and the stories of Corporal Menzies and Private Dixon; and that at least three were killed. That they did their duty is not in doubt.

If there are to be any last words they belong to those who were there:

I remember Johnny Field. He was RASC. A superb soldier, I would say he was twenty. He was a shining example..
Robert Peatling, 2nd Parachute Battalion

It was a terrific shock to me...to find out the number of my pals who had not returned. Amongst these was the lad who had been with me ever since we first volunteered for parachuting. We did our first jump together,

The debris of war, panniers lie broken open with their contents scattered in the meadows along the river. Courtesy Airborne Museum 'Hartenstein'

Legs Wattam. His name, though, still lives in the memory of all those that returned – and we still, especially on exercises, find it hard to realise he is not with us. He was last seen swimming the Rhine – but his chances were little of reaching the other bank... all I can say is 'We did our best'.

Lance Corporal J. L. Hughes RASC

My most poignant memory will always be the time I spent watching the supply aircraft coming over and dropping their containers, on an area not under our control. They were met by a screen of flak, and it was awe-inspiring to see them fly straight into it, straight into a flaming hell. We had thought that some of them would not face it and would jettison their cargoes, in which case we should get them for they would fall short and therefore in our lines. But they all stuck to their course and went on, nor did they hesitate.

Lieutenant Colonel M. St J. Packe RASC

Driver Stuart Brooking RASC.
Author's Collection

It was OK before we got over Arnhem, but after that it was bloody murder, and when we returned they would not believe what the Jerries were throwing at us. I did three trips and it was the same each time. I was one of the lucky ones.

Sergeant H. Eckersley RASC, 223 Air Despatch Company RASC

I'm still very upset at the loss, at that late stage, of the fine men of our little unit who had performed so well throughout the operation.

Major C. C. Chidgey RAOC

And finally, from Stuart Brooking, on 26 September 1944:

We boarded the Dakota. The pilot started the engines ready for take-off. Then the engines stopped, and the pilot said it was all over at Arnhem.

Driver S. Brooking RASC

1. This almost certainly makes him a 63 Company man, for this was their dress when despatching; unlike other companies who wore more conventional military attire.
2. As told in 'Without Tradition, 2 Para 1942-46' by Robert Peatling

A lone Horsa stands forlorn among the wreckage on the Landing Zones. Courtesy Bundesarchiv Bild 101I/590/2331/22A.

Annex 1

Their Name Liveth For Ever More

The records of those from the Royal Army Service Corps, the Royal Army Ordnance Corps and the Army Catering Corps killed at the Battle of Arnhem are taken from *The Roll of Honour* 4th Revised Edition 1999 compiled by J A Hey and published by the Society of Friends of the Airborne Museum Oosterbeek. I am grateful to Mr Hey for his permission to reproduce them here. There are no specific records of deaths in the Seaborne Echelon or the AFDAG.

Basic information only is given here. Further details, including, in many cases, the location of the field grave prior to internment in a formal cemetery, can be found in the *Roll of Honour*. The names are arranged within the units with which they were serving, thereby demonstrating the wide range of tasks undertaken by the airborne logisticians. Within the unit, names are sorted alphabetically and then by recorded date of death. Where a known grave exists the reference is given.

Mr Hey records the death of seventy-five air despatchers. It is however, felt certain that seventy-nine died, all of whom are recorded on the Air Despatch Memorial at Oosterbeek. The four who do not appear in the Roll of Honour are marked with a * at the end of their personal details.

Royal Army Service Corps

Headquarters 1st Airborne Division

Jones, Leslie D;	Driver;	T/10702368;	age 21;	20 September 1944.	Oosterbeek 16.A.12.
Cheeseman, Douglas H;	Driver;	T/181502;	age 23;	22 September 1944.	Oosterbeek 17.B.12.
Smith, Bernard B;	Lance Corporal;	S/248717;	age 28;	22 September 1944.	Oosterbeek 17.B.13.
Devonshire, William G;	Private;	S/14537921;	age 19;	23 September 1944.	Oosterbeek 17.B.15.

Headquarters 4th Parachute Brigade

Wattam, Cyril;	Private;	S/197199;	age 24;	25/26 September 1944.	General Cemetery at Amerongen, Grave 1.
Whyte, George R;	Driver;	T/81814;	age 23;	25/26 September 1944.	General Cemetery Amerongen, Grave 6. (Special memorial with the inscription: 'Buried Near This Spot')

11th Parachute Battalion

Brennan, Thomas;	Driver;	T/10690465;	age 34;	25 September 1944.	Oosterbeek 29.B.4.

133 Parachute Field Ambulance RAMC

James, John H;	Driver;	T/10703025;	age 22;	18 September 1944.	No known grave.
Parker, Joseph;	Driver;	T/14664599;	age 19;	18 September 1944.	No known grave.

181 Airlanding Field Ambulance RAMC

Dadswell, David;	Lance Corporal;	T/210869;	age 23;	22/23 September 1944.	Oosterbeek 5.B.20.

250 Airborne Light Company RASC

Bondy, Robert C;	Driver;	T/202762;	age 35;	17 September 1944.	Oosterbeek 8.B.7.
Bennett, Wilfred;	Driver;	T/244904;	age 24;	18 September 1944.	No known grave.
Kennell, John J;	Driver;	T/14665291;	age 19;	18 September 1944.	No known grave.
Plant, Leonard;	Lance Corporal;	T/83849;	age 22;	18 September 1944.	Oosterbeek 15.A.3.

Thomas, Robert J;	Driver;	T/247030;	age 23;	18 September 1944.	Oosterbeek 6.B.2.
Butten, John S;	Driver;	T/176187;	age 30;	18/25 Sept 1944.	No known grave.
Whittet, Henry G;	Corporal;	T/234512;	age 35;	18/25 Sept 1944.	No known grave.
Field, Martin J;	Driver;	T/7955403;	age 20;	19 September 1944.	No known grave.
Kavanagh, Desmond T;	Captain;	204081;	age 25;	19 September 1944.	Oosterbeek 6.B.1.
McKinnon, James G;	Driver;	T/121840;	age 26;	19 September 1944.	No known grave.
Walford, John A;	Driver;	T/191884;	age 28;	19 September 1944.	No known grave.
Wiggins, Albert;	Corporal;	T/264820;	age 22;	19 September 1944.	Oosterbeek 6.B.12.
Geere, Kenneth J;	Driver;	T/10696905;	age 20;	20 September 1944.	Heverlee War Cemetery, Near Louvain, Belgium, plot 8.E.5.
Burns, Joseph D;	Driver;	T/263384;	age 22;	21 September 1944.	Oosterbeek 17.A.19.
Hill, Frederick W;	Driver;	T/135184;	age 27;	21 September 1944.	Oosterbeek 22.B.14.
Huggins, Stanley A;	Driver;	T/152874;	age28;	21 September 1944.	No known grave.
Peacock, Leonard;	Driver;	T/170811;	–;	21 September 1944.	Oosterbeek 1.A.10.
Snelling, Robert J;	Staff Sergeant (Mechanic);	T/83558;	age 28;	21 September 1944.	Oosterbeek 21.B.6.
Davies, Henry C;	Lance Corporal;	T/174786;	age 29;	22 September 1944.	Oosterbeek 1.A.9.
Morton, James;	Private;	T/222698;	age 33;	22 September 1944.	No Known Grave.
Docherty, Archibald F;	Lance Corporal;	T/236791;	age 38;	23 September 1944.	Oosterbeek 16.A.9.
Doubleday, Robin;	Corporal;	T/120468;	age 26;	24 September 1944.	Oosterbeek 21.B.16.
Hatton, Douglas;	Driver;	T/10706563;	age 22;	24 September 1944.	Oosterbeek 21.B.14.
Law, Albert;	Driver;	T/177730;	age 25;	25 September 1944.	No known grave.
Walsh, John;	Sergeant;	T/187114;	age39;	25 September 1944.	Oosterbeek 25.A.3.
Sharp, Walter R;	Corporal;	T/151611;	age 31;	25/26 Sept 1944.	No known grave.
Preston, William R;	Driver;	T/235810;	age 31;	1 October 1944.	Oosterbeek 24.B.14.
Bell, Robert F;	Lance Corporal;	T/47328;	age 37;	2 October 1944.	General Cemetery Lochem, Row 1 Grave 1.
Judd, Leslie J G;	Corporal;	T/191738;	age 28;	15 October 1944.	Oosterbeek 24.A.17.
Olsson, Arthur O;	Driver;	T/205285;	age 31;	27 February 1945.	Berlin War Cemetery, Germany, 10.D.8.
Johnson, Edward G;	Corporal;	T/163717;	age 29;	5 March 1945.	Hanover War Cemetery Plot 15.F.14.

48 Air Despatch Column RASC

223 Air Despatch Company RASC

Davis, Herbert;	Driver;	T/14703038;	age 38;	19 September 1944.	Ath (Lorette) General Cemetery, Belgium, Plot 5.B.32.
Grace, James;	Lance Corporal;	T/843117;	age 28;	19 September 1944.	Oosterbeek 4.B.15
Thompson, Henry W;	Driver;	T/1836995;	age 22;	19 September 1944.	No known grave.
Austin, Herbert A	Corporal	T/124054	age 26;	21 September 1944	Erith (Brook Street) Cemetery, Kent UK. Sec M, Grave 1283*
Edwards, Herbert A;	Lieutenant;	311098;	age 27;	21 September 1944.	Oosterbeek CG 4.C.2.
Morgan, Owen;	Driver;	T/14300375;	age 20;	21 September 1944.	No known grave.
Pilson, James;	Lance Corporal;	T/192235;	–;	21 September 1944.	Uden War Cemetery 1.H.5.

Robinson, Joe;	Driver;	T/14339807;	age 34;	21 September 1944.	Oldham (Greenacres) Cemetery, Lancashire, UK. Sec C Row 13, Grave 17*
Roscoe, Eric;	Lance Corporal;	T/1736143;	age 36;	21 September 1944.	Oosterbeek CG 4.C.2.
Sleet, George P;	Driver;	T/1579884;	age 23;	21 September 1944.	No known grave.
Taylor, Jack;	Driver;	T/1538535;	age 27;	21 September 1944.	Oosterbeek CG 4.C.2.
Welham, Ben;	Driver;	T/14707104;	age 38;	21 September 1944.	Oosterbeek CG 4.C.2.
Abbott, Lionel H S;	Driver;	T/14439683;	age 19;	21 September 1944.	Overloon War Cemetery 4.C.10.
Abbott, Roy;	Driver;	T/14438865;	age 22;	21 September 1944.	Overloon War Cemetery 4.C.9.
Chisholme, George;	Lance Corporal;	T/3710623;	age 26;	21 September 1944.	Overloon War Cemetery 4.C.8.
Baxter, Thomas H;	Corporal;	T/4853953;	age 35;	23 September 1944.	Oosterbeek 17.C.6.
Beardsley, Frederick W;	Driver;	T/4981126;	age 29;	23 September 1944.	Oosterbeek 17.C.5.
Clark, Leslie J;	Corporal;	T/1751089;	age 37;	23 September 1944.	Oosterbeek 17.C.4.
Newth, Richard C;	Driver;	T/14662728;	age 35;	23 September 1944.	Oosterbeek 6.D.2.
Williams, Paul;	Driver;	T/14426212;	age 18;	23 September 1944.	Oosterbeek 17.C.7.

799 Air Despatch Company RASC

Adams, Reginald A;	Lance Corporal;	T/3911832;	age 29;	21 September 1944.	Roman Catholic Cemetery, St. Oedenrode, Grave 29.
Claxton, Rowland J;	Driver;	T/5770427;	age 31;	21 September 1944.	Roman Catholic Cemetery, St. Oedenrode, Grave 28.
Hall, Albert E;	Corporal;	T/187220;	age 32;	21 September 1944.	Bergen op Zoom War Cemetery CG24.c.1-3.
Rhodes, George H;	Corporal;	T/10694070;	age 33;	21 September 1944.	Roman Catholic Cemetery, St. Oedenrode, Grave 27.
Tite, Donald F;	Driver;	T/14418031;	age 19;	21 September 1944.	Roman Catholic Cemetery, St. Oedenrode, Grave 30.
Woodward, Harold;	Driver;	T/1455222;	age 30;	21 September 1944.	Bergen op Zoom War Cemetery 24.C.4.
Yeo, Frederick G W;	Driver;	T/14673529;	age 19;	21 September 1944.	Bergen op Zoom War Cemetery 24.C.5.

800 Air Despatch Company RASC

Adamson, James;	Lance Corporal;	T/249802;	age 29;	21 September 1944.	No Known Grave*
Clements, Ronald N;	Lance Corporal;	T/189176;	age 29;	21 September 1944.	Roman Catholic Cemetery, Ravenstein, Grave 3.
Crooks, Robert W;	Driver;	T/857964;	age 32;	21 September 1944.	General Cemetery Woensel, Eindhoven, Plot KK.130.
Dellanzo, Joseph;	Corporal;	T/10684750;	age 30;	21 September 1944.	General Cemetery Woensel, Eindhoven, Plot KK.125.

Sharpe, Robert;	Lance Corporal;	T/4806032;	–;	21 September 1944.	General Cemetery Woensel, Eindhoven, Plot KK.129.
Van Ingen, George;	Driver;	T/14508172;	age 20;	21 September 1944.	General Cemetery Woensel, Eindhoven, Plot KK.126.

49 Air Despatch Column RASC

63 Airborne Composite Company RASC

Ashton, Richard E;	Driver;	T/161755;	age 29;	19 September 1944.	Oosterbeek 4.C.16.
Bowers, James;	Driver;	T/14662693;	age 41;	19 September 1944.	No known grave.
Chaplin, William J;	Driver;	T/839827;	age 35;	19 September 1944.	Rheinberg War Cemetery, Germany, Plot 13.C.25.
Cross, William D;	Driver;	T/14663327;	age 33;	19 September 1944.	No known grave.
Harper, Leonard S;	Driver;	T/14562999;	age 29;	19 September 1944.	Oosterbeek 15.B.15.
Hodgkinson, Robert;	Driver;	T/14230247;	age 33;	19 September 1944.	No known grave.
Nixon, Philip E;	Corporal;	T/176341;	age 29;	19 September 1944.	Oosterbeek 15.B.16.
Ricketts, James;	Driver;	T/169028;	age 27;	19 September 1944.	Oosterbeek 15.B.14.
Rowbotham, Arthur;	Driver;	T/169195;	age 28;	19 September 1944.	Oosterbeek 15B.13.
Smith, Frederick G;	Driver;	T/10684001;	age 33;	19 September 1944.	No known grave.
Weston, George L;	Driver;	T/14663278;	age 23;	19 September 1944.	No known grave.
Neale, Gordon;	Driver;	T/14435628;	age 18;	20 September 1944.	Oosterbeek 1.C.1.
Pescodd, Alfred W J;	Corporal;	47580;	age 38;	20 September 1944.	Jonkerbos War Cemetery, Nijmegen, 4.E.4.
Pragnell, Robert F;	Driver;	T/61437;	–;	20 September 1944.	No known grave.
Armand, Stanley V;	Driver;	T/14636618;	age 26;	21 September 1944.	Oosterbeek CG 4.A.2-5.
Harris, John R;	Driver;	T/5628455;	age 27;	21 September 1944.	Oosterbeek 15.A.11.
Law, Stanley;	Lance Corporal;	T/3776418;	age 28;	21 September 1944.	Oosterbeek 30.C.1.

398 (Airborne) Divisional Composite Company RASC

(Twelve Individuals were attached to 63 Airborne Composite Company RASC on 2 September 1944, and participated in their sorties)

Heckford, Ernest V;	Driver;	T/14430032;	age 19;	20 September 1944.	No known grave.
Waring, John;	Lance Corporal;	T/14238064;	age 35;	20 September 1944.	Groesbeek Canadian War Cemetery CG12.C.9-12.

253 Airborne Composite Company RASC

Barker, Alfred E;	Corporal;	T/180513;	age 31;	18 September 1944.	General Cemetery Roosendaalen Nispen, Grave 3.1.
Breading, Denis;	Driver;	T/14264139;	age 29;	19 September 1944.	Oosterbeek 22.B.8.
Cadle, George C;	Private;	T/203481;	age 22;	19 September 1944.	Mierlo War Cemetery Grave 6.E.12.
Courtney, James;	Private;	T/199044;	age 33;	19 September 1944.	Mierlo War Cemetery Grave 6.E.11.
Enderby, Norman;	Driver;	T/10679621;	age 21;	19 September 1944.	No known grave.
Holdsworth, Francis C;	Driver;	T/14394044;	age 33;	19 September 1944.	No known grave.
Taylor, Frederick;	Driver;	T/14506917;	age 21;	19 September 1944.	Oosterbeek 22.B.7.

Fowler, George A;	Corporal;	T/185692;	age 29;	20 September 1944.	Jonkerbos War Cemetery, Nijmegen, 20.H.8.
Hadley, John T;	Driver;	T/5623132;	age 25;	20 September 1944.	No known grave.
Leech, Joseph F;	Driver;	T/10663588;	age 22;	20 September 1944.	Oosterbeek 29.C.1.
Rexstrew, Frederick;	Lance Corporal;	T/179420;	age 30;	20 September 1944.	Oosterbeek 29.C.8.
Abbott, Albert E;	Driver;	T/217689;	age 30;	21 September 1944.	Canadian War Cemetery, Groesbeek, 22.F.2.
Caldecott, Leslie H;	Lance Corporal;	T/80730;	age 22;	21 September 1944.	Oosterbeek 18.B.11.
Churchyard, Sidney L;	Driver;	T/10693855;	age 22;	21 September 1944.	Oosterbeek 27.C.8.
Gregory, Harold;	Driver;	T/152672;	age 28;	21 September 1944.	Oosterbeek 18.B.7.
Johnston, James F;	Driver;	T/188996;	age 28;	21 September 1944.	Jonkerbos War Cemetery, Nijmegen, 20.J.8.
Thompson, William G;	Driver;	T/84459;	age 25;	21 September 1944.	No known grave *
Jones, George E;	Driver;	T/170974;	–;	22 September 1944.	Jonkerbos War Cemetery, Nijmegen, 19.H.5.
Noble, Ernest;	Driver;	T/157697;	age 24;	21 September 1944.	Oosterbeek JG 18.B.9-10.
Parker, Colin;	Driver;	T/175876;	age 31;	21 September 1944.	Oosterbeek JG 18.B.9-10.
Crossley, William T;	Driver;	T/2184109;	age 41;	23 September 1944.	No known grave.
Simpson, Francis W R;	Lance Corporal;	T/10693502;	age 34;	23 September 1944.	No known grave.
Hayton, Robert W;	Driver;	T/10698386;	age 22;	23 September 1944.	Oosterbeek 15.A.5.
Lightwood, Cyril W;	Driver;	T/14285926;	age 21;	23 September 1944.	General Cemetery, Heteren, Grave 2A.13A.
Reardon, Gerard;	Lance Corporal;	T/185097;	age 31;	23 September 1944.	Oosterbeek 16.A.3.
Shore, Reginald;	Driver;	T/10689983;	age 21;	23 September 1944.	Oosterbeek 31.A.1.

Royal Army Ordnance Corps

Headquarters 1st Airborne Division

Gibson, Victor;	Private;	7612322;	age 25;	18 September 1944.	No known grave.
Brown, Robert D;	Staff Sergeant;	7596110;	age 25;	25/26 Sept 1944.	No known grave.

1st Airborne Division Ordnance Field Park

Grantham, Frederick W;	Corporal;	10541663;	age 26;	25 September 1944.	Oosterbeek 1.A.2.
Andrews, Kenneth C W;	Corporal;	14216620;	age 38;	25/26 Sept 1944.	No known grave.

Army Catering Corps

Headquarters 1st Airlanding Brigade

Toms, William H;	Corporal;	3447531;	age 24;	21 September 1944.	Oosterbeek 5.D.9.

156 Parachute Battalion

Creasy, Cecil H;	Private;	5826176;	age 27;	25 September 1944.	Oosterbeek 32.B.10.

Unknown Units

Maddocks, Sidney;	Private;	403493;	age 37;	22 September 1944.	Oosterbeek 21.B.8.

Annex 2

Those Present

It would have been marvellous to have been able to publish a list of all those who went to Arnhem, but the records simply do not exist in any acceptable form; save for the RAOC whose participation is set out in an Army publication entitled '21 Army Group Ordnance' written by Major J Lee-Richardson RAOC and printed and published in Germany in February 1946. Even then, research has shown that the fate of some individuals as shown by Major Lee-Richardson was not correct and this has been put right where possible.

The following, therefore, is the complete nominal roll of RAOC at Arnhem. It is with deep regret that the RASC and ACC are not reproduced, but such lists as exist are incomplete and would be misleading.

Headquarters RAOC 1st Airborne Division

Lieutenant Colonel G A Mobbs	POW, wounded
WO1 (Sub Conductor) G E Jenkins	Glider landed south of Arnhem. Escaped October 1944
Staff Sergeant R D Brown	Missing, killed

Headquarters RAOC Personnel Detached to the Ordnance Field Park

Sergeant C Bennet	Escaped by swimming the Rhine, 25/26 September 1944
Private Hodges	POW*
Private V Gibson	Killed. Date disputed, either 18 or 25 September 1944
Private Browning	POW*

Brigade Ordnance Warrant Officers

WO1 (Sub Conductor) F F Eastwood	Glider landed south of Arnhem. Escaped October 1944
WO1 (Sub Conductor) Halsall	POW, wounded*
WO1 (Sub Conductor) Higham	POW, wounded*

1st Airborne Division Ordnance Field Park Gliderborne Element

Major C C Chidgey	POW, wounded
Staff Sergeant R Wilson	POW*
Sergeant K C W Andrews	Missing, killed. Substantive rank: corporal
Sergeant R Plowman	Escaped, means unknown, 25/26 September 1944
Corporal F W Grantham	Killed, 21 September 1944. Headstone date incorrect
Corporal Thompson	POW*
Corporal Longley	Escaped, means unknown, 25/26 September 1944
Private S G Harsley	Escaped by boat, 25/26 September 1944
Private Pooley	POW, wounded*
Private Wright	POW, wounded*
Private Wynn	POW, wounded*

1st Airborne Division Ordnance Field Park Forward Parachute Detachment

Captain B V Manley	POW
Staff Sergeant H Walker	POW, wounded
Private E V B Mordecai	POW, wounded
Private F R G Pugh	POW, wounded
Private McCarthy	POW, wounded
Private K Heaney	POW

* Indicates direct transcript from Major Lee-Richardson's work, reproduced without additional substantive evidence.

ANNEX 3

Memorials

There are three known memorials to the airborne logisticians, all of them associated with the Royal Army Service Corps. The smallest, and least well known, is to 250 Airborne Light Company. It is situated at Long Hills Hall near West Field Farm at Branston Heath near Branston in Lincolnshire. It is reached by driving out of Branston along the B1188 in the direction of Sleaford. Some six miles from Branston is Long Hills Hall, surrounded by farmland and it is here that the memorial can be found. Approach the gate, with its lodge, and the memorial is straight ahead.

The land on which to build the memorial was donated by Bentley Nelstrop of West Field Farm, and the cost of the structure was found from money raised by the veterans of 250 Airborne Light company.

The details which follow on the air despatch memorials in Oosterbeek and at Down Ampney are taken from the Memorials Register published by the Institution of the Royal Army Service Corps and the Royal Corps of Transport, with whose permission they are reproduced here.

Arnhem Air Despatch Memorial Oosterbeek Cemetery

COUNTRY: *HOLLAND*
LOCATION AND BRIEF DESCRIPTION: *This Air Despatch Memorial stands within Arnhem on a site close to the Oosterbeek Cemetery where so many of those whom it commemorates are buried.*
17 September 1994 marked the fiftieth anniversary of 1st Airborne Division's landing at Arnhem. On Sunday, 18 September 1994, fifty years to the day from when the first resupply flights took place, a new memolrial was unveiled at Arnhem, which states:

> *To the memory of the Air Despatchers of the Royal Army Service Corps who, together with the aircrew of the Royal Air Force and the Royal Canadian Air Force, gave their lives in valiant attempts to resupply the airborne forces during the Battle of Arnhem.*

The names of the Air Despatchers who died, seventeen of whom have no known grave, are listed on the monument's panels.

The memorial was dedicated by the Reverend E.J. Phillips who was the Padre of The 3rd Battalion the Parachute Regiment at Arnhem. At the end of the Service of Dedication wreaths were laid on behalf of the companies of the fallen soldiers. A wreath was laid by 47 Air Despatch Squadron, Royal Logistic Corps, at the time the only remaining Air Despatch unit in existence.

The memorial was designed by Mr A. C. Wheeler of Swindon. The stone for the monument is called Hopton Wood from Derbyshire. It was sculptured by Mr D. Greaves of Cirencester. The monument was transported to Holland and erected by members of 47 Air Despatch Squadron RLC.

Ownership: Air Despatch Association
Stewardship: Air Despatch Association.

Down Ampney Memorial Window

COUNTRY: *ENGLAND*

LOCATION AND BRIEF DESCRIPTION: *This memorial window commemorating the RAF, the 1st and 6th Airborne Divisions and the Air Despatch Groups RASC can be found within All Saints Church, Down Ampney, Wiltshire.*

The Memorial Window was dedicated on Sunday, 9 June 1974 at the Down Ampney Parish Church of All Saints by the Right Reverend Basil Guy, Bishop of Gloucester. The window is dedicated:

IN MEMORY OF THE MEN AND WOMEN OF THE ROYAL AIR FORCE
THE FIRST AND SIXTH AIRBORNE DIVISIONS AND
AIR DESPATCH GROUP ROYAL ARMY SERVICE CORPS
WHO TOOK PART IN OPERATIONS FROM DOWN AMPNEY-1944-1945

Research indicates that in 1971 a Mr Alan Hartley, a Second World War flight mechanic with 271 Sqn RAF, visited his wartime base and realised that unless some permanent reminder was introduced the efforts of those who had served at Down Ampney would soon be forgotten. He gained permission from the vicar and church council for a memorial stained-glass window. Goddard and Gibbs provided the designs and were subsequently given the contract for the manufacture and fitting.

271 Squadron was part of No 46 Group Royal Air Force which within Transport Command specialised in supply by air, paratroop dropping and glider towing.

The first recorded military air supply drops took place at Kut el Amara in 1916, but it was during World War II that this method of resupply became of major significance. The responsibility for packing, installing and despatching loads was assumed by the RASC air despatch units. Since 1942 air despatch units have lived, worked and died alongside their RAF colleagues. The Operations from Down Ampney, in particular Operation MARKET GARDEN, typify this close co-operation.

Christopher Hibbert in his book *Arnhem* wrote:

> *The sight of the Stirlings and Dakotas flying unhesitatingly into the German barrage where sometimes, although hit and on fire, they continued to circle above the German lines while the Royal Army Service Corps Despatchers threw out the supplies before the aircraft crashed into the earth, was so moving that for many of those who witnessed it no more poignant memory of Arnhem remains.*

As a result of their part in the operation the air despatch units were awarded the right to wear a formation sign of their own. The now familar, yellow Dakota on a blue background is depicted in this memorial window. The dedication included the following:

Brigadier and Mrs D.N. Locke
Colonel (Retd) and Mrs S.W. Walsh
(Sam Walsh commanded 48 Air Despatch Regiment during D-Day and Arnhem)
Colonel (Retd) and Mrs A.F.J. Kingsmill

Annex 4

Hamilcar Loads

The loads for the three Hamilcars full of stores which landed with the second lift were as follows:

<u>Glider Number One:</u>

75-mm High Explosive Fuzed M54	20 Panniers	For the 1st Airlanding Light Regiment RA
6-pounder Anti-Tank APCBC [1]	15 Panniers	
3 -inch Mortar High Explosive	5 Panniers	
17-pounder Armour Piercing Shot	60 Rounds	

<u>Glider Number Two</u>

RE 10[2]	16 Panniers
75 mm High Explosive Fuzed M54	10 Panniers
6-pounder Anti-Tank APCBC	10 Panniers
3-inch Mortar High Explosive	6 Panniers
17-pounder Armour Piercing Shot	30 Rounds
Barbed Wire	4 Rolls
Mines Anti-Tank Mark 5	40
Mine Tape	4 Rolls
Pick Shafts	4
Pick Heads	2
Mine Signs	4
Screw Pickets	16

<u>Glider Number Three</u>

RE 10	9 Panniers
6-pounder Anti-Tank APCBC	5 Panniers
3-inch Mortar High Explosive	4 Panniers
Ordnance Stores	30 Panniers

1. APCBC: Armour Piercing Capped Ballistic Capped – a particular design of armour piercing shot
2. Assorted Royal Engineers' stores.
3. Mine Tape: White tape, usually made of linen, for marking the boundaries of friendly forces' minefields
4. Screw Pickets: Corkscrew-shaped steel pickets, usually 6 feet in length, used to support barbed wire entanglements.

ANNEX 5

List of Stores Dropped on 1st Airborne Division During Operation Market Garden

Weapons [1]

Sten Carbine Mk V c/w Bayonet	18
2″-mortar, Airlanding	162
3″-mortar (with modified baseplate)	52
Tripod, folding Bren LMG	170
Rifle No 4 Mk 1 (T)	12
PIAT	87
.303″ Rifle	52
Vickers LMG .303″	30
Vickers GO, No 1	6

Ammunition and Grenades [2]

Grenade Hand No 82	10,240
Grenade Hand No 79	6,840
Signal 2-Star (Red-Green) Mk 1	14,616
75 mm Pack How	19,170
20 mm Polsten	6,552
Sten Carbine Mk V	1,272,200
.303″ Bandolier	1,641,630
.303″ Mk VIIIZ	1,641,630
.303″ Tracer	823,756
PIAT	16,902
2″-mortar	50,332
3″-mortar	30,276
.45″ Automatic	24,000
.38″ Revolver	12,528
17-pounder	1,114

Signal Equipment [3]

Wireless Station No 76(/109/A(Para))	6
Wireless Station No 22 (Para)	29
Wireless Station No 18 (Airlanding)	55
Wireless Station No 68P (Airlanding)	17
Wireless Station No 8 Mk II	57

Engineer Stores

Warsop Drills	4

Packing Sets

Cushions Packing 3″ Mortar Bombs Set A	648
Cushions Packing 3″ Mortar Bombs Set B	648
Cushions Packing 3″ Mortar Bombs Set C	648
Packing for W/T Set No 76	6
Packing for W/T Set No 22	29
Packing for W/T Set No 18 or 68	72
Packing for W/T Set No 38	57

Vote 8 Stores [4]

Stretchers Folding Airborne	1,272
Valises Rifle	32
Bags Sleeping Airborne	366
Equipment Carrying 3″ Mortar and) Sets 1	52
Bombs) Sets 2	52
Sets 3	52
Sets 4	52
Shelter Portable No 12 (Workshop shelter)	31
Crosses distinguishing hospital airborne	30
Ladders Rope 22 Ft	2
Ropes Climbing 125 ft	6

1. These weapons would normally be expected to go to the OFP for cleaning and preparation for issue.
2. Ammunition would normally be collected by 250 Company and taken to the DAA
3. Signal equipment would normally go to the OFP for stock
4. Known in modern parlance as 'General Stores', one element of 'Ordnance Stores', the other two components of which are 'Technical Stores' and 'Motor Transport' Stores

ANNEX 6

Tonnages of Resupply Collected Daily[1]

Date	Net Approximation of Tonnages Collected	Percentage Collected out of Total Dropped	Source
D+1	14	66	3 Bulk Loaded Hamilcars
18 September	12	14	33 Stirlings
D+2 19 September	21	5.4	Stirlings and C47
D+3	3	10.6 from all 41	First drop from a few C 47
20 September	38		Mostly rations from Stirlings and C47
D+4 21 September	11	4	Stirlings and C47
D+5 22 September	Nil	–	No Drop
D+6 23 September	7	2.4	Stirlings and C47
D+7 24 September	Nil	–	No Drop
D+8 25 September	Nil	–	4 Dakotas only

Total supplies collected – 106 tons. Total percentage collected 7.4%.

Notes:
1. It is estimated that another 100 tons approximately fell in unit lines and was collected and used by them, especially in the case of units in the neighbourhood of the river. But there are no figures to support this estimation.
2. The rate of collection towards the end fell off steeply as the number of jeeps and trailers available for collection decreased. By D+4 the effective availability had been reduced by half, and on D+8 only two jeeps and trailers remained serviceable. The shrinking of the perimeter towards the end also contributed to a reduced rate of recovery.
3. Nearly everything recovered was eventually issued with the exception of some 300 galls Pet (sic), 17 - pounder and 2″ Mor Smoke. There was (sic) also a quantity of RE minefield panniers left in the dump.

Gun Amn (sic)

Date	75 mm	6-pounder	17-pounder
18 September	80	30	24 rounds between 18
19 September	250	80	and 21 September
20 September	330	140	
21 September	400	170	
22 September		No Resupply	
23 September	160	80	
24 September		No Resupply	
25 September		No Resupply	
Total	1220	500	24
Composition	M48 – 960 M54 - 50 Smoke – 120 Armour Piercing – 120	APCBC – 250 DS[2]–180 High Explosive – 70	APCBC – 24

1. Taken from 1st Airborne Division Post Operational Report Part II Appendix E
2. DS: Discarding Sabot, a type of armour piercing shot

ANNEX 7

Air Despatch Equipment

The information in this annex is drawn from: *The RAF Airborne Forces Manual.* It is the official air publication for RAF Paratroop Aircraft and Gliders 1942 to 1946. It is Volume 8 in the RAF Museum Series and was published by Arms and Armour Press. It is out of print, but copies are in the RAF Museum at Hendon and the Airborne Museum 'Hartenstein', where they are available for research. I am grateful to the curator of the RAF Museum for permission to draw on the manual for this annex and elsewhere in the book and to reproduce Crown Copyright information. The manual contains exhaustive detail on Air Despatch equipment, with only a flavour being offered in this annex.

Supplies Dropping Apparatus

The appartus described here was for use in supplementary supply dropping operations as distinct from dropping supplies with a paratroop section, the two types of operation requiring, in most instances, different apparatus.

The Mark VB apparatus comprised a percussion cap on the nose, a cylindrical container for the supplies and bucket to house the parachute. The container could be adapted to carry either a liquid load, a load of ammunition or a load of food and other supplies. The whole apparatus could be slung from a 500-lb bomb carrier or from some other type of universal bomb carrier. For liquids it had a volume of 2.07cu ft, which permitted the carriage of 11.25 gallons filled through a filler cap in the lid, which was sweated in position to provide a seal. The Mark VI apparatus was known as the pack and harness. It comprised a webbing harness in which the package of supplies was wrapped to be dropped as a 'parcel'. It could be slung from the same bomb carriers as the Mark VB.

There were also a range of specialist containers, examples of which are pictured in Chapter 1 of this book, tailored for use with specialist equipment, especially communication equipment.

Wicker panniers were made in the form of two rectangular hampers telescoping one into the other, with closed dimensions of 36x20x16 inches. A piece of 5-plywood was wired to the base of a

Panniers, configured for 'daisy chain' dropping, ready to exit.
Courtesy RAF Museum Hendon

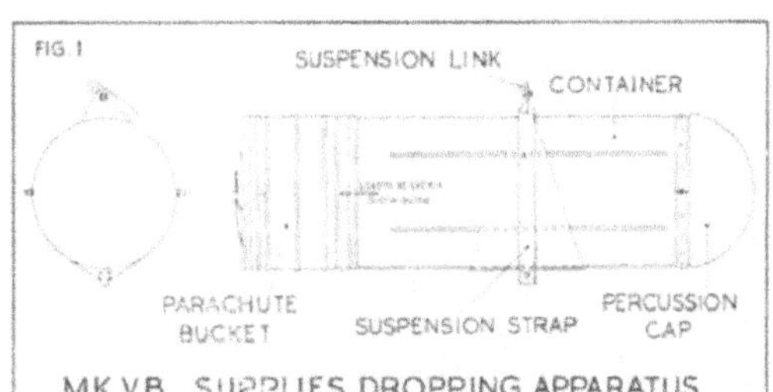

Mk VB Supplies Dropping Apparatus.
Courtesy RAF Museum Hendon

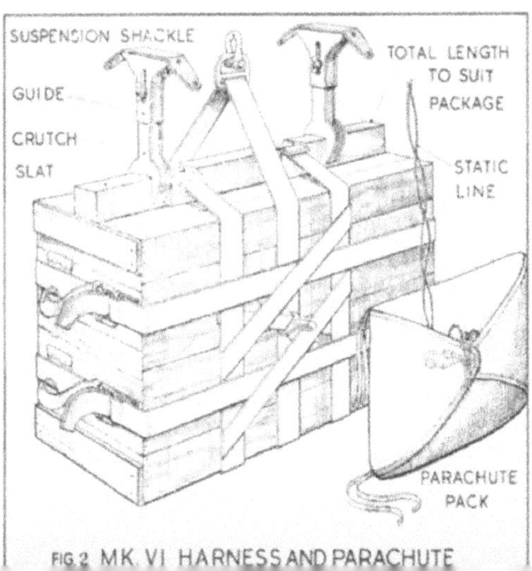

Mk VI Harness and Parachute.
Courtesy RAF Museum Hendon

single pannier or a pair of panniers in order to speed their despatch. Each pannier, whether for despatch singly or in pairs, was secured in a modified form of the Mk V1 harness used in conjunction with a parachute suitable to the load carried.

Panniers were either despatched singly or as a pair, and in the latter case the 'daisy-chain' method was used. This involved two panniers being placed one on top of the other and held together by four ties made of 100-lb silk cord, the ties being made between the leather straps on the panniers with two ties at each side. A parachute was attached to each pannier, with the static line of the bottom pannier, 5ft 6in long, being attached to the leather strap at the parachute end of the top pannier. The static line of the top parachute, 15ft 6in long, was attached to a snap hook on the static line cable of the aircraft.

Panniers were despatched through the side door of the Dakota, using roller runway. The only arrangement shown in the RAF Airborne Manual is a single runway fed from side bays, also constructed of roller runway. However, there was also a double track system, and this is shown clearly in the Chapter 2 picture of panniers being manhandled into a Dakota. Since the double track could take sixteen panniers, whilst the single is only shown in the manual with a maximum capacity of fifteen, the double track would appear to have been more effective.

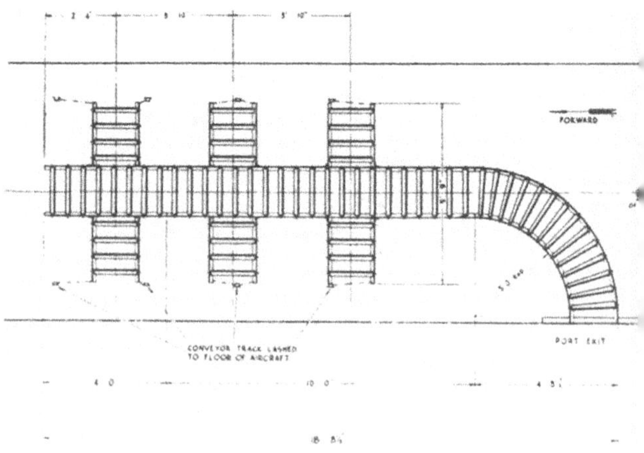

The single-track roller runway. Courtesy RAF Museum Hendon

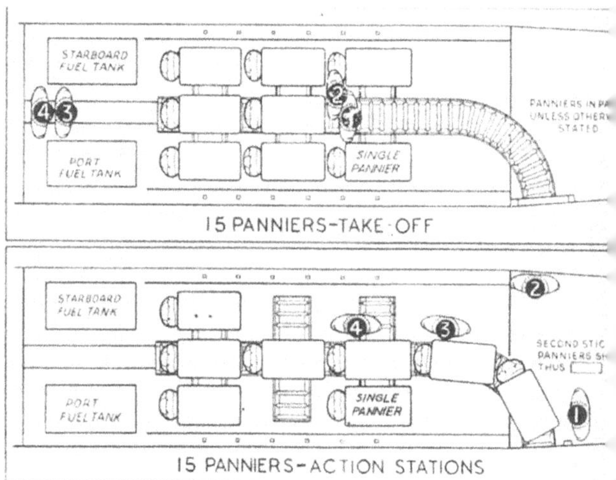

An example of crew and pannier positions, in this case for fift panniers. Courtesy RAF Museum Hendon

Where two panniers were despatched as a single load they fell as one object until the partial development of the top parachute caused to jerk which broke the four ties between the panniers. As the bottom pannier fell away its static line was pulled by the top pannier whereupon it broke free and descended as a separate single item. The clear advantage of this method was that twice as many panniers could be despatched for a single pass.

ANNEX 8

Ration Packs

The information in this annex is drawn from: *The Second World War 1939–1945 Army Supplies and Transport* Volume II. Appendix IX, held in the RLC museum. I am grateful for the curator's permission to reproduce Crown Copyright detail.

Wherever possible the Army sought to feed soldiers on fresh rations, resorting to packed rations only when neccesary. This was not only to offer a better, more balanced, diet, but also to preserve precious and expensive ration packs for when they were most needed. Arnhem was, clearly, a case where ration packs would be used, and the two in question were the 24-hour ration pack and the Composite (14-Men) Ration Pack, known as Compo.

The 24-Hour Ration Pack

The 24-hour ration was primarily a landing or assault ration for use in temperate climates. Its purpose was to provide the highest possible calorific value, in this case 4,000 calories, with minimum weight and space. This was achieved largely by eliminating the use of tin plate. The outer pack was of waterproof and gasproof waxed cardboard. The complete ration in its cardboard box fitted into the large half of the mess tin, and where 48 hours' subsistence was catered for then the other would need to be stowed elsewhere. The gross weight was 2lb 3oz. There was, for assault troops, a special pack called the 24-hour ration (A). which fitted into the smaller half of the mess tin, and this was very helpful where 48 hours' rations were issued. It is not clear which type was issued for Arnhem.

It was stressed in the instructions that these rations must not be sampled prior to arrival or men would go hungry after landing. Officers were directed to make it their duty to ensure that rations were intact, and to impress on men that this was it and there would be no more. When used for 48 hours it was issued with a special flat tin of twenty cigarettes. Cooking was by means of tablets either of hexamine or solidified alcohol. It comprised:

Item	Number	Weight (Ounces)
Biscuits	10	9
Oatmeal	2 blocks	3.5
Tea, sugar and milk blocks	Several wrapped together	
Meat block	1	4
Raisin chocolate	2 slabs	4
Chocolate (Vit)	1 slab	2
Boiled sweets		4
Chewing gum	2 packets	
Meat extract cubes		0.5
Salt	1 packet	0.25
Sugar	4 tablets	0.5
Latrine paper	4 pieces	

The tea-sugar-milk blocks could each produce 2 pints of tea.

Composite (14-men) Ration Pack

The 14-men pack was to feed troops for periods not exceeding six weeks. It comprised tinned commodities, with variations to allow for change of diet. It was intended for centralised cooking under unit arrangements. There were two categories: one with biscuit and comprising seven varieties identified as Types 'A' to 'G'; and one without biscuit for issue when fresh bread was available and comprising three types, designated Types 1, 2 and 3. Full details of the contents of all these Types are in Appendix IX to *Army Supplies and Transport*. However, they all contained selections from a variety of preserved meat, sausages, bacon, luncheon meat, sardines and salmon. There was also baked beans, tinned fruit, soups, cigarettes, margarine and chocolate together with vegetables, jam, tea, sugar, milk, biscuits, puddings, cheese and soap as well as eighty-four sheets of toilet paper.

For airborne operations the 14-Man ration could be packed with three cases, forty-two rations, per pannier. For use with the bomb type container twenty-eight rations to the precise scale of the compo ration could be dropped in the Mark I or Mark III container. To achieve this fourteen rations at the Compo scale were packed, less biscuit, into a wooden keg with one 7.5lb tin of biscuits to complete the ration. Two kegs and two tins of biscuits were then fitted into each container.

Free dropping was considered an option for rations, but experience had shown that doing so with cased supplies often incurred considerable loss due to breakage of containers on impact with the ground. Losses could, however, be minimised if free-dropped rations were 'dry' items as opposed to processed items and were packed in hessian sacks of 80-lb capacity, but only loaded to 40-lb weight.

There was also an invalid pack capable of being air dropped, for use in hospitals. In addition to the normal contents one might expect there were two bottles of brandy packed in a wooden box. Whether these were for consumption by the patients or the medical staff is not made clear.

Sources

Airborne Museum Hartenstein, Oosterbeek
Airborne Forces Museum, Aldershot
Bundesarchiv, Koblenz
Imperial War Museum, London
Museum of Army Flying, Middle Wallop
The Royal Logistic Corps Museum, Deepcut
Regimental Headquarters The Royal Logistic Corps
The Institution of the Royal Army Service Corps and the Royal Corps of Transport
The Royal Army Ordnance Corps Secretariat
The Royal Pioneer Corps Association
The Army Catering Corps Association
The Defence Postal and Courier Agency
47 Air Despatch Squadron RLC, RAF Lyneham
RAF Museum, Hendon

Persons:
R G Adams (Whitchurch), Lt Col (Retd) D A Armitage (Andover), W F Bater (Paignton), B Blaxley (Chudleigh), W Boersma (Oosterbeek), S Brooking (Ashburton), D Brown (Stockton on Tees), A S Brown (Aldershot), L Burns (Bodmin), Lt Col W M Carlisle (London), W H Chedgey (Bridgenorth), N Cherry (Nottingham), C C Chidgey (Bruton), R A Clancy (Northampton), K W Clarke (Leicester) now deceased, Christine Clarke nee Bradshaw (Leicester), R Collins (Birmingham), S H Cooper, D Cutting (Newmarket, Ontario, Canada), A Dawson (Weston-Super-Mare), P R R de Burgh (West Lavington), R Dent (Milton Keynes) now deceased, H Eckersley (Bolton) now deceased, S Fenton (Prestwich), W V Gell (Seaford), R M Gerritsen (Duiven), J H Gifford (Monmouth), N G Griffin (Amesbury), A Groeneweg (Doorwerth), S G Harsley (Peterborough), R P Hilton (Aldershot), P W H Jay (Cheltenham) now deceased, T Jones (Isle of Man) now deceased, Lt Col (Retd) B T Kavanagh (Warley), B V Manley (Blackwater), Marie Manley (Blackwater), C Marshall (Cochrane, Alberta, Canada), Betty Maskell, previously Grace (Cinderford), Susan Mitchell (Brucken Germany), Sir Nigel Mobbs (Slough), E V B Mordecai (Harrogate), R G Pearce (Bristol), R Peatling (Wimborne Minster), E Pepper (Bilston), Beryl Pickles-Eastwood (Barnoldswick), F R G Pugh (Winchester), Freda Pugh nee Burgess (Winchester), I Renwick (Bognor Regis), J R Roberts (Chester), R N Sigmond (Renkum), H C Simmonds (Weymouth), T Smith (Gateshead), J Staple (Parkestone), J Taylor (Branston), C van den Bosch (Arnhem), J van Slooten (Oosterbeek), R Voskuil (Oosterbeek), F Weatherley (Rotherham), J J G White (Bishop's Stortford), J Wild (Heighton), E Th A Wijnhoud (Arnhem), L W Wright (Ipswich).

Public Record Office
WO/171 393 War Diary (WD) HQ 1st Airborne Division, WO/171 400 WD HQ CRASC 1st Airborne Division (Airborne Element), WO/171 402 WD RAOC OFP Airborne Detachment, WO/171 394 WD HQ 1st Airborne Division Seaborne Echelon, WO/171 395 WD HQ 1st Airborne Division (A/Q Branch) 2nd Seaborne Echelon, WO/171 399 WD Commander RASC 1st Airborne Division, WO/171 403 WD RAOC OFP Seaborne Echelon, WO/171 2378 WD 93 Coy RASC Seaborne Echelon, WO/171 2416 WD 250 Coy RASC Seaborne Echelon, WO/171 2177 WD HQ Air Despatch Group RASC, WO/ 171 2371 WD 63 Coy RASC, WO/166 15581 WD 49 Air Despatch Column, including Annex B.
Diary Lcpl J L Hughes RASC, HQ RASC 1st Airborne Division Standing Operational Instruction of 8 August 1944, HQ 1st Airborne Division Post Operational Report of 10 January 1945, Part II - Administrative Aspects of the Operation.

Published Sources:
The Day Gone By; An Autobiography Richard Adams (Hutchinson London 1990)
Arnhem 1944 The Airborne Battle Martin Middlebrook (Penguin Books 1995)
First IN! Parachute Pathfinder Company Ron Kent (B Batsford Ltd London)
The Story of the Royal Army Service Corps 1939 - 1945 (The Institution of the Royal Army Service Corps)
A History of the Royal Army Ordnance Corps 1940-1945 Brigadier A H Fernyhough (William Clowes and Sons, Limited, London and Beccles)
It Never Snows In September Robert J Kershaw (Ian Allen Ltd, Shepperton, Surrey)
Remember Arnhem John Fairley (Peaton Press)
Airborne Carpet Operation Market Garden Anthony Farrar-Hockley (MacDonald and Co)
A Bridge Too Far Cornelius Ryan (Simon and Schuster)
Arnhem Major General R E Urquhart CB DSO (Cassel London 1958)

Regimental Publications:
The Journal of the Royal Army Service Corps - various editions
The Royal Army Ordnance Corps Gazette - various editions
The Royal Army Service Corps Review Volume 1 No 5 1952 Lieutenant Colonel M StJ Packe RASC
The Story of the Army Catering Corps and Its Predecessors H N Cole (1984)
The Royal Pioneer, the regimental journal of the Royal Pioneer Corps, No30 Volume 7 March 1952
A Great Adventure (The Story of a Sub-Conductor RAOC) WO1 (Sub-Conductor) G E Jenkins RAOC RAOC Gazette January 1945
Mailshot, A History of the Forces Postal Service Edward Wells (Defence Postal and Courier Services)

Unpublished Sources:
The Personal Memoirs of His Eight Days at Arnhem T/10667508 Sergeant K W Clarke RASC
The History of Air Despatch Lieutenant H O'N Drew RASC
21 Army Group Ordnance Major J Lee Richardson (Printed in Germany; February 1946)
Personal Memoirs of Arnhem 10584589 Private E V B Mordecai RAOC
Personal Memoirs of Arnhem Private K J Heaney RAOC
Ministory XXXV11, Supplement to Friends of the Airborne Museum Newsletter No 49, by R M Gerritsen
Without Tradition 2 Para 1941 - 45 Robert Peatling
Roll of Honour Fourth Edition 1999 Jan Hey (Friends of the Airborne Museum)
Who Was Who 2nd Revised Edition Chris van Roekel (Society of Friends of the Airborne Museum)

Index

The preface, list of maps, tables and annexes are not included. Page numbers followed by 'p' denote that a photograph forms part or all of the subject matter.